The First Sikh Spiritual Master

Timeless Wisdom from the Life and Teachings of Guru Nanak

Harish Dhillon

Walking Together, Finding the Way ®
SKYLIGHT PATHS ®
PUBLISHING
Woodstock, Vermont

To
Ashok Chopra

The First Sikh Spiritual Master:
Timeless Wisdom from the Life and Teachings of Guru Nanak

2006 First SkyLight Paths Quality Paperback Edition
© 2005 by Harish Dhillon
Original edition published in English by Indus Source Books, P.O. Box 6194, Malabar Hill P.O., Mumbai 400006, India. www.indussource.com

Library of Congress Cataloging-in-Publication Data
Dhillon, Harish.
[Guru Nanak]
The first Sikh spiritual master : timeless wisdom from the life and teachings of Guru Nanak / Harish Dhillon. — 1st Skylight Paths quality pbk. ed.
    p. cm.
Reprint. Originally published: Guru Nanak. Mumbai : Indus Source Books, 2005.
Includes bibliographical references.
ISBN-13: 978-1-59473-209-6
ISBN-10: 1-59473-209-4
1. Nānak, Guru, 1469-1538. 2. Sikh gurus—Biography. I. Title.
BL2017.85.N36D55 2006
294.6092—dc22
[B]

                                                                                        2006019891

10 9 8 7 6 5 4 3 2 1

Manufactured in the United States

Cover design: Jenny Buono

Walking Together, Finding the Way®
Published by SkyLight Paths Publishing
A Division of Longhill Partners, Inc.
Sunset Farm Offices, Route 4, P.O. Box 237
Woodstock, VT 05091
Tel.: (802) 457-4000   Fax: (802) 457-4004
www.skylightpaths.com

CONTENTS

INTRODUCTION

The life of Nanak, the founder of Sikhism, which is among the youngest religions of the world, has always fascinated would-be biographers. This fascination arises from the desire to probe the mystery of a remarkable life—a man who revelled in his ordinariness, who denied that he was in any way a saint, a saviour, or a redeemer, and who never claimed any divine inspiration. Yet, through his teachings, his personal example, and his influence on mankind, he attained great divinity.

Nanak was admired, loved and respected even in his lifetime. His name was inscribed as "Hazrat Rab-i-Majib, Baba Nanak Faqir Aulia" (Anand Acharya, *Snow Birds*, [London 1919], p. 182), on a memorial in Baghdad. In the Punjab, his Hindu disciples called him Satguru Nanak Dev while his Muslim followers referred to him as Hazrat Nanak Shah. To the *yogis* he was Nanak Nath, while to the Buddhists he was Nanak Lama. Bhai Gurdas said of him: "God the Bountiful heard the wail of suffering humanity and sent Guru Nanak to the world" (*Var* 1:23).

Mehrban writes: "He does not look like a man of the world—to our good luck, we are meeting in him God Himself" (Sodhi Mehrban, *Janamsakhi: Shri Guru Nanak Dev*, 1620 [Amritsar, 1962], p. 296). The chronicles also tell us that whosoever met Nanak said "never in their lives had they met a man so near God" (Sham Singh, *The Seekers' Path*, p. xiv).

Perhaps the most comprehensive summing up of Nanak's personality, his role in the social and religious reform of his period, and his lasting and continued influence on the people who believe in him, is by Sujan Rai Bhandari, a contemporary of Aurangzeb, writing 150 years after Nanak's death: "Guru Nanak was the chosen man of the world.... During this time he was the leader of the caravan on the Path of Truth, a torch bearer on the way of real religion. In his verses, written in the vernacular, he has inculcated an explicit language and with brilliant similes, the reality of God, His Omnipresence and Absolute Unity.

"Most of the disciples and devotees of Baba Nanak are men of real attainments, of God-fearing saintliness. The worship of these people consists of the reading of the hymns of their Guru, which they read in soft and sweet singing tones and sing in concert to heart-melting and charming tones. Having removed all hatred from their hearts and lifting the curtain of doubt, darkness and narrowness from their minds, they look upon their relatives and others alike. Friends and foes are equal to them. The service of stranger and traveller in the name of their Guru, which they always keep on repeating, they regard as the greatest devotion. If a person were to come at midnight and mention the name of Baba Nanak, however unfamiliar he may be, say even if he were a thief, a *sadhu*, or an evil-doer, they look upon him as a brother and a friend and serve him to the best of their ability." (Ganda Singh, *The Punjab Past and Present*, vol. III, p. 361–363)

In our own times, Sadhu T. L. Vaswani, the well-known philanthropic social reformer, who has come to be regarded as a saint, called Nanak "a prophet of the people" and said of him: "At rare intervals in history does appear a man like Nanak ... whose life opened an era in the history of India and Asia, in the history of humanity" (Vaswani, Sadhu T. L., *A Prophet of the People*, p. 15).

In spite of all this admiration and respect which Nanak continues to command five hundred years after he lived, the would-be biographer faces a daunting task because there is little source material available whose historical validity has been proved beyond doubt. We have only the brief biography written by his near-contemporary, Bhai Gurdas, and the little that we can glean from his teachings. Little wonder then that the first attempts at writing Nanak's biography, the janamsakhis, draw heavily upon oral tradition. These janamsakhis were written over a hundred years after Nanak's death. By this time Nanak had well and truly been established as a legend and many myths had grown around him. The janamsakhis are replete with stories of Nanak performing miracles and displaying supernatural powers, stories that most people have come to believe implicitly, forgetting that the only supernatural power Nanak acknowledged was the power of the Supreme Reality and the only miracles he believed in were the miracles performed by God. In fact, he went so far as to say:

"Dwell then in flame uninjured,
Remain unharmed amid eternal ice,

> Make blocks of stone thy food,
> Spurn the solid earth before thee
> With thy foot,
> Weigh the heavens in a balance
> Then ask thou that Nanak perform wonders."
> (*Raga Sree*. Trans. Cunningham J.D., *History of the Sikhs*)

Because of the lack of historical details and the myths that shroud our perception of him, Nanak seems to us further back in the mists of time than he really is. We think of him as belonging to the mythical times of King Arthur rather than, as Navtej Sarna so pertinently points out in his excellent *The Book of Nanak*, someone who lived at the time when Columbus discovered America, Magellan completed his first voyage around the world, Martin Luther began his reform of the Christian Church, and the printing press was invented. We forget that Nanak founded this young religion 1400 years after the birth of Christ and about 900 years after the birth of Islam.

There have been numerous efforts to correct the balance, all resulting in biographies of Nanak. Historians like Karam Singh looked for hitherto undiscovered documents containing references to Nanak. They visited old families and antique dealers, examining private collections and looking for new source material on Nanak's life. They sifted through traditional and legendary accounts and looked for corroboratory evidence in Bhai Gurdas' account and in Nanak's *bani*. From this, they built up a fairly comprehensive account of Nanak's life which served as a basis for the numerous biographies that have been attempted since, both as individual works and as part of more comprehensive histories of the Sikh religion and people. "Nevertheless, when we put together all the material, check one with the other, discard the miraculous, delete the accretion of the credulous, we are still left with enough to recreate a life story with a fair degree of authenticity" (Singh, Khushwant, *A History of the Sikhs*, vol. I p. 303).

Roopinder Singh, at the beginning of his remarkable book *Guru Nanak: His Life and Teachings*, asks: "Why another book on Nanak?" My only justification for retelling a story that has already been told so often is the firm belief that a story as beautiful and inspiring as Nanak's needs to be retold as often as possible. I have tried to write in simple language and in an easy, readable style, culling from the work of other writers before me. If a fraction of the great charm of this story can communicate itself to the reader, the effort will have been worthwhile. The world has far greater need of Nanak's example and of his teachings now than it ever did before.

THE TIMES

At the time of Nanak's birth, the Punjab was a much bigger geographical unit than the modern Punjab. On the northern boundary were the massive Himalayas. These acted as a barrier between the Punjab and Tibet. The western boundary of the Punjab was marked by the Indus, from the point where it enters the plains to its confluence, after approximately 1500 miles, with the five rivers which give the area its name—Punj-ab (the land of five rivers). West of the Indus lie the Hindu Kush and the Sulaiman Mountains, which have formed an effective geographical barrier. It was through several passes in this chain of mountains that invaders from Afghanistan came into the Punjab. There was no geographical feature to clearly define the eastern boundary of the Punjab and it was here that the Punjab seemed to merge into the Gangetic plain. The Punjab is a region that is essentially a flat plain through which flow the Indus and its five tributary rivers: Jhelum, Chenab, Ravi, Sutlej, and Beas. These rivers make the Punjab an extremely fertile land.

Now, of course, the Punjab is considered the granary of India, but at that time a large portion of the land was covered with dense forest. Not only were these forests home to a wide variety of wild life but they also gave the people of the Punjab a hideout from the oppression and bloodthirsty cruelty of wave after wave of invaders who swept through their land.

It is no wonder that a land so rich and fertile should have been home to one of the oldest civilizations of the world. Sir Mortimer Wheeler, in *The Cultural Heritage of Pakistan*, writes that stone implements have been found, which carbon dating has established as being over 500,000 years old. Copper and bronze implements too, which go back 25,000 years, have been excavated from along the riverbank. In addition to the ruins at Harappa and Mohenjo-daro, many Harappan and pre-Harappan sites have been excavated, most notably near Ropar and Ludhiana. From the artefacts dug up at these sites it is obvious that the

1

Punjab was the home of a people who had reached a very high degree of civilization long before the coming of the Aryans.

This civilization was finally destroyed by the onslaught of the Aryans—people from Central Asia, who were the first recorded invaders to sweep into the Punjab. The Vedic religion, as such, evolved in the Punjab and it was here, in their adopted land, that the Aryans created the great works which symbolise everything that is glorious in the Vedic and Sanskrit period.

The Aryans, in coming to the Punjab, showed the path to other conquerors. They were followed by the Persians, led by Darius. Darius' successors ruled northern Punjab for a hundred years after his death in 485 BC and when Alexander and his armies marched to the banks of the Beas in 326 BC, they found many traces of the Persian rule still intact. Alexander, as we know, stayed in India only for a short while and the political might of the Greeks he left behind was stamped out by the Mauryas. Yet the Greeks left a permanent impression on the culture of the region. In museums in Peshawar, Taxila, Lahore, New Delhi, and Mathura, and in private collections, pieces of exquisite sculpture from the Gandhara school, shaped under the strong influence of the Greeks, can be seen.

Greek political influence in the Punjab was extinguished by the Mauryas, who, in turn, were eclipsed by Bactrian invaders led by Menander. The Bactrian invasions were soon followed by marauding Scythian tribes. After this, there was a period of respite for a few centuries which saw the Golden Period of ancient India under the Guptas. They were, through careful strategy and military strength, able to keep invaders from coming into the Punjab. But once the Gupta dynasty went into decline, the Mongoloid Huns poured in. Again, for a short while, the invaders were held at bay by Vardhana and his son, Harsha. Harsha was the last great Indian ruler of the Punjab and after his death in 647 AD, his empire disintegrated and once again the Punjab was invaded in quick succession by different tribes from across the mountains. There was one difference, however, between the invaders of this period and those that had come earlier: the new invaders were all united by one faith—Islam.

With Mahmud Ghazni's first invasion in 1001 AD, the stage was set for the influx of Afghan tribes. The Ghaznis, the Ghoris, the Tughlaqs, the Suris and the Lodhis—each tribe penetrated further into the hinterland, staying longer in its adopted home than its predecessors.

In between these invasions was the scourge of the Mongols, led by Taimur, the effects of whose visit it took Northern India many centuries to recover from.

These repeated invasions finally ended with Babar, a descendant of Ghenghiz Khan from his father's side and of Taimur from his mother's side. He overthrew Ibraham Lodhi at Panipat in 1526 and established the powerful Mughal Empire, giving the Punjab much needed respite from foreign conquests.

Though most of these conquering races, especially the earlier ones, had not regarded themselves as empire builders and had come as plunderers lured by the fabled wealth of Hindustan, many of them settled down in the area now known as the Punjab. There was a consequent mingling of races, as also of language, culture and faiths. The conqueror had either been assimilated into the mainstream of life in the Punjab or had quietly faded away, leaving behind a people and a culture that were richer because of the new and varied influences they had been exposed to.

The coming of the Muslim conquerors introduced a new phenomenon in the Punjab. The process of assimilation gave way to a crisis of confrontation which was to persist for over six hundred years and give birth to the youngest of the great religions of the world—namely Sikhism.

Where earlier the conqueror and the conquered had adopted an attitude of give and take as far as their way of life, their customs, and even their religion, was concerned, Islam by its very nature precluded assimilation of any kind with the native inhabitants who were, by and large, practising Hindus. There was a sharp divide between the philosophies of Islam and of Hinduism, their mode of worship, and the attitude that laid down the rules for their conduct and their social structure.

The Muslim faith was staunchly monotheistic and abhorred the worship of idols while the Hindus believed in many gods and goddesses and their religion revolved around the worship of the physical manifestation of these gods and goddesses.

The Muslim invaders came into India with a firm belief that all fellow Muslims were equal and there was a total absence of any feeling of distinction along the lines of profession or social position. The concept of caste was completely alien to them. As such they were bound to come into conflict with the Hindus for whom social order and social conduct were determined by the caste system. The Muslims were meat

3

eaters and consumed beef, whereas the Hindus were essentially vegetarian and venerated the cow. It was only natural that the Hindus should regard the Muslims' consumption of their sacred animal with horror.

Both the Hindus and the Muslims practised congregational prayers but there was a marked difference in their prayers. The Muslims bowed to the west, in the direction of the Ka'aba while the Hindus bowed to the East. Music, in the form of the singing of *bhajans*, was an integral part of the Hindu worship while the Muslims forbade all forms of music within the precincts of the mosque. Bhai Gurdas emphasises the difference: "The Hindus turn to the Ganges, the Muslims to the Ka'aba in Mecca. The Muslims take to circumcision, while the Hindus stick to their thread. The Hindus worship Ram, they Rahim" (Bhai Gurdas, *Var* 1:21).

The Muslims believed in the Day of Judgement, when the dead would rise from their graves and be judged by God for their deeds. With this in mind the Muslims buried their dead. The Hindus believed in the transmigration of the soul and the theory of *karma*. Just as a man discarded an old and worn out set of clothes, so too did the soul abandon this body upon death. Rebirth was determined by the actions in man's previous birth. If he had accumulated good *karma*, he would be reborn in a higher plane. If not, he would be condemned to a life of hardship and suffer the effects of his bad *karma*. The Hindu was thus encouraged to engage in meritorious deeds and evolve to an ever-higher plane, so that ultimately his soul would be granted *moksha* or freedom from the cycle of birth and death. Since the body was merely like a discarded set of clothes, it was cremated after death.

Even with these basic differences it would perhaps have been possible, as it had been in the past, for the conqueror and the conquered to come to terms with each other and evolve a way of life where their differences of belief and faith could be accommodated comfortably. But the new religion, by its very nature, precluded such an accommodation. The Muslim leader or ruler firmly believed that it was his sacred duty to root out heresy and spread Islam, even if it meant waging *jehad* and carrying out conversions at the point of a sword. Since the Prophet's philosophy had forbidden all idol worship and had resulted in the destruction of the idols that the Semitic tribes before him had worshipped, the Hindus, with their emphasis on idolatry as an integral part of their faith, were especially abhorrent to the Muslims. The conquerors also felt that if the natives were compelled to change their religion to Islam, their subjugation would be complete and permanent. The Hindus were considered a threat to Muslim rule and they were subjected to every kind of humiliation and brutality in an attempt to force them to convert to Islam. "Islam generates more passion among its follower than any other religion. It does not believe in turning the other cheek but in hitting back. To be a Muslim means to accept that your life is well lost if it is in defence of your faith. You become a martyr with an assured place in paradise." (Singh, Khushwant, *This above All: Why Islam is different* [Tribune, May 21, 2005])

Islam is unlike any other religion; it does not believe that one's belief is one's personal business. Islam looks upon religion as a social obligation and does not approve of separating religion from politics or government. For Islam, the state and religion are inseparable. "It must not be forgotten that the very essence of Islam is both a religion and a system of governing a church state" (Titus, Murray, *Islam in India & Pakistan*, p.14).

For almost five hundred years the Hindus groaned under the yoke of Muslim rule—the cruelties and barbarism heaped upon them in the name of religion were beyond anything that they had had to endure in the past. Islam recognised only two kinds of people: the *Ahal–i-Islam* or Muslims and the *Ahal–i–Kitab* or those who believed in the revealed book, to which category belonged the Christians. The rest were regarded as *Dar-ul-Harb* or infidels, and it was the duty of the true Muslim to convert these to Islam. Islam tolerated the non-idolaters among the infidels but subjected these *zimmis* to a special tax, called *jeziya*. After the first brutal efforts to forcibly convert all Hindus to Islam, the rulers recognised the sheer impossibility of the task they had undertaken. As a compromise, even though the Hindus were idolaters, they were categorised as *zimmis* and subjected to the *jeziya*. It is a different matter that, more often than not, the *jeziya* levied on the Hindus was so high that the poorer amongst them chose to convert to Islam rather than starve to death.

Visits to places of pilgrimage were an essential part of the Hindu tradition. In an attempt to destroy this tradition, a heavy tax was levied on every pilgrimage, while a poor Muslim was encouraged to go on the mandatory *Haj* to the holy cities of Mecca and Medina by an extremely generous state subsidy. The irony of the situation could only have made the Hindus more belligerent in their opposition to Muslim rule. Hindus were also debarred from holding positions of high office, no matter how intelligent and capable they were. So much so, that many Muslim rulers laid down a law that Hindus were not allowed to wear fine clothes or even ride horses. They were not allowed to build new temples or repair old ones which had fallen into disrepair. In other words, the undeclared effort was to let time and the weather destroy all places of Hindu worship. "Hindu temples were razed to the ground and at those very places and with the same material mosques were raised" (Bhai Gurdas, *Var* 1:20).

Certain religious fairs, which provided an opportunity for the mass-scale gatherings of Hindus, were prohibited. Any Hindu who showed signs of becoming a political or militant leader was immediately looked upon as an enemy of the state and every effort was directed towards destroying him at the earliest.

In spite of all these repressive measures, the Muslim conquerors did not achieve notable success in the conversion of the vast Hindu majority. In fact, the Muslims who had succeeded in converting the entire populations of Arabia, Iraq, Turkey, Egypt, Iran, and Afghanistan were apparently frustrated in their tremendous and brutal efforts at the conversion of the Hindus. One of the main reasons for their failure was the personal nature of the religion of the Hindus. Hinduism was not an organised religion. It had not been founded by any one spiritual leader nor was there a governing body that wielded influence over the entire community. Some of the lower castes, hoping to find an escape from their inhuman existence, were easily persuaded to convert to the new religion. There were also those who succumbed to the lure of material benefits while a large number of those converted were forced to do so at the point of a sword. But these were scattered populations, and the majority of the people remained true to their faith.

There was a tremendous and bitter hostility between the Muslims and Hindus—a hostility that led to blood-curdling cruelty on the part of the conquerors with increasing frequency. The more they failed in their efforts at conversion, the more determined they became to decimate the resisting natives.

The time was ripe for reformist movements, which would provide some kind of bridge between the two faiths, ease tensions, and permit the followers of Islam and Hinduism to live side by side in a state of harmony. The Sufis had tried to resolve the divide between Hinduism and Islam and had succeeded to some extent. Sufism was the mystical branch of Islam that stressed on intuition rather than any reasoned argument.

The first Sufi orders to be established in India were the Chisti and Suhrawardy orders. The Sufis preached a deep and personal love for God and laid emphasis on the mystical experience that arises from such a love. They believed that just as there was deep anguish in separation from the beloved (God), there was ecstasy of the highest order to be attained through union with God. For the Sufis, God was omnipresent and a true Sufi would remember Him at all times. Tolerance, piety, and equality were essential edicts of the Sufi faith. In Nanak's time, the important centres of the Suhrawardy sect were Lahore and Multan, while the Chisti sect had centres in Thanesar, Jhansi, Narnaul, and Panipat. But the most important centre of the Sufi tradition was at Pak Pattan, where Sheikh Fariduddin Ganj-i-Shakar had his seat.

The religious tradition of the Hindus had been subjected to reform from the earliest times. Buddha and Mahavira had established the heterodox schools of Buddhism and Jainism almost two millennia before Nanak. The widespread acceptance of their doctrine led Sankara, in the 8th century AD, to spearhead the revival of Hinduism. He enunciated the philosophy of *Advaita* or Monism, declaring that *Brahman*, the all-pervasive spirit in the universe, was the only true Reality and that the individual soul, *atman*, was but a manifestation of this eternal being.

Sankara was followed by Ramanujacharya, who taught that man was a part of God but not identical with Him, in his philosophy of *Vishishta Advaita*, or Qualified Monism. Madhavacharya proclaimed, however, that man was forever a devotee or servant of God and he established a dualistic school within the folds of Hindu philosophy.

The Bhakti movement, which commenced with the Alvars in Tamil Nadu, was an important religious and social movement that gave an impetus to change. "Bhakti" implies intense love for God and, according to Hindu philosophy, is the simplest path to salvation. The proponents of Bhakti preached equality, doing away with the rigid barriers of caste and creed. Emphasising that anyone could reach the Almighty by surrendering to Him, the movement had a profound impact on the people. Over time, the Bhakti movement gained momentum and spread all over India, bringing much-needed reform in the Hindu religion.

In Northern India, the first truly reformist sect was established by Ramananda, in Benaras about 1400 AD. Ramananda was a *bhakt* of Lord Rama, an incarnation of Vishnu. His followers were called

7

Vaishnavas because he preached total devotion and surrender to Vishnu. Like all the Bhakti saints, he believed in the equality of man and welcomed followers from all classes of society. During the same period, Gorakhnath, a follower of Lord Shiva, preached the doctrine of yoga. He taught that by sustained mental concentration, anyone, whatever his caste, could be liberated and united with the Great Soul. His doctrine prescribed extreme discipline and an austere life. These two movements sought to destroy distinctions of race or caste by preaching faith and the abandonment of the pleasures of life.

Kabir, the mystic weaver, was the foremost proponent of the Bhakti movement in the North. He emphasised a loving devotion to God and preached that salvation was achieved not through knowledge but through the grace of one's Guru and through a faithful adherence to the faith. He was the first to attempt to break the stronghold of the learned mullahs and erudite pandits who regarded themselves as custodians of all religious knowledge and learning. His teachings were largely drawn from those of Ramananda but he addressed both Hindus and Muslims alike. He attacked the worship of idols and the total authority that the Qur'an and the *Shastras* wielded over the spiritual life of the people. In an attempt to reach out to the masses, he deliberately avoided the use of learned language and even today, one of the most endearing qualities of Kabir's teachings is that he employs metaphors and imagery drawn from the day-to-day life of the ordinary man. He called upon both Hindus and Muslims to strive continually for inner purity. He referred to this world as *maya*, an illusion. *Maya* was a deceitful mistress, working constantly to entrap man in her wiles. However, Kabir limited the application of his preaching by his assertion that the most desirable condition for man was to reject this material world and so escape the allurements of *maya*. Other leading proponents of the Bhakti movement of the time were Ramdas, Mira, and Tulsidas.

Chaitanya, a Brahmin from Bengal, followed the Bhakti movement in asserting that it was love for the divine that led to salvation but he did not preach detachment from the world. His disciples lived the lives of householders and found a balance between the spiritual and the material worlds.

Thus, by the time Nanak evolved his philosophy, the Hindu mind was used to debate, questioning, and reform. It had been awakened by the work of the reformists and was also influenced by some radical ideas from Islam. Ramananda and Gorakhnath had brought the

8

message of equality in religion, a message that was further strengthened by Chaitanya. Kabir had denounced idol worship and the dictatorial authority of the religious texts. He had further destroyed the stranglehold of Arabic and Sanskrit on religion by preaching in a language which the simplest and most illiterate of men could understand.

"But all these reformers were so impressed with the nothingness of life that they did not feel that improving man's social condition was worthy of thought. They aimed chiefly at freedom from priesthood and from idolatry and polytheism. They gave themselves up entirely to contemplation in the hope of future bliss and freedom from the cycles of birth and death. They did or preached nothing that would give their disciples freedom from social and religious bondage and from the debasing corruption of the ages. They perfected forms of dissent rather than planted the germs of nations. As a result, over the following centuries their sects remained as they had left them." (Cunningham, J.D., *History of the Sikhs*)

In their purest form, both Sufism and Bhakti focussed on the individual's private experience and did not have the attributes to become commonly accepted religions. It was left to Nanak to preach precepts that would provide the foundation of a new religion which would be acceptable both to the Hindus and the Muslims.

BIRTH AND CHILDHOOD

Talwandi is a little town about sixty miles from Lahore and twenty miles from Wazirabad, on the road to Lahore. It is now known as Nankana Sahib, in honour of Nanak who was born here, and is an important centre of pilgrimage. But it remains essentially a small town of little strategic importance. It was otherwise in the years preceding Nanak's birth. Its location in central Punjab, almost halfway between the rivers Ravi and Beas, placed it directly in the path of all those who came to India. Because it lay on the route followed by traders, it quickly became prosperous. But because it also lay on the path of the numerous invading hordes, it attracted their greed and wrath, and was pillaged, ravaged, and often destroyed altogether. But the village refused to die. Each time it was burnt or reduced to dust, it resolutely rose again in defiance of the invader's might, very much like the legendary Phoenix. Thirteen times Talwandi was destroyed and thirteen times it rose stronger and more beautiful than before.

The last time it was rebuilt was under the supervision of a new chieftain named Rai Bhoe. Rai Bhoe was a Bhatti Rajput by birth, but like many military leaders of the time, he had converted to Islam. While "Raja" denoted a king, no matter how small, "Rai" was a title that denoted a prince or a chieftain of a district, a little town, or even of a village. Considering the feudal system that prevailed during those times and the large degree of autonomy that each administrative unit enjoyed, "Rai" was far from being merely an honorific title. It carried with it much authority and power. Rai Bhoe exercised such authority. He made sure that Talwandi was rebuilt along well-planned lines. He built a fort strong enough to withstand any future invasions. He set up an administrative structure that encouraged growth and provided the basis for the well-being and prosperity of the inhabitants. It was only a matter of time before Talwandi became a popular stop for caravans on the trade route to Delhi. The prosperity and security of Talwandi attracted more and more people, who sought to make a permanent home within its walls.

Among these people was a Bedi family that had migrated from a village close to Amritsar. The head of the family was Shiv Ram Bedi, an honest, hard-working man, who made his living as a grain merchant. He was determined to do well by his family and give them a decent home in Talwandi. It was not long before his honesty and industry earned him an enviable reputation, word of which soon reached the ears of the chieftain.

Rai Bhoe would often come to observe Shiv Ram at work and to pass the time of day with him. He soon realised that Shiv Ram had a remarkable facility in money matters, especially in keeping accounts. He requested Shiv Ram to come in once in a while to monitor the keeping of his revenue records. Shiv Ram's monitoring resulted in such a remarkable improvement in efficiency, and consequent increase in revenues, that Rai Bhoe offered him the post of Chief Accounts Officer at a salary far in excess of his earnings as a grain merchant.

So it was that Shiv Ram became an important and influential member of the Rai's staff. Before long, the Bedis had one of the biggest houses in the village, extensive tracts of agricultural land and a large herd of cows and buffaloes. They were looked upon as a family of repute and influence in Talwandi.

Although Shiv Ram was an employee, there was an ease and camaraderie that developed between the two men because of their mutual respect for each other. Sometimes of an evening, the Rai would wander down to the Bedis' house and the two men would sit together on a rope cot in the courtyard and exchange views. The evening hours would glide away, the shadows dissolve into the dark. Often a message would arrive from the Rai's household summoning him back and, much against their will, the two men would take leave of each other.

The relationship forged such deep bonds of affection and friendship that it was as if they had now become part of each other's families. In spite of belonging to different, almost hostile, religions, they participated in each other's festivals and family functions. With this kind of affinity and mutual respect, it was only natural that when Shiv Ram died, his son Kalyan Chand step into his father's shoes in the employ of Rai Bhoe.

Kalyan had done a long apprenticeship with his father and observed him closely while he worked. He was an intelligent boy who emulated

his father and had learnt to appreciate the value of hard work. Kalyan
Chand proved to be an even greater asset to the Bhatti family than his
father had been. He and Bular, Rai Bhoe's son, had played together as
children and had grown up into manhood together. After Rai Bhoe's
death, Bular assumed the position of the Rai of Talwandi, and the
Bhattis and the Bedis were linked even more closely than before. When
Kalyan Chand was married to Tripta, daughter of Rama of Chahalwala,
a village south of Lahore, there was great rejoicing in both the
households.

But as the days lengthened into months, and the months into years
and Tripta remained without child, a strange uneasiness descended
upon the Bedi household. Rai Bular consoled his friend by assuring him
that although God sometimes deemed it fit to hold back the gift of a
child for a long period of time, he almost always rewarded the years of
waiting. But as the years stretched on, Kalyan found it increasingly
difficult to wait patiently for God's benevolence. He became restless and
moody. He would wake up from his sleep and pace the courtyard till
dawn broke in the eastern sky. He lost interest in food and often left his
meal unfinished to go for long walks in the fields.

Tripta tried everything she could to coax her husband out of his
melancholy and when she failed, a deep sadness descended upon her.
She was destined to be barren, she told herself. She had failed in one of
her major responsibilities as a wife; she had failed to provide a son and
heir to the Bedi family. In her despair she turned more and more to
religion, in the hope of finding some solace in prayer. On a hillock about
a mile out of Talwandi was a picturesque temple that was approached by
a flight of steep, white-washed steps. Tripta took to visiting this temple
often. After making her offering to the deity, she would sit under a
spreading *pipal* tree to contemplate the countryside that stretched into
the distance. Sometimes she would lose track of time and the priest
would have to gently prod her to return home. One day, as she sat under
the *pipal* pondering over her plight, she suddenly knew what she had to
do. She had to convince Kalyan to take another wife—a wife who would
give him a child. This was a step that was common in those days—when
the first wife could not conceive, a second wife was brought into the
household. What was not common was that the first wife herself should
make this suggestion. When Tripta broached the subject to her husband,
he drew her to his breast and wept like a child. He loved her too much
to even think of relegating her to a secondary position in his life.

Rai Bular, too, worried for his friend. He suggested a step which he felt might bring Kalyan some measure of peace: Kalyan Chand should go on a pilgrimage to the five *dhams* and beseech the gods to be merciful to him and Tripta. And so it was that Kalyan or Mehta Kalo, as he was popularly known in Talwandi, set out on his pilgrimage as a wandering mendicant.

After two months of arduous travel, he reached the second pilgrimage centre. Over the years, this centre had grown into a little township around the main temple. In the compound stood two ancient trees, protecting pilgrims from the fierce heat of the sun. Radiating from the temple was a maze of steep cobbled streets lined with shops and *dharamshalas*. In spite of the throng of pilgrims and the lively hustle-bustle of the bazaar outside, an ineffable peace and quiet pervaded the temple complex.

Kalo had covered vast distances on foot, suffering the heat and the rain. He had lived like the *fakirs* on whatever food he could obtain through begging. Now, when he reached the holy shrine, he had been without food for four days. When he stopped to rest his weary limbs at the entrance to the shrine, he caught the eye of a well-to-do pilgrim, who sat with his family under a huge sprawling tree, finishing his evening meal. The pilgrim looked closely at the dishevelled and travel-worn *fakir*; it was obvious to him that the man had not eaten for many days. He picked up the little food he had left and offered it to the *fakir*. "Forgive me, Baba, for this meagre offering. Perhaps I could give you a small gift of money to buy yourself some food."

Kalo smiled up at him through the dust and grime that lined his face. "It is most kind of you—but I cannot accept any money." He looked down at the packet of food, meagre by any standards, and said, "I assure you that this is more than enough for my needs."

He watched the pilgrim walk away, herding his small group of children along. Then he turned and found his way to a well at the rear of the temple compound. Placing his packet of food and his bundle of spare clothing in a safe corner, he bathed and washed his dusty, sweat-streaked clothes and hung them out to dry. Donning fresh clothes, he settled down on a little brick platform to enjoy the food the pilgrim had given him. But before he could put the first morsel of food in his mouth, he became aware of someone watching him closely. He looked up and saw an old *fakir*, thin and gaunt, with a long, grizzled beard, and matted hair coiled around his head.

13

Kalo smiled and held out the packet of food. The *fakir* accepted it gratefully and seating himself on the platform next to Kalo, began to eat. It was obvious from the way he wolfed down the food that he too had not eaten for many days. There was little food and it was soon finished

"You are not really a *fakir*," he said to Kalo. "What is it that brings you on this pilgrimage? What great boon do you seek that makes you live the life of a mendicant, subsisting on the generosity of others?"

"I seek the boon of a child. God, in his wisdom, has not seen fit to bless my wife and me with a child, even though we have been married for many years now. So I come as a mendicant, a beggar, to the five *dhams*, to seek divine intervention."

The *fakir* smiled, "You do not need to seek divine intervention. It will come to you of its own accord because there is already great divinity in you. Only a true man of God would give away the little food that he has, even when he himself has known hunger for many days." He touched Kalo's shoulder in a gentle gesture of blessing. "Go home, son, and be with your wife. She needs you more than ever in these difficult times. God is only testing you. Your life, in its goodness, is itself a pilgrimage, and will bring the blessings that you seek. Go home now; I know that God will give you the gift of a child."

So Kalo abandoned his pilgrimage and returned home, a strange radiance emanating from his face, and a stillness permeating his spirit. Tripta, seeing her husband so much at peace, felt a deep, warm happiness descend upon her and harmony was at last restored to the Bedi household.

It was as the *fakir* had predicted. A year after Kalo's encounter with the strange old *fakir*, Tripta found herself heavy with child. As was the custom in those days, when her time was near, she returned to her parents' home in Chahalwala, and it was there that a beautiful, healthy daughter was born to her. It was also a custom in those days that a boy or a girl born in the maternal grandparents' home, or *nankeh*, was often named Nanak or Nanki. Kalo and Tripta's little girl was thus named Nanki.

She was a happy, cheerful baby who grew into a gregarious child. She won the hearts of all those who came into contact with her. Her parents doted on her, and the Bhatti household, happy that the Bedis had at last been granted this great boon, made much of her. Nanki had everything that her little heart desired; everything, that is, except a sibling. As she grew older, she would throw tantrums and insist that her parents bring home a baby brother for her. When she watched other brothers and sisters at play, she would break into uncontrollable weeping and pray that God would give her a brother too. She did not have long to wait—God, in his mercy, answered the little child's prayer, and when Nanki was four years old, Tripta was again heavy with child.

Early in the pregnancy, Daulatan, the midwife, read the signs that only midwives can, and predicted firmly that the child would be a boy. As the months passed, the elderly women of the neighbourhood endorsed the midwife's prediction. Mehta Kalo, who had so desperately wanted a male child, found his heart filling with hope. He could not bear to let Tripta out of his sight. Four times a day, he would abandon whatever he was doing and rush home to see if his wife was all right. Rai Bular, who had been witness to his friend's long years of suffering, was an indulgent employer and did not hold this against him. So great was Kalo's anxiety that when it was time for Tripta to leave for Chahalwala, he made a departure from tradition and insisted that the child be born in Talwandi. He requested Tripta's mother to stay with her in Talwandi during the difficult time, a request she readily acceded to and which brought great comfort to the expectant mother.

And so it was that on the night of *Vaisakha Sudi* 3, corresponding to April 15, 1469, Tripta went into labour. With Daulatan and her mother in attendance, Tripta was confident and at ease. Not so her husband Kalo, who paced up and down the moonlit courtyard, imagining all kinds of things that could go wrong. Rai Bular had looked in on his friend once and tried to reassure him. Realising that this was an anxiety that Kalo had to deal with alone, he told Daulatan "send for me if anything is needed" and went quietly home.

Now Kalo agonised over his decision to keep Tripta in Talwandi for her delivery. What if something went wrong? Then he dismissed the thought as a weak one, born out of a desire to absolve himself of responsibility. He knew he could not have borne the suspense of not knowing if he had indeed been blessed with a son. Suddenly, a sharp cry broke the stillness of the night. But it was not the cry of a newborn baby—it sounded more like a peal of laughter! Kalo stopped in his tracks, his heart missed a beat, and he could feel the blood drain from his face. Then, after what seemed an eternity, Daulatan appeared at the doorway, a little swaddled baby in her arms. "Congratulations Mehta Sahib—it's a boy!" she announced, enunciating each syllable clearly in her old quavering voice. "He is a very special child. In all my years as a midwife, I have never seen a birth like this one. Did you hear him laugh?" The blood had rushed back to Kalo's face. In one leap, he climbed the two steps of the courtyard. He took a gold coin out of his pocket and, waving it around the baby's head, gave it to Daulatan. The aged midwife held up the swaddled baby for the father to see. The light of the moon fell upon the little face. The eyes were closed, the cheeks were puckered, and the face was red and mottled. Yet, to Kalo, he was the most beautiful baby the world had ever seen. He swept the baby into his arms. "Only for a moment," Daulatan cautioned. Kalo held the baby close to his heart, overcome with gratitude at God's bounty, and turned away so that the midwife could not see the tears glistening in his eyes. When Daulatan reached out for the baby, it was with the greatest reluctance that Kalo handed him back.

In spite of the unearthly hour, Kalo knew what had to be done immediately. He hurried through the streets, stumbling in the dark, till he came to the house of one of the most respected inhabitants of the village—Pandit Hardayal. The pandit was a highly erudite man. He had made a deep study of the religious texts, not only of the Hindus, but also of the Muslims. Yet he had none of the arrogance or impatience that characterised men of great learning and intellect. If there was any display of his learning, it was only in his efforts to practice what he had studied and learnt. Unlike most priests and mullahs of the time, Pandit Hardayal showed great tolerance for all faiths and castes. He lived a simple life, demanding or expecting nothing from those who sought his help in performing rituals, in casting horoscopes, or in resolving day-to-day problems. His advice, drawn as it was from his deep study and long years of experience, was always practical and down to earth, and within the realm of practice of the simple villager.

Kalo hesitated at the doorway, loath to knock, loath to disturb the sleep of the elderly pandit. But then, the need for casting an accurate horoscope came upon him with pressing urgency, and raising the heavy iron ring, he knocked on the door.

"Just a moment. I am coming," answered a voice, and a few moments later, Kalo saw the tall, gaunt figure of the priest framed in the doorway. The flickering light of his oil lamp showed a man who, though stooped with age, had bright and clear eyes, and who sported a luxuriant walrus moustache that gave him an air of distinction. He recognised Kalo and smiled. "So it is a son! I was expecting you," he said, as he turned and led his nocturnal visitor into a small room where he carefully placed the lamp in an alcove. Sitting cross-legged at a low desk, he drew out a sheet of handmade paper.

"When was he born?" he asked.

"Just a few moments ago, Panditji. I have come directly to you," replied Kalo.

The pandit began drawing tables on the sheet of paper and filling them in with numbers as Kalo watched with bated breath. He felt a wave of affection well up within him. Through his personal example, the pandit had been a role model for most of the villagers. His simple life, his total lack of attachment to material things, the absence of desire from his life, his equal concern for the Hindus and Muslims—all this endeared him to the villagers who had nothing but respect and kind words for the pandit.

At last, after what seemed an eternity, the pandit looked up. His face had a look of awe and when he spoke, his voice, though soft and gentle as always, had a hushed quality to it—he knew he was imparting tidings of great import.

"You are truly blessed Kalo—a great and divine soul has taken birth in your house today. Your son is born to a greatness that comes to this world but rarely. His light will spread far and wide, bringing radiance to these dark times. Your son will be revered by both, the Hindu and the Turk." He folded the horoscope and handed it to Kalo. "Keep this carefully. I will read it for you and explain the signs whenever you feel the need."

Kalo hesitated, wondering what offering he could make without offending the pandit. Sensing his hesitation, Pandit Hardayal smiled. "I have given you great tidings and you must make a special offering. Send me a sack of wheat and a *seer* of *mishri* when it is daylight. Go home now. I will come on the thirteenth day to name the child. May God always bless him and your fortunate household." Kalo touched the pandit's feet and returned to his house.

The next day, when the village awoke to the news of the birth of Kalo's son and the wonderful prediction that Pandit Hardayal had made for his future, there was great rejoicing in Talwandi. All through the day, the villagers converged on Kalo's house to congratulate him on his good fortune, and all day the household was kept busy providing sweets and other refreshments to the visitors. Messengers were sent out to friends and relatives in the neighbouring villages to tell them the good news and to invite them to the naming ceremony.

The days that followed were filled with lots of activity and preparation for the ceremony. Through all the excitement, little Nanki sat cross-legged, her baby brother on her lap, giving him up reluctantly only to be fed, bathed and cleaned. If people asked to hold him, she would shake her little head and say "no, he is mine" and everyone began to refer to him as "Nanki's baby."

On the auspicious day, Kalo's house was filled with noise and laughter as his guests arrived and exchanged greetings. The courtyard was filled to capacity and people spilled over on to the terrace, braving the strong April sun to witness the ceremony and to hear the name the pandit would give to the baby for whom he had predicted such a tremendous future. At last the pandit came and a hush fell over the courtyard. He recited the mandatory prayers, as Kalo and Tripta sat opposite him across the sacred fire, performing the prescribed rituals. When the prayers were done, he took the baby from the reluctant Nanki's lap. He looked carefully at the baby's face, and then held him up for all to see. "He is truly Nanki's baby and to ensure that he always remains so, I name him 'Nanak'."

There was a collective sigh from the crowd and though it was difficult to tell whether people were pleased or disappointed, the broad, dimpled smile on Nanki's face clearly revealed her joy.

Other than Nanki, the person who was most delighted by Nanak's arrival was Kalo's neighbour—Sayyad Hassan. He had come but recently to Talwandi and, strangely for those times, had chosen to take a house in the Hindu quarter of the village. It is true that in spite of the great hostility that existed between the people of the two faiths, there were often bonds of friendship and affection that crossed the divide, the most notable being the mutual respect and affection that existed between the Bedis and the Bhattis. But, in spite of these bonds, when it came to a choice of residence, people preferred to live among their own. So when Sayyad Hassan and his wife first moved into the house next to Kalo's, there was much raising of eyebrows and mutterings under the breath. The Hindus living in the quarter gave him a wide berth. Even the good-natured Kalo and Tripta, after their initial visit to welcome their new neighbour, had kept their distance.

Sayyad Hassan was a quiet, unassuming man, who lived a simple, unpretentious life. He was obviously a great scholar because he had a large library—more books than the people of Talwandi had ever seen. He was clearly a man of some means, always elegantly turned out, with his hair and beard immaculately kept. If he noticed the suspicion and wariness of his Hindu neighbours, he did not show it. He did not seek interaction with them but he did not actively avoid it either. Gradually, he established his goodwill and his neighbours came to see him for what he was—a quiet, well-meaning individual who respected the privacy of others and their way of life. In his unobtrusive way, he was ever-willing to help, whenever it was required.

Now, with the arrival of Nanak, Sayyad Hassan was reticent no longer. He and his wife spent hours in Kalo's household, looking into the baby's face and playing with him whenever Nanki would permit them. They even took to bribing Nanki to bring the baby to their house. Tripta saw the radiant smiles on their faces as they played with her son and she sent up a silent thanks to heaven, for her child had brought joy and happiness not only to her own household, but also to the childless home of her neighbours. She liked to feel that the state of blessedness that Pandit Hardayal had predicted for her son was already at play.

The excitement of those early days soon faded into the humdrum routine of everyday life in the village. In the first few years of his life, there was little to mark Nanak with the extraordinariness and greatness that Pandit Hardayal had predicted for him. It is true that those who came into contact with him came away with a favourable impression and a desire to meet him again. But this was not unusual and could be said of many little children in their infancy. By the time he was five, however, he began displaying the traits that would mark him out for the rest of his life. He was unfailingly gentle. Children often got into fights with each other or quarrelled over each others' possessions, but not Nanak. He never raised his voice, never used abusive language, and if another child coveted one of his toys, he gladly gave it to him. Innumerable were the wooden carts and balls that Nanak parted with and innumerable were the efforts that Tripta made to instil in him a sense of possessiveness about his belongings.

"It was your toy, Nanak," she would say with gentle firmness. "It was bought for you to play with. Ram Rakha has his own toys. You must hold on to what is yours—if you keep giving away what belongs to you, you will soon have nothing left and what will you do then? No one will give you what is theirs."

He would listen intently but the very next moment he would give away the *pinni* that Tripta had made for him. He was never able to learn the concept of "mine" and "yours" and soon Tripta, though still disapproving, gave up her lectures in despair. Nanki, however, observed her brother's generosity with admiration. She would watch with glowing pride as he parted with yet another toy or sweet, her pride blossoming in spite of the shadow of her mother's disapproval.

Nanak showed equal respect and affection for all, irrespective of age or caste or creed. One day, he returned from play and when they sat down for the evening meal, he declared he was not hungry. Tripta put her hand to his forehead to see if he had a fever. "Are you feeling well?"

"I am fine, Mother. I was passing Shambhu's house and saw him eating his meal. I was so hungry that when he asked me to join him, I sat down and shared his meal. My stomach is full now and I can eat no more." Tripta and Kalo exchanged glances. Tripta waited for Kalo to speak and when he didn't, she took it upon herself to explain things to her son.

"You must never eat in Shambhu's house again," she said.

"Why? He eats here when his mother comes to clean and sweep," said Nanak, puzzled.

"That is different. They are Shudras, untouchables, and you are a Khatri. Their food is polluted, unclean, and you will defile your caste if you eat with them."

"But the food was not unclean," Nanak protested. "In fact, it was very tasty. There was *allu vadi* and it was more delicious than the *allu vadi* that you make. Shambhu's mother even put a little ghee on my *chapatti*."

Tripta was perturbed. It was going to be an uphill task to teach Nanak to observe caste rules. When would the boy ever learn? If he continued like this, he would become an outcaste among his own people and they would be shunned by all their friends and relatives. She sighed and shook her head.

She needn't have worried. With his affable nature and his concern and respect for all those around him, Nanak was forgiven this apparently strange behaviour. He would outgrow this, people said indulgently, he would soon learn the distinction of caste.

Nanak had a special corner in his heart for Sayyad Hassan and his wife. Perhaps, even as a child, he had sensed the loneliness of the childless couple and sought to spend as much time as he could with them, because it brought them happiness. Perhaps he was fascinated by the wealth of knowledge—literature, philosophy, history, astronomy— that was contained in Hassan's library. But from his conversation it was soon apparent that Sayyad Hassan exerted a tremendous influence on his young mind—an influence that could not but broaden the child's mind and make him aware of a world beyond Talwandi, long before people much older than him became aware of that world.

"Tell me, Hassan Sahib," Nanak asked his mentor one day, "I have heard talk of *jehad*, the fight that Muslims are called upon to fight against all enemies of Islam. Does it mean that every Muslim has to kill anyone who is opposed to him?"

Sayyad Hassan smiled at the earnestness in the boy's eyes and in his voice. He ruffled the little boy's hair. "You must understand the difference between an enemy of a Mussalman and an enemy of Islam. Each Mussalman, or even Hindu for that matter, is bound, through his conduct and his speech, to make some enemy in his life. It is not this enemy that a true Muslim is called upon to fight against. *Jehad*, or holy war, is to be fought against any force that interferes with a Muslim's practice of Islam. And *jehad* must first be fought within a Muslim's soul. The forces of both good and evil exist in our souls and the forces that interfere with our following the right path are evil. Islam calls upon its followers to subdue and conquer these evil forces within us by waging a *jehad* against them ... only then can we be true Muslims."

Nanak pondered over Sayyad Hassan's words for a while and then, in a perplexed voice, he said, "But this is true not only of Muslims. Hindus, too, must subdue and conquer the evil within them before they can hope to become true Hindus." Sayyad Hassan was pleased by Nanak's perception. "Exactly, my son. So you can see there is not that much of a difference between the real practice of Hinduism and Islam as our *maulvis* and pandits would have us believe."

But there was stirring of gossip in Talwandi, disapproval at a Hindu child spending so much time in a Muslim household. Would Sayyad Hassan try to convert the Bedi child to Islam? But nothing that the child did or said suggested that Hassan had been proselytising. And when they saw him participating in all the Hindu prayers and rituals with enthusiasm, this suspicion was stilled and put aside. Once again Nanak's regard for the Hassans was accepted as something that he would outgrow.

Very early on, Nanki recognised this special quality in her little brother—his ability to treat all people equally: the Shudra and the Khatri, the Hindu and the Mussalman, the friend and the foe. She knew that this was a very unusual quality and recognised in it the greatness that had been predicted for her brother.

There was someone else who saw and recognised what the little girl had sensed. That was Rai Bular. He had a special fondness for Nanak. The little boy sometimes came with a message for his father and the Rai would draw him into conversation. While walking through the streets of Talwandi, he would often stop to watch Nanak play with the other children. Yes, the boy's attitude and behaviour were so mature for his years that they almost seemed precocious. There was no denying that he was an extraordinary child who merited special attention and special treatment.

Another quality of Nanak's that drew attention and comment was the fact that he appeared to be totally self-contained. He could be by himself for hours without the need to interact with other human beings, without the need for toys and playmates. Even when he allowed himself to be drawn into play with the other boys, there was an element of aloofness in his participation. He seemed lost in his own thoughts, following a stream of consciousness that was entirely his own, living in a private world which he was unwilling to share with others. And yet, his gentleness, his kindness, and his affable nature made everyone forgive him this strangeness and put it down as something he would outgrow.

His aloofness did not preclude the companionship of two boys from the village. One was Bala, a Sandhu Jat, and the other was Mardana, who belonged to a family of Muslim Dums, who were singers and *rabab* players. They, more than any other boys of the village, were tolerant of Nanak's moods. When he wished to be left alone, they let him be. Nanak often visited Mardana's house and listened to him while he practised. By now the entire village had accepted that the boy would always ignore caste distinctions and no comments were made at the constant companionship of Mardana and Nanak. With his sharp mind and his ability to absorb everything around him, Nanak soon developed an understanding of the nuances of classical music. He recognised and learnt the various *ragas* and often, when Mardana or other members of his family practised the singing of religious songs, Nanak too would join in. In this way, not only did Nanak build up knowledge of classical music but also a repertoire of devotional music which would stand him in good stead in the future.

Mardana was the same age as Nanak and had a similar build. When strangers saw them together, they often mistook them for brothers. Mardana had always been a carefree, happy-go-lucky child; his lack of seriousness and garrulousness were a perfect foil to Nanak's quiet, introverted nature. If there was one thing that Mardana took seriously, it was his music. His father never had to enforce the strict regimen of the *riyaaz* on Mardana. He happily spent hours studying and practising the intricacies of each of the *ragas* that his father taught him.

Initially, Mardana had been embarrassed by Nanak's presence in his house and his participation in the singing of devotional songs

"Are you not afraid of what your father will say?" he asked, when Nanak had been coming to his home for a month or so.

"What will my father say?"

"He will say that you lose caste by hobnobbing with a family of *marasis* and that you shame him by doing so. He will say that as a Khatri you demean yourself by learning how to sing, that it is an occupation meant only for the lowly *marasis*."

Nanak looked closely at his new friend. "Perhaps you are right. Perhaps my father will, some day, say this to me. But it will not be the truth. The truth is that there is only one caste in the world and that is mankind. As far as singing is concerned, it elevates my spirit and uplifts my heart. There is nothing demeaning about this." He paused to catch his breath. "There can never be any fear in following the truth." And Nanak's friendship with Mardana continued to blossom.

Kalo was perturbed by the growing signs of Nanak's detachment from the world around him. "What will he do in life," he asked Rai Bular, "if he does not interact with people around him? Though he sometimes plays with his friends, he is becoming increasingly aloof and spends hours by himself, wandering through the thick forests and groves around the village. The only activity he seems to take interest in is the music in Mardana's house. What good will these interests do him? Help him to earn a living as a *marasi*? I fail to see how he will achieve the greatness that Pandit Hardayal has predicted."

"Be patient with him, Kalo," Rai Bular advised his friend. "I have observed Nanak closely and have nothing but admiration for him. He has an extremely sharp mind and understands things far more easily than boys much older than he. He is polite, kind, and compassionate, and has no attachment to material things. I have never seen these qualities in one so young before."

"I wish I could share your certainty about his future," replied the anxious father.

They were quiet for a while and then Rai Bular suggested, "Why don't you give him something to occupy his mind? He is seven years old now, old enough to pursue a course of study. Send him to Pandit Gopal so that he can learn to read and write."

And so it was that at the age of seven, Nanak commenced his studies with Pandit Gopal who ran a small school for the village children. On an auspicious day, Nanki and Mehta Kalo took Nanak to Pandit Gopal. Nanak touched the pandit's feet and Mehta Kalo gave the pandit a tray with sweets, rice, betel nut and a silver coin, which Nanki had carried carefully from home.

Nanki would walk her brother to school everyday and then sit quietly to one side while Pandit Gopal conducted his lessons. It was a source of great pride to her that Nanak was the brightest little boy there and was soon able to answer questions which even the older boys could not. In the afternoon she would walk back with her brother, stopping by the *beri* tree to see if it had begun fruiting. Nanak loved to gather a fistful of *bers* and the two would skip their way home, munching on their treat, humming a little tune Nanak had picked up at Mardana's.

Nanki was eager to encourage her brother to study and made sure he revised his lessons everyday. She would take his *patti*, or wooden slate, wash it and give it a coat of *gachni*, the special clay that is used for this purpose, and put it where he would find it dry and ready for use the next morning. She would wash Nanak's clothes, repair the frequent tears that their tree-climbing had caused and stitch on any buttons that had fallen off. She would sit patiently beside him, working on a *phulkari* while he studied. Occasionally, she would ask him what he had been studying and then surprise him by asking questions about that topic. Nanak found comfort in her presence and was motivated to work harder at his studies.

While the other boys were still struggling with their alphabet and the intricacies of grammar, Nanak had, in the space of a year, gone far ahead and was composing poems and writing essays on a variety of subjects. While his classmates had difficulty with multiple digits, Nanak could work the most complex sums in his mind. But Rai Bular's hope, that once he began going to school Nanak would be drawn back into the world of men and would display a desire for social interaction, was belied. If anything, Nanak became more and more withdrawn and spent ever-increasing time in the wooded area around Talwandi. This area was frequented by holy men drawn from all faiths and denominations. There were *fakirs* and dervishes, *sadhus* and ascetics, monks and *tantriks*. Each of them drew a small following from Talwandi and the neighbouring villages. Both Bala and Mardana were amazed to see that when they had finished their discourse and the small congregation had melted away,

Nanak alone sat on to ask questions about what had been said, to seek to understand the significance of the sermon in greater depth.

On occasion, Rai Bular would steal softly into the thicket and listen to his young protégé in earnest debate with the holy men. He would later accompany him to Sayyad Hassan's house, where the boy Nanak sought to understand even further the finer nuances of what he had heard in the forest. Soon, like Nanki, Rai Bular too found his affection and admiration for the young boy transform into a feeling akin to reverence.

At the end of two years Nanak amazed his teacher by composing a poem on his *patti*. The poem had thirty-five stanzas which began serially with each of the thirty-five letters of the Gurmukhi script. Each stanza dealt with a universal truth—like the omnipresence of God, the illusionary nature of the world that surrounds us, and the spiritual value of meditation.

> "… O foolish heart, why do you forget Him?
> When you render your account, O brother,
> Then alone will you be among the educated."
> (*Raga Asa*, Trans. Sarna, Navtej, *The Book of Nanak*, p. 32)

Years later, when Guru Arjun Dev compiled the *Guru Granth Sahib*, this poem, popularly referred to as the *Patti Likhi*, was included in the sacred text. Pandit Gopal, proud of the spiritual depth of his young student's composition, admitted to himself that there was nothing more he could teach the little boy. So when Nanak dropped out of school altogether, Pandit Gopal did not insist that he be made to attend.

The next step in Nanak's education was prompted by his desire to delve deeper into sacred literature. In his discussions with the *sadhus* in the forest, the argument, more often than not, veered to the holy texts, and Nanak found his understanding hampered by his ignorance of Sanskrit. He discussed this with his mentor Sayyad Hassan, who suggested that he take up the study of Sanskrit under the renowned scholar Pandit Brijnath Shastri, who had made Talwandi his home a few years before. Kalo accepted Sayyad Hassan's suggestion with a marked degree of reluctance. He didn't think much good could come from the study of Sanskrit and of the ancient religious texts, but at least Nanak would be gainfully employed and not while away his time roaming around the village and its environs.

As always, Nanak proved to be an adept student and the pandit was delighted to have the opportunity to teach such a bright boy. For a while an element of stability was once again restored to Nanak's life and to the Bedi household.

The Punjab, during the Sultanate period and during the Lodhi rule, did not form one administrative unit. It was divided into smaller units such as Multan, Dyalpur, Lahore, Jallandhar, Sirhind and Samana. Each of these units had its own governor who was directly accountable to the ruler in Delhi. At the time of our story, the governor of Jallandhar was Nawab Daulat Khan Lodhi, with his capital in Sultanpur. He was a powerful and capable ruler and under him there was no laxity in collecting revenue from the villages and towns of the region. During these years, the governor's *Amil* who came to collect the revenue from Talwandi was a handsome, intelligent young Khatri by the name of Jai Ram. Jai Ram was the son of Parmanand Patta, a minister with Daulat Khan Lodhi. Though he sometimes displayed flashes of the arrogance and impatience that often comes from being close to the seat of authority and power, he was a genial, polite man with a great sense of humour. As a result he was well-liked by the people he came into contact with in Talwandi. Rai Bular had occasion to observe him at close quarters and was drawn to the young man. When they sat together of an evening, talking about sundry matters, Rai Bular felt the years slip away from him. Soon the level of familiarity and friendship achieved permitted them to discuss matters of a very personal nature.

Thus it was that Rai Bular felt free to ask his friend why he did not marry and start a family, now that he was so well-established in his job.

"My parents have not been able to find a suitable Khatri girl for me," he replied with a laugh. "Well, actually, they did find a few girls but at that time I wasn't ready for marriage and now that I do want to get married, they refuse to find me one. They were so embarrassed by my refusal to even meet the girls they had found for me that they do not want to get involved again. It seems I must find a girl myself."

"Then why don't you?"

"My job keeps me busy—besides, I cannot trust my judgement in so serious a matter." Both the friends laughed at this and then Jai Ram said, "But *your* judgement I do trust. Why don't you find a girl for me?"

"And if you refuse to see her?" Again there was laughter.

But long after Jai Ram had left for Sultanpur, his remarks, jocular as they were, stayed on the Bhatti's mind. It was time for Jai Ram to get married and start a family. He was sure that in Talwandi there would be a Khatri girl who would make a suitable bride. His thoughts turned immediately to Nanki and his heart leapt with joy. Yes, she would make a perfect match for the *Amil*. He had seen Nanki often when she came with a message for her father and on his own, not infrequent, visits to the Bedi household. He had seen the sweet little girl grow into a beautiful young woman who was selfless and content with very little. She always found the time to bring a little warmth to the lives of the old and the infirm. As a result, her face glowed with the inner radiance that comes when people give freely of themselves. Yes, she would make a highly suitable bride for Jai Ram.

It was a time when girls were married very young and according to the prevailing social norms, it was time to find a match for Nanki. Kalo occasionally commented on how Nanki was now grown up and how it was time to find a bridegroom for her. But Rai Bular knew that he was not really in a hurry to find a match for his daughter—he wished to keep her with him for the extra year or two that social convention permitted. But now, thinking of how perfect a pair Nanki and Jai Ram would make, Rai Bular wasted no time in broaching the subject to his accountant. Though Kalo had not anticipated that his daughter would go away so soon, he couldn't help but be thrilled at the prospect of such a good match. He had interacted with the young man on many occasions and admired him greatly for his qualities of heart and mind, but never in his wildest dreams had he thought of him as a prospective groom for his daughter. There was great rejoicing in the Bedi household, and in Talwandi at large, when a message came back from Sultanpur to say that Jai Ram's family too favoured the proposal. After Pandit Hardayal had declared that the two horoscopes matched perfectly, a day for the wedding was set.

Though they were people of some means, Jai Ram's family, like Mehta Kalo's, did not favour ostentatious and vulgar displays of wealth. It was a small *barat* that came to the wedding and, except for a token exchange of gifts, there was no demand or expectation of dowry. Rai Bular took an active part in all the preparations for the wedding. After all, not only was he a loyal friend, he had been instrumental in arranging the marriage.

The ceremony was performed by Pandit Hardayal according to Vedic rites and everyone in Talwandi commented upon what a wonderful couple Nanki and Jai Ram made. Soon it was time for the *doli* to leave and a sudden hush descended on the gathering. The joy and festive spirit gave way to a mood of deep poignancy. Even though both Nanki and Nanak conducted themselves with dignity, it was obvious to everyone that the impending separation weighed heavily on the brother and sister. Nanak's lack of worldliness had always rendered him extremely vulnerable and Nanki had often protected her brother. Her eyes burned bright with unshed tears as she bid him good bye. Nanak, on his part, knew how dependent he was on his sister, from whom he drew so much emotional strength. He was going to miss her terribly but he forced a little smile to his lips as he led her to her *doli*. He watched the *doli* wend its way towards Sultanpur. When it was out of sight he rushed into the forest to find a secluded place to vent his grief.

After Nanki's marriage, life in Talwandi returned to its routine and Nanak went back to his Sanskrit studies with Pandit Brijnath Shastri, throwing himself whole-heartedly into his work. Within two years he had achieved remarkable fluency in the language and not only understood all the ancient texts but also knew many of them by heart. But he also realised his mastery of Sanskrit and of the religious texts was only a skill that would enable him to understand what the *rishis* and saints of the past had said about this world, about life, and about the world of the spirit. He had learnt whatever he needed to further his quest. He saw no point in pursuing his studies in this field any longer. So, as he had with Pandit Gopal, he dropped out of his studies with Shastriji. But the shastri could not accept this breach of discipline with the same equanimity as Pandit Gopal. He confronted Nanak with his continued absence from class. Nanak politely but firmly told him that he had learnt the Sanskrit he needed, and would not be coming back to study. The shastri strode straight to Rai Bular's residence and confronted Mehta Kalo in his little office.

"I have never seen such a cussed boy," he said. "He is a brilliant student, easily the best pupil I have ever had, and just as he is getting somewhere, he wants to abandon everything. You must ensure that he comes back to me. If he pursues his studies with the same vigour as he has been doing these last two years, I assure you that he will grow up to be one of the greatest scholars of our times. His fame will spread far and wide and people will come long distances to him to seek answers to their questions and to engage him in debate."

Rai Bular, who had come into the room on hearing of Shastriji's arrival, could not help smiling. Like all great scholars, the shastri nurtured a streak of vanity. He wanted the credit for having nurtured and created such a brilliant scholar. Kalo had a troubled frown upon his brow but could not find the words to express himself. It was left to Rai Bular to placate the shastri.

"Come, come, Shastriji, do not be so grievously troubled on young Nanak's account. Like all of Talwandi, you too know of his moodiness and eccentricity. Rest assured both Kalo and I will do everything in our power to reason with him—to convince him that the only good that can come to him is by pursuing his studies with you."

Mehta Kalo was influenced by Nanki and Rai Bular's attitude towards Nanak for a while—they looked up to him with respect bordering on awe. He found it increasingly difficult to chastise his son, even though he was greatly distressed by his giving up his studies. But as the days stretched on, he found himself growing impatient with his son's listlessness. Nanak spent all his time lost in his own thoughts, often spending hours in the forest discussing spiritual matters with the holy men who stopped there en route their pilgrimages. Sometimes he would also visit Sayyad Hassan, his neighbour, and the nature of their conversations did nothing to reassure Mehta Kalo about his son. From his point of view, all the activities Nanak engaged in were unproductive. He could see none of them leading in any way to the greatness that Pandit Hardayal had predicted for Nanak. As a result, whenever Nanki or Tripta reminded him of this prediction, he would snap back and say that Pandit Hardayal could, for once, have made a mistake in his calculations.

Eventually, the three who were most concerned about Nanak's future—Kalo, Sayyad Hassan and Rai Bular—put their heads together and it was decided that while they waited for destiny to step in, Nanak should begin attending Persian classes. Persian was the court language at Delhi and also at the administrative centres of the various governors and independent principalities. With a mastery over Persian, Nanak would have no trouble in finding official employment. This suggestion found favour with Kalo because he felt that state employment was definitely a step on the path to greatness. With diligence and sincerity, Nanak could rise to be the right hand man of the governor himself. Nanak, always eager to learn, greeted this suggestion with enthusiasm. So Sayyad Hassan introduced Nanak to Maulana Qutab-ud-Din. The maulana not only taught him Persian and Arabic, but also introduced him to the Qur'an and to the salient features of Islam.

Nanak had now reached the age of puberty. It was time for the performance of the *yagnopavitam*, a ceremony in which a Brahmin or

Khatri boy was invested with the sacred thread. This ceremony not only marked the coming of age of the boy, but also initiated him into the next stage of life. The thread was a symbol of his superior caste, which made him a superior human being. Pandit Hardayal was asked to set a date for the ceremony.

Invitations for Nanak's thread ceremony were sent to all friends and relatives in the neighbouring towns and villages. A special invitation went out to Sultanpur to Nanki and her husband Jai Ram. All arrangements were made. The courtyard was washed many times over and then sprinkled with holy water, *gangajal*, to sanctify it and make it pure. A special platform was constructed for the ceremony to seat the pandit and Nanak. The floor was decorated with auspicious signs made with coloured rice powder. Lamps were lit and placed along the edge of the platform, and the courtyard was well-illuminated. The perfume of incense pervaded the air and smoke from hundreds of incense sticks curled heavenwards through the late evening air. The priest chanted holy *mantras* as Nanak sat cross-legged opposite him, his back straight and his body bare from waist upward. Nanki sat close to the platform, her eyes fixed adoringly on her beloved brother. How handsome he looked and what an air of spiritual radiance there was about him! It seemed to her that he even wore a halo around his head!

Pandit Hardayal finished his recitation. He picked up the *janeu*, the sacred thread made of seven twisted and braided strands of yarn. He blessed the cord, and unwinding it, reached out to place it on Nanak's shoulders. Nanak held up his hand to stop him.

"What is the significance of this thread, Panditji?" he asked the priest.

"This is a sacred thread," the pandit explained patiently. "It marks you out, at all times, as an upper-caste Hindu. By wearing this thread you will become a pure Hindu."

"Does a person become pure merely by wearing a thread?" Nanak asked, in a voice loud enough to be heard by every person gathered in the courtyard. "Is it not our deeds, our actions, our commitment to truth and rightful living, which will mark us as being pure and set us apart as belonging to a superior group?" He paused for his words to sink in, and then, with a soft smile playing on his lips, he added, "What cleanliness or purity can this thread impart? The thread itself will become dirty and soiled. There is no permanency in it; it will wear out and break, while the thread of our good deeds will always remain with us. No! Take it away, I will not wear it!"

There was a collective gasp from the shocked congregation. No one had ever stood up against or rejected this ancient custom and here was Nanak, little more than a boy, refusing to wear the sacred thread. Pandit Hardayal could not control his anger. He stood up, shuffled into his wooden sandals, and made his way through the crowd to the door of the courtyard. First Kalo, then Rai Bular and Jai Ram, tried to stop him but he brushed them off and hurried out of the house. After this insult he would never again have anything to do with the Bedi family. He could not help remembering that fateful evening when Kalo had brought him the joyous tidings of Nanak's birth. For the first time in his life he admitted that he could have made a mistake in his calculations, been wrong in his prediction. After what the boy had just done, he could see no greatness in his future, only damnation.

In the meantime, there were horrified murmurs amid the crowd in the courtyard—murmurs that soon rose to a clamour. This was truly abominable behaviour; it was sacrilege to refuse the sacred thread. Not only had Nanak roused the anger of the pious and highly respected pandit, he had also brought great disgrace to his family. One by one the guests left the courtyard, not wanting to be party to this break with tradition and religion. Most of them did not even stop to say goodbye to Kalo or other members of his family. The feast that was to follow the ceremony did not take place.

Kalo was hurt and angry but he knew his son well enough to realise that no purpose would be served by trying to upbraid or chasten him. Tripta was frightened out of her wits—frightened for the safety of her son. She was sure that the gods too would be angry with her son and this anger would only bring him harm. Kalo stole to his bed, wrapped himself in his *chaddar* and pretended to sleep. The others decided it was best to leave him alone. Jai Ram and Nanki sat late into the night trying to comfort Tripta. Silence had descended on the house and the village, a silence that intensified with the deepening gloom of the night. The lamps still burned in the courtyard, though their light was now eerie, and smoke from the incense sticks still curled heavenwards.

Nanak sat alone on the platform, lost in thought, the abandoned *janeu* on the ground beside him. At last, Nanki came furtively through the stillness, draped a *chaddar* around his bare shoulders, and prevailed upon him to partake of the food she had brought for him. Though she was confused by what had happened and miserable at her parents' embarrassment and unhappiness, she could not find it in her heart to blame her brother. She admired him for standing up for his convictions. The wearing of the sacred thread was only an empty ritual and could not bestow purity on the wearer. The self could be purified only by walking the right path. Her brother was right to have eschewed the former and embraced the latter for it showed great strength of character.

What Nanak the boy said on this occasion is reflected in what he said later as a Guru, words that have found place in the Adi Granth:

> "From the cotton of compassion,
> Spin the thread of contentment,
> Give knots of continence and twists of Truth;
> This is the sacred thread of the soul –
> If thou hast one such, O Brahma, then put it on me.
> It will not snap, nor soil; nor will it be burnt or lost
> Blessed is the man, O Nanak,
> Who wears such a thread around his neck."
> (*Raga Asa*, Trans. Sarna, Navtej, *The Book of Nanak*, p. 35)

If Nanak was in any way affected by the consequences of his action, he did not show it in the days that followed. He continued to go to Maulana Qutab-ud-din for his Persian and Arabic lessons and for his study of the Qur'an and of Islam. He found great pleasure in discussing what he had studied with Sayyad Hassan. Then, as with every course of study he had pursued earlier, there came a moment when Nanak felt that he had gained everything that he would ever need from the subjects he had been studying. No purpose would be served by following this course of study any further. He spoke to the maulana about his feelings and in parting gave him a poem he had composed in Persian.

> "Know for certain in thy heart, this world perishes."
> (*Raga Tilana*, Trans. Sarna, Navtej, *The Book of Nanak*, p. 33)

The maulana smiled as he read the poem: the boy was right, there was nothing more he could learn from the maulana.

SEARCH FOR AN OCCUPATION

Kalo had lost all hopes and aspirations for Nanak's future. He despaired at the lack of continuity and perseverance in his son's efforts and he could not imagine how the boy was going to earn a living, leave alone achieve the greatness that had been foretold for him. Rai Bular's constant reminders about the boy's brilliance and sharp intellect did nothing to comfort him. If the pattern of his life was anything to go by, any sustained effort on his part did not last beyond a period of two years.

Though each of his teachers swore by his ability in the subjects that he had studied, Nanak showed no special aptitude which would indicate the path that he was going to follow in life. Worst of all, he showed no remorse or regret at his directionless life and certainly no desire to pursue a productive one. Kalo had been patient all these years but he could be patient no more. Nanak was fourteen years old and by this age all other boys had already begun an apprenticeship to the profession that they would eventually follow. In his son's case there seemed to be no profession in sight. All he seemed to do was spend time in the forest with *sadhus*, *fakirs* and *pirs*.

"If this is where his future lies, why does he not abandon home and join one of these mendicant groups who spend all their time going up and down the country from one pilgrimage centre to another, keeping body and soul together with whatever scraps of food are thrown their way? Who knows, the pandit's prophecy can still be fulfilled by his becoming the leader of one such group or even by gaining *tantrik* powers by which he can give children to the childless, bring separated lovers together, or help to discover where stolen gold has been hidden!" Kalo expressed his anger to his friend Rai Bular.

Rai Bular comforted him, saying, "Your concern and worry are understandable but do not allow this to make you so bitter and cynical. You know as well as I do that sometimes God's plans are not clear to us.

But believe me, it is only a matter of time. As a father, you have hopes and aspirations for Nanak but I have observed the boy objectively. I assure you that the potential I see in him is far beyond what I have seen in any other boy. Why, you have but to look at his face to see the spiritual radiance, the light that shines there. Be patient, my friend, I know it is easy for me to preach because I do not have the responsibility of seeing him settled in life. But believe me when I say with all my heart that I wish he were my son."

Kalo was touched by the Bhatti's sincerity. "I believe you, my friend. You have never said anything to me that is not sincere and true. But tell me, what should we do with the boy while we wait for this 'greatness' to come his way?" Rai Bular smiled at this wry comment and the sombreness of the moment was lifted.

"We must find him an occupation, an employment," he said thoughtfully.

"That is easier said than done. You know the boy's temperament. If he doesn't find joy in what he is doing, he will abandon it the very next day and no amount of cajoling or persuasion will make him take it up again."

Rai Bular pondered over this for a while. "You are right, my friend. We must give this careful thought. My little Nanak is very clear in his likes and dislikes and it is difficult to dissuade him once he has made up his mind."

Over the next few days the two friends deliberated over what kind of job Nanak could take up. Various possibilities were suggested and discussed, but each, after careful deliberation, was discarded. Finally it was Tripta who came up with a solution.

The answer had come to her as she lay awake mulling over their problem. She cast her mind over the activities that her son enjoyed the most. He was happiest spending time by himself in the wooded area around Talwandi, absorbed in his special thoughts, with no one to disturb him. If this could be harnessed to something productive, they would have found an occupation that Nanak would enjoy and pursue with a degree of enthusiasm. The answer to this too came in a flash. About six months earlier they had been short of a cowherd and Nanak had volunteered to look after the herd. Every day, as the sun gently set on the horizon, Nanak had returned with his herd, with a look of divine happiness on his face.

"Mother, can I still take the cattle to graze?" he had asked hopefully, when he heard of the cowherd's return. She had laughed then, amused at the prospect. Running her hand tenderly over his head she had replied, "Not tomorrow, you have your studies to attend to. But I promise that whenever we need a cowherd I will call upon you for help."

Now, in the face of the crisis that confronted them, sending Nanak to herd the cattle seemed the ideal solution. The more she thought about it, the more convinced she was. Unable to contain her excitement at her idea, she woke up her husband. Half-asleep and disoriented, it took him a few moments to understand his wife's proposal and he burst out laughing. But when he gave it some considered thought, he knew that his wife had found an ideal occupation for their son.

Next morning he voiced this suggestion to his employer. Initially, Rai Bular was shocked at the prospect of a boy from a prosperous Khatri family taking on such an occupation. However, keeping in mind Nanak's nature and the long hours that he spent in the wilderness, he too found it an ideal solution.

"And who knows," Kalo said, "he may end up becoming a champion cowherd with all the keepers of large herds vying for his services— offering him a fortune if he will work for them. And he may even go down in history as the first great cowherd!"

Rai Bular checked an angry retort at his friend's sarcasm. "Do not mock Pandit Hardayal's prophecy," he said quietly. "I do not have his learning or his skill in reading the stars; I do not know when and how your son's destiny will unfold. But I know that it will, and when it does, you too will hold him in reverence and acknowledge his greatness."

And so it was that Nanak, much to his delight, began to take his father's herd to graze in the grassy pastures on the outskirts of the village. He had always loved to be in the lap of nature, and now, from morning till night, Nanak observed the trees and the wild flowers, the butterflies and the insects, the birds and the wild animals in the jungle. He passed the hours in serene silence, from the time when the dew still glistened on the blades of green to the time that the birds flew in army formation across the evening sky to their nests and the herd lowed impatiently to be driven home. He revelled in their beauty and felt the pulse of the one Great Spirit that breathes through all creation. He observed the change of seasons and how nature copes with this transformation. The passage of time, the rise and fall of temperature, and the alternating dry and wet seasons were an allegory for the continuous changes in human life, he thought.

All these reflections were to find expression years later in his *bani*, most notably in the beautiful composition *Barah Mah*, which describes so graphically and completely the effect of the change of seasons on nature, and symbolically, on the mind and spirit of man.

His sojourn in the woods also gave him ample opportunity to indulge in his other favourite pastime—discussions on spiritual matters with holy men. He learnt a great deal about different religions and sects. It was here that he met the renowned Sufi scholar Sayyad Hussain and was first introduced to Sufism. And it was here that, at a very young age, he became aware of the various reformist movements in the Hindu religion and the efforts being made to build bridges between the Hindu and Muslim faiths.

Sometimes Nanak became so absorbed in these discussions that he forgot his herd. One of the janamsakhis tells of an incident when Nanak's herd wandered into a neighbouring field while he was engaged in conversation with some holy men. The irate farmer rushed to lodge a complaint with Rai Bular about Nanak's negligence.

"Lower your voice, Raj Kumar," Rai Bular said, drawing the farmer aside, so that Kalo who was busy with his accounts in an adjoining room would not hear the complaint. "What is the extent of the damage to your crop?"

"*Hazoor*, it is …" the farmer hesitated, unable to look Rai Bular in the face.

His manner infuriated the Rai and he shouted, "Tell the truth man, or I will skin you alive."

Hearing Rai Bular's raised voice, Kalo came into the room and asked, "What is the matter?"

"Nothing," Rai Bular said quickly. "Nothing at all."

"Then why did you raise your voice?"

Rai Bular could find no ready explanation and Kalo turned towards the farmer. "What have you done to arouse Rai Sahib's anger?" he demanded.

As the farmer narrated his woes, Rai Bular sensed his friend's anger quickening. He spoke up quickly. "But he has not told us the extent of the damage. Out with it then, Raj Kumar, tell us how much crop you have lost."

The farmer remained tongue-tied and then, in a rush, he confessed, "I did not stop to assess the damage. The moment I saw the cow grazing in my field I rushed to you, *Hazoor*."

"Then let us go and inspect the damage. You have my word; you will be compensated for it."

The three went together to Raj Kumar's field but they found no damage worth the name. Rai Bular was so relieved that there would be no trouble between father and son that he did not rebuke the farmer but sent him on his way, jesting that perhaps his eyes were failing him and Nanak's cow had not wandered into his field at all!

By and large, however, Nanak was conscientious in his work and even while debating with the *sadhus* and *fakirs*, he kept an eye on his herd to ensure that they did not wander too far. Nanak found great joy in this work and his enthusiasm spilled over to other spheres of his life as well. He spent more time with his father and mother, participating in the daily humdrum life of the family. He reached out to the villagers and became less of an introvert. He began to visit Mardana's home more often and to participate in the singing of devotional songs. His mother would often hear him singing while he bathed and was pleasantly surprised at the sweetness of his voice. People discovered to their surprise that Nanak had a sense of humour and that he had the wonderful ability to laugh at himself. As a son he became more devoted than ever before. He anticipated his father's every need and ran errands for him without being asked to. The parents were amazed at the transformation in their son but Tripta was a little afraid too.

"He laughs and he sings all day. I have never seen him so happy and I am afraid that someone will cast an evil eye on him."

"Do not ruin the happiness of the present with imaginary fears about the future," her husband advised. "If it is God's wish that this happiness should come to an end, there is nothing we can do to prevent it. Let us enjoy it while it lasts and thank providence that it was given to us, even if only for a short time."

When Nanki and Jai Ram came on their annual visit, they were overcome with happiness at the atmosphere that now prevailed in the Bedi household. Nanki was especially happy to see a bond developing between her father and her brother and she prayed that this state of affairs would prevail.

However, six months later, uncertainty began gnawing at Mehta Kalo's heart again. He could not imagine the boy herding cattle for the rest of his life. He was an intelligent, hardworking lad, honest and sincere; surely life had better things in store for him? He hoped that having found fulfilment and satisfaction in his current occupation,

Nanak would be willing to try his hand at something more challenging. He turned once again to Rai Bular for advice. It was decided that Nanak should be provided with an opportunity to try his hand at business.

Within walking distance of Talwandi was the little town of Chuharkhana. On market days it became a centre for the purchase of essential commodities like salt, turmeric, oil, and soap. Traders from nearby villages flocked to Chuharkhana to buy these at wholesale prices and sell them in their villages for a small profit. Rai Bular and Kalo drew up a plan to enable Nanak to take advantage of this opportunity. They gave Nanak a sum of twenty silver rupees, considered a minor fortune in those days. "Go to Chuharkhana, my son. Buy the commodities that you feel are most in demand and bring them back to Talwandi and earn yourself some profit."

Nanak was happy to comply with his father's instructions and took his mission seriously. He studied the market to assess the commodities most in demand and the prices they were retailing at. He drew up a list and decided the quantity of each commodity that he would buy in Chuharkhana.

On the next market day, he sought his parents' blessings and, accompanied by his childhood friend, Bala, set out for the town. There was a flush of excitement on his face. He was determined to carry out this business as successfully as he was carrying out his duties as a cowherd. He would make his father proud by earning a handsome profit. As the two boys hurried towards Chuharkhana there flashed in his mind an image of his father declaring to his friends: "My son is a successful businessman. I am truly proud of him."

The road to Chuharkhana skirted a forest but there was a much shorter path that cut directly through it. It was a bright, sunny morning and by the time they reached the outskirts of the forest, the two boys were perspiring profusely. The shady path running through the forest, with its overhang of tall trees, beckoned tantalisingly. It was an invitation that Nanak found difficult to resist. "Let's take that path, Bala; the trees will protect us from the strong sun. Not only will we reach Chuharkhana sooner but we will also be spared much discomfort."

Bala hesitated. They were carrying a large sum of money and they ran the risk of being waylaid by robbers. It would be embarassing to return to Talwandi and admit that they had lost their money. Bala also worried on another count. He knew there would be ascetics and holy men camping in the forest and his friend would be drawn to them like a moth to a flame. Bala was sure they would be debating philosophy long after the market hours of Chuharkhana were over. They would cut sorry figures if they returned to Talwandi without having transacted any business on their first day.

"No, Nanak, let us take the main road. It is not safe to go into the forest with the money we have," he cautioned.

"Who is to know that we carry so much money? It is safely hidden in my belt. Besides, who would dare to waylay a big, tough Jat like you?" He smiled at his friend and with one quick stride, turned off the road onto the path, leaving Bala with no option but to follow him into the forest.

All went well until they came upon a group of *sadhus* camping in a clearing. They were different from any *sadhus* that Bala had ever seen before—they were all stark naked and stood statue-like in various postures, absorbed in prayer and meditation. Nanak stopped in his tracks and Bala felt that his worst fears would be realised.

"Come, come, Nanak," he said, his voice sharp with urgency. "We have no time. The best bargains in the market are to be struck in the early hours. We can come back tomorrow to spend the whole day with the *sadhus*."

Nanak knew his friend was right but then he had never seen such peculiar *sadhus* before. They were obviously from a very esoteric sect and he could not resist the temptation of finding out more about them.

"It will only take a minute," he said. "I promise I will stop just long enough to find out what sect they belong to." He noticed his friend's hesitation and added, "Bala, I assure you, I'll only ask two or three questions and will not get into a discussion."

Seeing how much this meant to his friend, Bala gave in. "All right," he sighed, "just a few questions."

Nanak walked up to a *sadhu* who was much older than the others and was obviously the leader of the group. He sat cross-legged on a small mound, his eyes closed in prayer. Perhaps he became aware of the boy standing before him, perhaps he had actually finished his prayers at just that moment, but he opened his eyes and looked straight at Nanak. Nanak bowed to him and the holy man held up his right hand in blessing. Then he indicated the ground in front of him, inviting him to sit down. Nanak did as he was bid and after a moment's hesitation, Bala too sat down beside his friend.

"*Maharaj*, why do you not wear any clothes?" Nanak asked with his usual directness.

39

"We are Nirbanis. Our faith enjoins us to eschew anything that might bind us to this world. Wearing clothes would entail the need to procure them and this need would bind us to the material world. Besides, God created us in nakedness like he created all other species and we must live in nakedness like the other species do. In so doing we would recognise, and be one with, the universal spirit that inhabits all living species."

Nanak did not empathise with this philosophy but he could see that the old man believed implicitly in what he was saying and that his words were spoken with a high degree of conviction.

"What do you do when it gets cold?" he asked.

"The threshold of human tolerance, both of the body and the spirit, is limitless. By careful training, the body can be taught to tolerate a very high degree of cold. But till we reach that point in our training, we do what the birds and the animals do—we migrate with the change of seasons. When it is warm here in the plains, we move northwards to our shrines and centres in the hills and when it becomes cold there, we come down to the plains again. There is much one can learn from observing the animal world—most of all one learns that much that man deems essential for his survival is not really necessary at all."

"And what about food?" Nanak asked.

"We eat what nature provides—fruits, herbs, and nuts from the trees, or what God deems fit to provide in the form of gifts from other men."

Nanak sensed a contradiction in this—if the Nirbanis wanted to be free from dependence on others and from attachment to the material world, surely they should not accept gifts of food? "So ultimately you are dependent on alms for your sustenance, like most ascetics?"

"The difference is that we do not seek alms. We accept food if it is given to us but we do not go into the world of men to ask for food."

"And if no food is forthcoming, if there is nothing that nature provides?"

"We starve. Sometimes we die of starvation. But that is part of our faith, our way of life. And it is a moment of triumph for us when we face death knowing that we have not violated the tenets of our faith."

Nanak was horrified at what he thought was an extreme form of masochism. When he looked at all the *sadhus*, lost deep in meditation, and took in their emaciated, almost skeletal forms and gaunt faces, his heart went out to them.

"How long has it been since God last sent you some food?" he asked, deeply concerned.

"Seven days now. Two of our fellow-disciples have now gone into a state of unconsciousness from hunger. It is but a matter of hours before they find freedom from the fetters of this life and achieve a state of heavenly bliss."

Seven days, Nanak thought to himself in dismay, seven days with not a morsel of food. He looked around and saw the two *sadhus* who lay under a tree, their bodies curled up in the fetal position. They were so alarmingly thin that Nanak wondered how a breath of life could remain in their bodies.

"And you believe that God asks you to subject yourself to this extreme suffering?"

The holy man smiled. "You are not the first one to ask this question. We believe, like many others do, that fasting purifies the body and the spirit. The longer and more intense the fast, the higher the degree of purity one attains. If death comes while attaining this purity, then death is to be sought. If it is God's will, we will be provided sustenance."

There were many others who believed in the virtues of fasting. Muslims fasted for one whole month in a year as a penance, believing that it was a means of achieving nobility of spirit and proximity to God. The Hindus too were enjoined to fast on particular days. What Nanak found difficult to understand was the extreme to which the Nirbanis took this observance.

There were many other questions that Nanak asked, questions that the ascetic answered patiently. But Nanak's mind could not focus on the ascetic's words. His eyes went repeatedly to the two still forms who were breathing their last even as the old ascetic spoke to him. But there was not a crease of worry on this account on their leader's face. There must be some virtue in a faith that taught such total indifference to death.

He sensed Bala stirring restlessly beside him and he was reminded of the purpose of his mission. They touched the ascetic's feet and after receiving his blessings, quickly went on their way through the forest.

They reached Chuharkhana by mid-day, when the sun beat fiercely down upon the market place. Nanak went about his purchases quickly and Bala was puzzled to see him buying flour, millet, pulses, and even perishable vegetables which were available in plenty in the village.

"Nanak, we will not earn any profit if we trade in these commodities," Bala said, dismayed.

"Don't worry, my friend. We will earn a far greater profit than you have ever dreamed of. Trust me."

Bala was not convinced but held his peace. The sun was on the decline when they finally finished. Burdened with their purchases, their progress through the lengthening shadows was slow and Bala was glad when Nanak once again chose the shorter path through the forest. When they reached the clearing, Nanak placed his bundle of provisions at the ascetic's feet. All of a sudden Bala realised what his friend was going to do and he panicked. Nanak's father would never forgive them for this and he would be held responsible, for had he not been sent as much to keep an eye on Nanak as to assist him? He reached out and gripped his friend's wrist firmly and shook his head as Nanak turned to him enquiringly. But Nanak only smiled and gently released his hand. He turned once again to the ascetic.

"*Maharaj*, God has seen fit to end your seven day fast. He has sent you some food."

Bala sighed in resignation. The deed was done; there was no going back now. They would have to face the consequences.

"Come," Nanak said to Bala, and after a last farewell to the Nirbani and his group of ascetics, the two boys walked quickly out of the forest.

In the Bedi household the day had been one of pent up excitement. The success of Nanak's venture would prove to be the turning point of his life. Nanki and Jai Ram, who were visiting at the time, were sure that Nanak would be able to strike a fine balance between his quest in the spiritual world and the pursuit of a profession that would earn him respect. As the hours lengthened and the boys did not return, Mehta Kalo grew increasingly impatient. He and Rai Bular went up the ramparts of the fort from where they could see the countryside for miles around. It was the height of summer and even at six in the evening there was bright sunshine and no sign of the approaching dusk. The two men paced up and down, looking anxiously towards Chuharkhana. Finally they saw two figures emerge from the forest. As they came down the ramparts and hurried to meet the boys, they were astonished to find them empty-handed.

"Where are your purchases?" Kalo asked sharply.

"There is nothing left. We gave all our purchases away," Nanak answered.

Kalo and Rai Bular listened in disbelief as Nanak went on to tell them of the encounter with the starving Nirbanis. "Two of them were dying. We would have been guilty of their murder if we had not fed them."

"What am I to do with this boy?" Kalo cried in frustration. He beat his breast and wept in sheer helplessness. The loss of a huge amount of money was bad enough, what was far worse was his son's failure.

"I will be the laughing stock of the village," he said. "The father of a boy who is so stupid as to give away twenty silver rupees to a group of parasitical mendicants. Oh! I will never be able to live this down."

"Calm down, Kalo. It is not the end of the world."

"That is what you always say. How long can I remain calm and patient in the face of one debacle after another?"

Rai Bular took his friend aside and appealed to him yet again. "Just this once, my friend. I promise you I will not ask for your indulgence again. Nanak is not a worldly child. It is too much to expect him to conduct himself in an ordinary way. I think we belittle him by supposing that he could be drawn into the sordid business of buying and selling. Besides, the damage has been done—no purpose will be served by chastening the boy."

Kalo realised that his friend was right; no purpose would be served by chastening Nanak simply because it would have no effect on him. He would continue to go his own way, doing what was in his heart, oblivious to the praise or censure of the world.

"And the twenty silver coins—have no worry on account of their loss. I will give you twenty more to make up this loss."

Kalo looked at his friend in disbelief. Rai Bular never seemed to tire of defending the boy and was prepared to go to any length to make up for his lapses. But Kalo's anger reared up again as he looked at Nanak. "He could at least admit he has made a mistake and ask to be forgiven," he raged.

"I have made no mistake," Nanak said, turning to his father. "You wanted me to earn great profit and I have. You have repeatedly emphasised that we must never turn away a hungry man, a *sadhu*, or a mendicant when he comes to our door for alms. You have often said that in the eyes of God it is an opportunity to earn great profit by giving food to one who is hungry or in need. If there is profit in feeding one merchant or beggar, imagine how great a profit I have earned you in the eyes of God by using your money to feed a group of ascetics who had gone without food for seven days."

Rai Bular was impressed by Nanak's irrefutable logic and struggled to hide his smile. But from the corner of his eye he could see that his friend was still furious and they walked back to Talwandi in tense silence.

In the manner of grapevines in all small places, the grapevine in Talwandi too had been active and had already relayed the news of Nanak's debacle. People stopped in the street to stare after him, and a few youngsters even passed whispered comments and snickered at their own humour.

The Bedi household was gripped by tension. Nanki and Tripta were longing to put their arms around the boy and tell him not to worry, that the loss of the money didn't matter and that they admired him for what he had done. But they were afraid of igniting Kalo's smouldering rage into a fresh outburst. Taking their cue from the head of the family, they greeted Nanak in total silence. Only Nanki managed a surreptitious smile. Nanak was upset by their apparent lack of understanding and when Tripta placed a *thali* of food before him, he pushed it firmly aside. Tripta was about to coax him to eat when Kalo cut in brusquely, "There is no need to fuss over him. If he is not hungry, he need not eat. Go, Nanak, go to bed."

Much later, when the household was quiet, Nanki and Tripta brought Nanak some food. Once again he pushed it aside. "You have earned so much merit by feeding twenty hungry men; will you deny us the little we would earn by feeding one hungry boy?" Tripta smiled and caressed his hair. Nanak felt the sadness lift from his heart. He knew that his father's disappointment notwithstanding, he had done the right thing in feeding the holy men. He smiled at his mother and sister, and ate the food that they had brought him.

In spite of the unstinting support of Rai Bular, Tripta and Nanki, a strange mood gripped Nanak after this incident. He became more and more withdrawn and began keeping entirely to himself. Even his sister's words of affection and his mother's comforting touch elicited no smile from him. He would lie for hours on his rope cot, his face covered with a *chaddar*, lost in his own thoughts. He ignored all efforts to reach out to him. He ate little and that only when his mother and sister threatened to go on a fast. Sometimes his mother would find him sitting all by himself, tears coursing down his cheeks in soundless weeping. He would go off on long solitary walks in the middle of the night. He stopped communicating with Bala and even stopped visiting Mardana to participate in the singing of devotional songs. He no longer indulged in endless debates with the holy men camping in the forest, or in discussions with Sayyad Hassan. It was as if he had lost all interest in life. He grew frail and gaunt. The sleepless nights left their mark in the dark circles under his eyes. There was a feverish restlessness in all that he did and in the occasional monosyllable that he deigned to utter. His condition deteriorated so much that Kalo forgot his anger and disappointment and was consumed by anxiety.

Nanak's strange affliction became a subject of concern for everyone in Talwandi. There were some who said that he had been strange from birth—hadn't he laughed when all other newborns cry? In fact, everything he had done in his life was strange, so this behaviour was to be expected. There were others who said that this was divine retribution—God's way of punishing him for the crass arrogance that he had displayed towards the wise and pious Pandit Hardayal at the aborted *janeu* ceremony. Still others said that he was possessed by an evil spirit, and till this spirit was exorcised, neither Nanak nor the Bedi household would know any peace. Tripta and Nanki, unable to find a rational explanation for Nanak's condition, began to subscribe to the theory of the evil spirit as well. They would have sent for an exorcist if Rai Bular had not warned them that such a course might do more harm than good. Nanak's lack of faith in miracles and supernatural phenomena like ghosts and spirits was well known, and an exorcist attempting to drive away a so-called spirit might have pushed him further into despondency. A cure through the services of an exorcist was thus abandoned.

At last Rai Bular prevailed upon Nanak to let Hardas, the village physician, examine him for a physical ailment. Hardas was a renowned physician and well-liked by the inhabitants of Talwandi and the neighbouring villages. Not only was his diagnosis remarkably accurate but his treatment was simple and uncomplicated. In addition, Hardas had an engaging bedside manner and was able to draw his patients out to share their worries and anxieties with him. As a result, his patients received both medical treatment and counselling from the worthy physician and they looked upon him as a friend and confidant.

So it was with Nanak. When Hardas felt his pulse, Nanak remarked, "I am afflicted not with the pain of the body, but with the pain of the soul." Hardas had a number of sessions with Nanak and no one knew what transpired between them. All that Hardas said to the anxious friends and relatives was, "Do not worry about Nanak's health, he will soon be well. He is troubled by matters of the spirit but he will come to terms with them. As Pandit Hardayal predicted at the time of his birth, he is no ordinary mortal. He is destined to be great and Talwandi will be proud to claim him as her son."

Hardas proved to be right. Gradually, the restlessness passed from Nanak's soul. He began to sleep and eat regularly; the flesh came back to his bones. He lost the feverish, wild-eyed look and his face now often lit up with a divine smile. Though still not gregarious, he was friendly and affable enough and spent more and more time interacting with others. He began to seek the company of holy men again. He resumed his scholarly sessions with Sayyad Hassan and his practice of singing devotional songs with Mardana. In short, he was once again the Nanak that Talwandi had known before the strange illness had come upon him. Everyone in the village heaved a sigh of relief and Nanki, who had stayed back in Talwandi to look after her brother, was at last able to rejoin her husband in Sultanpur.

Life moved on placidly and things were quiet in the Bedi household. But Mehta Kalo's frustration at the apparent lack of direction and purpose in Nanak's life surfaced from time to time and found expression in regular conflicts with his son. Nanak was not unduly perturbed by his father's flashes of anger and continued to follow the routine he had set for himself. Tripta was grateful that her son's moodiness seemed to be a thing of the past. Though he continued to spend long hours in introspection and meditation, he was polite and affable with everyone he came into contact with. Most important of all, to Tripta's delight, his face had begun to regain its healthy glow.

The monotony of their routine was broken one sunny morning by Nanki, who arrived in a state of great excitement. She had brought a proposal of marriage for her brother! Nanak was now seventeen years of age and though his record of uncertain and erratic behaviour did not mark him out as the most eligible of bachelors, the economic stability of the Bedi family and Mehta Kalo's proximity to Rai Bular had elicited a few discreet enquiries. Though most boys of his age were already married, Nanak himself had shown no inclination towards matrimony and had ignored the hints that had been thrown his way. Not wanting to pressure him, Tripta too did not pursue any of the proposals.

But the proposal brought by Nanki could not be brushed aside—the girl was a distant relative of Jai Ram's. Her name was Sulakhni and she was the daughter of Mul Chand, the *patwari* of village Pakhoke near the town of Batala. Nanki knew her well and had struck up a warm friendship with the young girl. She spoke of Sulakhni in glowing terms to her mother.

"Not only is she extremely attractive but she is also polite, gentle, and soft-spoken. She is diligent in performing her chores and will make an excellent home-maker. Her quiet sensibility and pleasant disposition will keep the family well-knit and happy."

Tripta laughed good-naturedly. "In your desire to get your friend as a sister-in-law you are lauding her to the skies."

"But you haven't heard the best part, Mother," Nanki said, grinning from ear to ear. "Sulakhni knows of our Nanak. She has heard the story of the *sacha sauda*, the true bargain, when he fed the Nirbanis. And," Nanki paused dramatically, her eyes large and incredulous, "she says she would like a husband like him!"

Tripta was delighted. "How did she hear of this?"

"I guess someone from my husband's family must have told her. But she says she is so impressed by what Nanak did, she would be happy to spend her life with him."

The news gladdened Tripta's heart. She admitted to herself that the reason why she had not pursued the matter of Nanak's marriage was her fear that no girl would be able to cope with her son's unworldly ways and moody behaviour.

"The girl seems an ideal bride for your brother. But will he agree to marry her?"

"Don't worry, Mother," Nanki said. "Have faith in me, I do have some influence over my brother and I am sure I can make him accept this proposal."

Sure enough, Nanak accepted the proposal. Sulakhni's acceptance of his extraordinary behaviour and nature finally won him over!

Nanki took Nanak's horoscope back with her and when the pandit in Pakhoke declared that Sulakhni and Nanak were eminently suitable for each other, there was much happiness on both sides. Rai Bular was firmly convinced that marriage would bring about a great change in Nanak's attitude towards life. With the responsibility of a wife, and later of children, Nanak was bound to act in a more responsible and down-to-earth manner. If nothing else, he would at least be forced to find himself an occupation. Mehta Kalo could not share his friend's optimism. His hopes had been dashed to the ground once too often and he was not prepared to set much store by the therapeutic value of marriage. But it was customary for young men of seventeen to get married and Kalo decided to comply with the established tradition.

As the day of the wedding approached, Mehta Kalo too was swept along by the tide of infectious gaiety that flowed into the Bedi household. The marriage of a son was an occasion for great rejoicing, and in spite of his disappointment and frustration at his son, Kalo loved him dearly.

As in Nanki's case, Nanak's marriage was a simple affair. Both families were well off but the ceremony was quiet and understated, without any display of wealth.

Sulakhni moved into the Bedi household and within a matter of days it was as if she had always been a member of the family. Tripta discovered, to her delight, that the girl was all that Nanki had said she was, and more. Always ready with a smile, she took on the responsibility of running the household and Tripta was happy to be relieved of the heavier chores which she now found difficult to perform. She had even found a place in her father-in-law's heart and he said to his wife, "I know no one can take the place of Nanki in our home and in our lives—but with Sulakhni here, the void our daughter left does not seem so deep anymore."

Sulakhni won her mother-in-law's admiration through her unflinching devotion to her husband. A bond of mutual respect and deep friendship had grown between the young couple. The strength of this relationship was revealed in their quiet moments together, when Nanak shared his deepest thoughts and concerns with Sulakhni. She did not always understand his worries, especially when they pertained to his spiritual quest, but it gave him strength to know that she would always support him, no matter what course his life took.

One evening, he returned home in a rather subdued mood. He answered every question in monosyllables and after having pecked desultorily at his food, he went to his room. Tripta restrained Sulakhni from finishing the chores. "Go to him, he needs you," she said to the young bride. Nanak smiled at her as she stole in quietly. "Come and sit by me," he said. They sat together in silence for a long time, their souls in communion.

Sulakhni reached out to smooth a furrow on his brow but he took her hand and held it close to his heart. "I know that there is only one thing that bothers you," she said eventually. "You worry whether the path you seek will ever be revealed to you."

Nanak touched Sulakhni's hand gently to his lips and then looked into her eyes and smiled. " I have spent much time in study and discussion and struggled to find a path which will lead me out of the pain and sorrow of our times—a path which others too could follow to achieve salvation, but sometimes the light appears dim and I despair of the path ever being revealed to me."

"I do not know much about these matters—but it would seem to me that you are walking this path already. Your *sacha sauda* could only have been performed by a divine soul."

Nanak chuckled at her trusting innocence. "In your simplicity you regard anything even slightly out of the ordinary as being marked by divinity. Anyone would have done as much in similar circumstances."

They were quiet again and Sulakhni snuggled close to Nanak. "Do not despair. Haven't you often said that we must trust in God and abide by his will? If you are struggling to find the right path, it is because God has so desired. If the path is revealed to you, it will be because God desires to reveal it to you—if not, then that too is God's wish. You must bow to His will and accept it with equanimity." Nanak held her close and with the warmth of her nearness, the worry and despair flowed away and he was again at peace with himself.

Nanak continued to follow his own course in life and there was no sign that he was likely to get involved in any productive activity as a result of his marriage. But Mehta Kalo, for once, refused to be despondent on that score. They had gained a daughter and soon there would be the patter of little feet around the house. Nanak would live the life that destiny had ordained for him and though it was not a life that he would have wished for his son, he accepted it as the will of God.

SOJOURN AT SULTANPUR

I t was now Tripta's turn to be impatient with her son. His lack of worldliness, his detachment from material things, and his spiritual quest had been precocious and endearing while he was a boy, but he was now a man with the responsibility of a wife. How long could he remain dependent upon his parents for his material needs? And when they were gone, would he still continue to spend endless days in discussions with men of spiritual leanings? Would he still remain complacent in the belief that God would provide for him and his wife? Or would he end up becoming a wandering mendicant himself? He had to start earning a living. When she voiced her concern to Kalo he brushed it aside with an air of resignation. Tripta kept her feelings bottled up inside her but could not contain herself when Nanki came over for a visit.

"I am frightened, Nanki. He spends so much time with holy men and wandering mendicants that I am sure one day he will go off like them on continuous pilgrimages from one sacred place to another. And then, what will become of our Sulakhni?" Her voice broke and she began to cry softly in the dark.

Nanki reached out and hugged her mother. "Don't worry, Mother," she said, caressing her mother's work-worn hand. "We will find a way out." Nanki's touch brought comfort to Tripta and she found that her fear had, for the moment, been stilled.

A few days later Jai Ram came to take Nanki home to Sultanpur and Nanki shared her mother's anxiety with him. "My mother does not feel that the bond of marriage is strong enough to bind Nanak to the material world. He is still without occupation and refuses to get drawn into everyday life. Mother is worried about their future. How will they support themselves once our parents are no more? Worse still, she is afraid that he might abandon his home and family and wander off with the holy men he spends so much time with."

Over the years, Jai Ram and Nanak had become close friends and Jai Ram had come to appreciate that Nanak was different from other men. He was impressed by his brother-in-law's detachment from all material things and his absorption with matters of the spirit. But now, listening to his wife, he realised that Tripta's apprehensions were well-founded. It was quite possible that Nanak would decide that his spiritual quest could only be fulfilled by moving away from Talwandi in the company of *sadhus* and *sanyasis*. The hope that his marriage would bind him to the world had been belied. Though Nanak loved Sulakhni, he still did not display any of the deep commitment to hearth and home that married men did.

Jai Ram felt that if Nanak could be persuaded to come to Sultanpur he would be able to find gainful employment for him there and, through constant monitoring and advice, make sure that he did well enough in that employment. "I think Nanak should come back with us. Your mother's anxiety will subside when she knows he is with us, safe from the temptation to abandon the world and become a pilgrim. And who knows, we might even be able to find him an employment that suits his temperament."

"Oh, that is an excellent idea! But it would be better if you spoke to my parents. They might refuse me but they will not be able to turn down a request from you."

The next morning Jai Ram found an opportunity to be alone with his mother-in-law. Kalo had gone to work, Nanak was out in the forest as usual, and Sulakhni and Nanki were busy with the household chores. Tripta sat in the sun, spinning yarn on her spinning wheel and Jai Ram, taking a *piri* from the kitchen, sat down beside her. She looked up from her work and smiled at him—a smile full of affection. They were indeed fortunate to have such a son-in-law. He was unassuming and undemanding, more like a son than a son-in-law. He cleared his throat and launched into what he had to say. "Nanki has told me of your anxieties and fears and I feel they are well-founded. We cannot sit by and let the situation slip out of our hands. I know that everything that happens in our lives is pre-ordained; we all come into the world with our destiny already worked out for us. But this does not mean that when we find things going wrong, we should make no effort to correct them. The journey of life is as important as the destination and we must do the best we can even though the success or failure of our efforts is not in our hands."

Tripta continued with her spinning, not looking at Jai Ram. He was not usually given to long speeches. She knew that there was more to come and that he was unsure of her reaction. She held her peace and waited apprehensively for Jai Ram to continue.

"Both Nanki and I feel that he should come to live with us in Sultanpur for a while."

The thread snapped and her hand slipped off the spinning wheel. Jai Ram saw the glint of tears in Tripta's eyes and continued quickly, "This would remove him from the influence of the sages and the holy men; the influence that is causing you so much anxiety. And who knows, the sights and sounds of the big town may provide him much-needed distraction. He could be persuaded to take up suitable employment too."

When Tripta finally spoke, her voice was low and hoarse. "I know how much you and Nanki love and admire him. I am sure your suggestion has come from the bottom of your heart and is motivated only by concern for your brother's welfare. I know that this is the best way for him, that he will be safe and well with you. But ..." Tripta hesitated. "What will people say? How can a man live in his brother-in-law's home?"

Jai Ram had anticipated this objection. "You say this is the best thing that could happen to Nanak at this stage and yet you hesitate because you are afraid of social censure. Is the opinion of others more important to you than the welfare of your son?" He was quiet for a while, letting his remark sink in. As Tripta wavered, he worded his next remark carefully to clinch the issue. "Besides, he will be with us only for a very short time—just as long as it takes him to settle down and find suitable accommodation."

"You are right, of course," said Tripta. "His interests must be placed above everything else. But in all these years he has never been out of my sight, not for a single day. I am frightened by the thought of his absence. Without his angelic face, his gentle smile, the sound of his voice, I feel my heart will break." This time she made no effort to control her tears.

"You are a strong woman, Mother; one of the strongest that I have known. You will find the strength to bear his absence."

"Yes, I suppose I will learn to survive."

That morning, it was Jai Ram who carried the midday meal to his father-in-law. Kalo was surprised, certain that there was more to this than just affection and regard.

"You needn't have come. One of the servants could have carried the meal to me."

"I needed an opportunity to talk to you alone."

"Come and sit beside me," Kalo said, indicating the rug-covered floor. "Tell me what is on your mind."

Jai Ram told Kalo what he had planned for Nanak. Kalo was touched but, like Tripta, concern about the social repercussions held him back. But finally he too gave his consent. "God bless you, my son. My wife and I have always felt blessed to have you as part of our family. You have brought happiness and warmth into our lives. And now this proposal for Nanak's future ... it truly reflects your concern and compassion for us. I can only hope and pray that you will find success in this endeavour because, as you know, I myself have failed in all my efforts."

When it became known that Nanak was to go and live with Nanki and Jai Ram in Sultanpur, there were murmurs of disapproval among the residents of Talwandi, murmurs which soon reached the ears of the Bedi family. Mehta Kalo was perturbed and he spoke about this to Rai Bular.

"It is a foolish convention to begin with—a convention designed to further isolate a girl from her family once she is married," Rai Bular tried to soothe Kalo. "The sooner it is broken and done away with the better. In any case, you know that this is the best thing you can do for Nanak—in fact the only hope that you have for your son. You cannot forego it because of social disapproval. Your son's interests are more important than acceptance by the community." Kalo was comforted by Rai Bular's advice and hoped that the change of place would do Nanak good.

Nanak had never been to Sultanpur and looked forward to the opportunity of being with Nanki and Jai Ram. If he had heard the shocked whispers or was aware that he was defying a common convention, he did not show it. Besides, even though Mehta Kalo had long given up berating him, Nanak was aware of his father's strong disappointment in him. He hoped that in Sultanpur he would find an opportunity that would provide him with a suitable means of livelihood. His one regret was being parted from Sulakhni, whom he had come to depend upon. She would be able to join him in Sultanpur only once he had established himself and set up home.

On the day of Nanak's departure a large crowd of friends and well-wishers assembled in the Bedi household to bid him goodbye and to wish him good fortune in this new phase of his life. The most difficult of farewells was the first to be made. In the privacy of his room, Nanak bid farewell to his wife Sulakhni. This scene is vividly and poignantly described in the *Puratan Janamsakhi*: "The news of Nanak's leaving for Sultanpur saddened his wife. Addressing him, she said, 'You have never expressed much affection for me here, and when gone, what is there to bring you back?' Nanak answered affectionately, 'O, guileless woman! I have not been doing much here, and do not know what I shall do there. I am of no use to you (here)'. Then she again supplicated, 'When you are even just sitting at home, it is like I possess the sovereignty of the whole world. Without you this world is not worth living.' Nanak was touched by these words and said, 'Do not be sad. Day by day, your sovereignty shall prevail.' Then she said, 'I do not want to stay back alone. Take me along with you!' But Nanak said, 'O, woman-of-god, let me go now. When I am able to secure some livelihood, I shall call you there. Pray agree to it.' She then silently acquiesced." (Trans. Macauliffe, *The Sikh Religion*, p. 32)

The parting from Sayyad Hassan was poignant too. He was old and frail and it was evident that he did not have much longer to live. No one knew when Nanak would return to Talwandi again and if Sayyad Hassan would still be alive then. He gave Nanak an old and valuable commentary on the Qur'an and when Nanak bent to touch his feet, he put his hand on his head and said, "Always remember, my son, that the cornerstone and the goal of all faiths, all religions, is one. Only the paths deviate from time to time. You are being sent to Sultanpur to find employment which will give you success in the material world. I have no doubt that your greater success will be in the world of the spirit and when you achieve the greatness you are destined to, my child, remember this frail old man who believed in you."

Nanak was overcome and turned away. One by one the farewells were made—Bala, Rai Bular, his father, his mother. But there was one goodbye that still needed to be said. He looked around for Mardana but there was no sign of him. Nanak smiled to himself. He was aware that Mardana could not bear to say goodbye. But no matter; the road to Sultanpur went past Mardana's house. He would meet him there.

On seeing Nanak, Mardana fell at once to weeping and wrung his hands in despair, saying, "Why don't you take me with you? You know I cannot live without you."

"I know that, my friend, and I too will find it difficult to be away from you. Give me a few months to settle down and then you can come to live with me in Sultanpur and together we will sing all those devotional songs which have brought us so much comfort and joy."

It took the party five days to make the journey from Talwandi to Sultanpur. On the way they had to cross the Ravi near Lahore and the Beas near Goindwal. Sultanpur was a prosperous town located on the banks of the Bein, a minor stream which is a tributary of the Beas. Cunningham, in his *History of the Sikhs*, says that Sultanpur was originally called Tamasvana and was very famous as a Buddhist settlement. Over the years it had become a picture of decay and neglect. It was restored partially by Sultan Khan, a general of Mahmud Ghazni. The Governor of Lahore at the time was Tatar Khan Lodhi, a cousin of Behlol Khan Lodhi, the founder of the Lodhi dynasty. Tatar Khan Lodhi had given the area of Sultanpur to his son Daulat Khan as a *jagir* in 1504. Daulat Khan would later become the governor of Lahore. But even after he moved to Lahore, he retained Sultanpur as the capital of his personal *jagir*.

During Nanak's entire sojourn in Sultanpur, Daulat Khan Lodhi lived only in Sultanpur. He took on the title of Nawab and proved to be a truly intelligent and enlightened ruler. He encouraged trade with neighbouring *jagirs* and Sultanpur soon earned a reputation as a rich and prosperous town. Many young and enterprising men came there to make their fortune and then stayed on, contributing further to the town's prosperity. Daulat Khan strengthened the fortification of the town and beautified it by laying out many gardens which soon became famous in the entire region. In addition, he encouraged art and scholarship and set up many schools, both Islamic and vocational. These drew teachers and scholars from all over the Punjab. In fact, Sayyad Hassan had taught for a while in one of the Islamic schools and many were the wondrous tales he had told Nanak of Daulat Khan's support and patronage of all branches of learning.

Nanki's cup of joy was complete. She had her adored brother all to herself and, in the days that followed, she and Jai Ram did everything in their power to make him comfortable. The three spent a happy time going around Sultanpur, enjoying the sights and the splendour of the town.

Jai Ram was a trusted official of the Nawab's court and held a place of privilege and favour. He soon found an opportunity to put in a word for his brother-in-law and ask for suitable employment for him. The Nawab agreed to meet the youngster to assess his abilities and skills.

Then, just as Jai Ram took his leave, the Nawab called out to him, "Isn't this the boy who spends all his time in debates with holy men? The boy who once spent twenty silver rupees on feeding hungry ascetics?"

"Yes, my lord, it is he," Jai Ram said, wondering whether the Nawab would hold this act of generosity against Nanak.

"I have heard of him and have wished to meet one who has shown so much compassion, such a marked inclination towards spiritual matters at such a young age. Tell him I look forward to our meeting tomorrow."

This remark reassured Jai Ram and he realised that the Nawab too looked upon Nanak's *sacha sauda* with admiration.

The next morning Nanki fussed over Nanak's dress. "You did not fuss so much when I dressed for my wedding," Nanak teased her. "I knew that your bride did not attach any importance to clothes—the Nawab's court does!" Nanki retorted spiritedly.

As he left the house Nanki held out a bowl of sweetened yoghurt— a custom designed to bring good luck, it was eaten before going on a journey or embarking on a venture. Nanak ate it without a fuss but then asked, "Do you really believe that eating sweetened yoghurt can ensure the success of a venture? If it were so, no one would need to work and milkmen would make a fortune."

Nanki smiled at this gentle chastisement. "I know your abhorrence of superstition, your distrust of the supernatural and the miraculous. But I am not made of such stern stuff. I would have regretted not feeding you the yoghurt if, God forbid, you returned without success." Nanak smiled affectionately at his sister and caressed her hair as he said goodbye.

Nanak walked into the Nawab's palace quite oblivious to the grandeur of his surroundings. The Nawab noticed the confidence of the handsome young man who walked beside Jai Ram and the total lack of wonder and awe on his face. It was obvious that what he had heard about the young man was true—he had detached himself from material things.

"This is my brother-in-law Nanak, the one I spoke to you about," Jai Ram made the introduction as they bowed and greeted the Nawab.

"We welcome you to our *durbar*," the Nawab said and indicated that they should be seated. "We have heard many good things about you," he went on without preamble. "Your reputation has preceded you. We had a very learned Islamic scholar from Talwandi—Sayyad Hassan—who taught in one of our schools some years ago. He often spoke of you."

The meeting went off well. The Nawab questioned Nanak about what he had learnt of Sanskrit and Persian and about the various religions and sects. Nanak answered all the questions with confidence and humility. It soon became obvious that the Nawab was impressed by the depth of the young man's knowledge and had developed an instinctive liking for him.

The very next morning Nanak assumed his appointment as the Nawab's storekeeper. This was an extremely important and highly coveted post in the Nawab's court. In those days, all revenues and taxes were collected in kind, mostly in the form of grain. A daily quota of grain was distributed to the Nawab's employees, his soldiers, and his servants, as part of their salary. In fact, very few officials were paid their salary completely in cash. The collection and distribution of grain was therefore a very important duty in the Nawab's court and it was of vital importance that the storekeeper be a man of impeccable honesty and integrity. From what he had heard about Nanak and his own assessment of Nanak, the Nawab was convinced that he had found an honest and dependable man, who would make an excellent storekeeper, the in-charge of the *modikhana*.

Nanak was expected to supervise the measurement of all the stocks coming in and leaving the *modikhana* and to maintain an account of all transactions. Periodically, there would be an audit and a physical stock-taking, to ensure that the records had been accurately maintained. In addition to a salary, Nanak was given a daily quota of grain. In spite of devoting himself to his work, Nanak still retained his preference for *fakirs*, ascetics and other holy men. Whenever one of them came to the store and begged for some grain, he would find it impossible to turn down the request. But he would always seek his employer's permission, weigh out the grain carefully, and record this too in his ledger.

The job suited Nanak because it was of a banal nature and left him plenty of time for meditation and introspection. There is a popular story that once, while weighing out grain to be distributed, he began counting the measures as they were weighed and put into a sack. When he reached the figure thirteen, or *tera* in Punjabi, he got stuck on it and counted "*tera, tera*" over and over again. It is said that he was lost in meditation and was addressing God: "Thine, Thine, all is Thine."

Once Nanak had settled down in his job, he decided to set up his own home. Nanki knew she would miss him but she helped him find a suitable house within walking distance both from her own house and from the *modikhana* where he worked. The Nawab gladly offered to take care of all the monetary arrangements pertaining to the house and Nanki procured the simple furnishings that would meet Nanak's needs.

It was about a month after Nanak had moved into his house that he had a most welcome visitor. Having eaten his evening meal, he had recited his prayers and was preparing for bed. Just as he covered himself and curled up in a comfortable position, he heard a knock on the door. He wondered who it could be at that late hour. Throwing off his blanket, he shuffled into his *juttis*. The knocking became more persistent.

"I am coming. I am coming." Nanak hurried across his small courtyard. When he opened the door the most wonderful surprise greeted him—the nocturnal visitor was none other than his dear friend Mardana!

"How wonderful to see you again!" he exclaimed.

"I missed our music sessions together and knew I had to come," Mardana said emotionally.

"Come, come," said Nanak, a little overcome himself. "You must be tired and hungry after your long journey." He too had missed his friend enormously.

Mardana quickly took charge of managing the house and Nanak no longer had to worry about household matters. With Mardana to look after him, Nanak's life soon settled into a well-ordered routine. He would wake early at the break of day and bathe in the Bein, which flowed close to his house. After an hour of meditation and prayer, he would eat the breakfast that his friend Mardana had prepared. Then he would go to the *modikhana* and the day would pass quickly in recording the scores of transactions that took place. Before the evening meal, he and Mardana would sit down together to compare notes on the day's happenings. Sometimes they would be joined by some learned men and discussions pertaining to religious and spiritual matters would ensue. Occasionally Nanak and Mardana would visit Nanki and Jai Ram. After Mardana's arrival, they had resumed singing devotional songs together and gradually this activity had become a daily affair. Nanak now took to composing hymns in praise of God, which the two friends would then sing together.

Nanak had established a reputation for great diligence and had impressed his employer with his sincerity, honesty, hard work, and the scrupulousness that he brought to all his transactions. The Nawab would sometimes ask Nanak to stay on after work and engage him in discussion. He became very fond of Nanak and it was obvious to Jai Ram that Nanak had at last found a suitable vocation. He had been able to strike a balance between the necessity of earning his livelihood and the desire to pursue his spiritual quest. There was a measure of stability that had come to Nanak's life. Jai Ram spoke about this to Nanki, who, on her next visit to her brother's house, suggested it was time for him to send for his wife. And so Sulakhni came to Sultanpur and resumed her responsibilities as Nanak's wife.

Close to Sultanpur, in the village of Malvian, lived a man named Bhagirath, who, like Nanak, spent a great deal of time in the company of *yogis*. It was only a question of time before Bhagirath heard that in Nanak, the keeper of the Nawab's *modikhana*, there was a kindred spirit. He was sure that making the acquaintance of one who had attained a high level of learning and saintliness would benefit him greatly. So one evening, he made the short journey to Sultanpur. As he approached the house, he heard strains of the most divine singing to the accompaniment of the *rabab*. He peeped in to find two men absorbed in their performance of devotional music. Not wishing to disturb them, Bhagirath waited outside, listening ecstatically. When they had finished he entered and introduced himself. Nanak bade him welcome and Sulakhni brought him a glass of warm milk.

Bhagirath was so impressed by Nanak that he returned again and again, sometimes to listen to his hymns, sometimes to take part in the discussions. Eventually, he took a house close to Nanak's, and moved there permanently. Bhagirath was Nanak's first disciple. Soon others followed and Nanak found himself giving discourses on all kinds of spiritual matters.

Late one evening, at the end of the *kirtan*, Nanak noticed a group of shabbily dressed men sitting at his doorstep even when there was sufficient place for them in the courtyard. He beckoned to them to come closer. They hesitated but when Nanak persisted, they came reluctantly into the courtyard to take their place in the congregation. As they sat down, Nanak saw that some of the others drew carefully away, as if to avoid contamination. Nanak smiled a small, sad smile—it would be generations before the "upper castes" learnt to shun the stigma of impurity attached to the "lower castes". But this stigma would only be discarded if people began to speak out against it. In a loud, ringing voice Nanak said, "We often look with distaste and horror at things we consider unclean. We make a distinction between the pure and the impure. For example, our brothers who follow professions that bring them in contact with what we consider unclean, are themselves looked upon as unclean and we shun their company. So much so that there are those among us who must bathe if the mere shadow of such a man falls upon them. But let me ask you, my friends, what is clean and what is unclean? We all work to ensure that the kitchen of our home is kept spotlessly clean, not only for the sake of our health but on religious grounds too. But are we really able to ensure the purity of our food? There are worms and maggots in the firewood and cow dung cakes that we use for fuel. There are tiny insects in the corn that is ground to make flour for our bread. The water we drink has a greenish hue because it is teeming with miniscule organisms." Nanak looked around at the audience. "My friends, we do not become unclean by being in contact with those whom we call 'low castes'. We become unclean if we do not protect our hearts and minds from polluting thoughts. We become impure if we allow greed and untruth to creep into our hearts. We become impure if our eye covets the wealth or wife of another. We are impure if we allow our ears to listen to calumny."

Nanak's discourses were powerful and passionate and his listeners were struck by his reasoned arguments. It was no wonder that those who heard him once, came back for more.

Now the pattern of his evenings changed. Everyday, there would be a group of visitors to Nanak's house. They would first listen to his discourse, engage him in discussion, and then request him and Mardana to render a few hymns. Sulakhni provided a simple meal for those who came to visit her husband and they all ate together, caste and creed forgotten. Once Nanki and Jai Ram came to visit and found themselves drawn into the spirit of the discourse and into the congregational singing. Both found such fulfilment from this visit that they came regularly to attend these sessions and soon became ardent disciples of the young Guru.

Shortly after Sulakhni joined her husband in Sultanpur, the marriage of Mardana's daughter took place. Bhagirath, who was a tradesman by profession, was entrusted the task of making all the purchases. He went to Lahore as the best bargains were reputed to be available in the markets there. During the course of his stay there he met a tradesman by the name of Mansukh, who shared his interest in spirituality. The two talked late into the night and, as expected, the talk veered to Nanak and his teachings. Mansukh was so impressed by what he had heard about the Guru that he made the trip to Sultanpur at the earliest opportunity. He wrote down many of Nanak's hymns and brought them back with him to Lahore. He collected a small group of like-minded people and they spent a few hours every evening singing Nanak's hymns. In the months that followed, people in Lahore became familiar with Nanak's *bani* and some of them, enthused by what they had learnt, travelled to Sultanpur to meet the Master.

Nanki and Jai Ram felt their hearts swell with pride at the growing congregation, the increasing number of disciples who came from faraway places to listen to Nanak's discourses and to participate in his sessions of *kirtan*. They both knew that this was the beginning of the fulfilment of Pandit Hardayal's prophecy. Nanki wished that her parents could know of Nanak's growing reputation as a learned and spiritual teacher. But they decided not to inform them, to let Nanak's reputation reach them of its own accord, as they knew it eventually would.

Professionally too, Nanak was doing exceedingly well. He had developed an enviable reputation for meticulousness and transparency in the conduct of all his transactions and in the maintenance of his records. Pleased with his work, the Nawab conferred many favours upon him which Nanak, in turn, immediately passed on to others, winning himself greater respect and esteem in the Nawab's eyes.

In 1494, Nanak and Sulakhni were blessed with a son, whom they named Sri Chand. Sulakhni was overjoyed. For Nanki too the birth of Sri Chand provided a sense of fulfilment. She was childless and the birth of her nephew filled a vacuum in her life. She doted on the child, often chiding Sulakhni for not looking after him well. Sometimes she would take the baby home for days at a time. Sulakhni, more friend than sister-in-law to Nanki, understood her need and treated her attachment to Sri Chand with indulgence.

The birth of Sri Chand provided an opportunity for the Bedi family to be together again, even though for the briefest of time. Kalo and Tripta were not in a position to come to Sultanpur to see their grandson. So Nanak made the five day journey to Talwandi with Sulakhni, Mardana, Nanki, Jai Ram, and little Sri Chand. The joy of the family reunion was clouded by the news that Nanak's mentor, Sayyad Hassan and his wife had recently passed away.

Nanak spent a few days in Talwandi. His parents, and all their friends and acquaintances, were now fully convinced of Nanak's greatness and his spiritual strength. They plied him with questions and Nanak gladly shared his knowledge and his insights with them. He was both amused and touched by their reverence.

In the evenings he sang his compositions and preached a simple sermon to his large congregation. "I have no miracles except the name of God. Through *naam* you can subdue your ego, your *haumain*, and this will result in the conquest of the five sins—lust, anger, greed, pride and attachment. Their conquest, in turn, will lead you to salvation and give you *mukti* or freedom from the cycle of birth and death." He paused and smiled at the familiar faces around him. "But you must be careful how you recite the *naam*. It is not the mere ritualistic mumbling of prayer; it is the recitation of prayer with understanding and its subsequent translation into action in your daily life. *Naam* must first be realised in your heart. It is then and only then, that we experience complete stillness of the mind and oneness with the Almighty." His fame spread and people walked great distances to hear him preach. The days passed quickly and soon it was time for Nanak and Mardana to return to Sultanpur.

Two years later another son was born to Nanak and Sulakhni, and was named Lakhmi Das. "Now I do not need to share Sri Chand with you," Nanki teased her sister-in-law. "You have a son of your own."

While his domestic life was happy, Nanak had trouble brewing at the court. Nanak's growing reputation and his exalted standing with the Nawab aroused tremendous jealousy and there were those who sought to destroy him. Soon malicious stories were circulating in court circles. It was rumoured that Nanak was stealing grain from the *modikhana* and falsifying records to cover up this theft. As proof of this accusation they pointed to the daily *langar*, the open kitchen that was organised in Nanak's house. "How else," they asked, "can Nanak afford to feed so many people everyday?" Some of these jealous courtiers made sure that these stories reached the Nawab's ears but he believed implicitly in Nanak's unimpeachable honesty and chose to ignore the rumours. But Nanak could not ignore them. He went to the Nawab and held out the keys of the *modikhana*.

"What is this?" the Nawab asked. "Are we to presume that you are giving up your job?"

"Not yet, my lord. It would only fuel the gossip and give my detractors something to hold up as proof of my guilt. I am offering you the keys so that you can order a special audit to establish the truth."

"We know that these stories are false and that you are incapable of doing what you have been accused of," the Nawab said, in a gentle and reassuring voice.

"I know that, my lord, and I am grateful to you for your unswerving trust in me. But I am afraid I must insist on an audit."

The Nawab looked at Nanak, saw the determined look on his face and went along with Nanak's demand. "All right," he said. "We will ask for an audit. We know that you sometimes give out more than the sanctioned amount of grain to the poor and the needy, which is perhaps what has led to these accusations. But we also know that you record this in your ledger and make it up from your own daily ration. We know that your *langar* too is run entirely on contributions from your disciples. But yes, you are right, it is important that these rumours should be quashed by conducting an audit."

The treasurer was called in for stock-taking. The stock and the accounts were found to be perfectly in order and Nanak was absolved of the charges levelled against him.

In spite of the unpleasant events at work, Nanak continued to remain calm. He immersed himself even more deeply in meditation, radiating an aura of profound peace. It was then that a momentous incident occurred.

One day, Nanak did not return home after his morning bath. Sulakhni sent Mardana down to the river to look for him. "I have never known him to take so long. He must have met another holy man at the stream and lost track of time. Please tell him to hurry; his breakfast is getting cold."

Mardana went down to the river and searched far and wide but there was no sign of Nanak. All he found were Nanak's neatly folded clothes behind a boulder on the riverbank. Mardana's eyes desperately searched the surface of the water for any sign of his friend but there was none. As the hours slowly passed, everyone lost hope and concluded that Nanak must have developed a cramp in the cold water and drowned.

When the Nawab heard the news, he rushed to the spot. He ordered a thorough search, asking his men to obtain fishermen's nets to drag the river. But even though the river was dragged for miles downstream, the body was not found. Sulakhni was beside herself with grief. Fortunately, her sons were too young to understand the tragedy that had befallen them. It was Nanki alone who refused to believe that her brother had died. "No," she said. "This can never happen. He has a destiny to fulfil. Besides, my brother is a strong swimmer and very familiar with this river. Mark my words, he will return to us." The Nawab, too, found it difficult to believe that Nanak could have drowned. He refused to abandon the search, ordering his horsemen to comb the area.

Nanki was finally proved right. While the search party dragged the river for Nanak's body, one of the soldiers, exhausted by the relentless effort, stole into the forest to catch a short nap. There, in the densest part of the forest, he was astonished to find Nanak sitting cross-legged, lost in deep meditation! They had all given him up for dead and here he was, safe and sound, apparently in perfect health! He ran to convey the glad tidings to the Nawab.

The *Puratan Janamsakhi* describes the incident: "People said, 'Friends, he was lost in the river; from where hath he emerged?' Nanak came home and gave away all he had. He had only his loin cloth left on him and kept nothing besides. Crowds began to collect. The Khan also came and asked, 'Nanak, what happened to you?' Nanak remained silent. The people replied, 'He was in the river and is out of his mind.' The Khan said: 'Friends, this is very distressing,' and turned back in sorrow.'

Nanak went and joined the *fakirs*. With him went the musician Mardana. One day passed. The next day he got up and spoke. 'There is no Hindu, there is no Mussalman.' Whenever he spoke, this is all he would say: 'There is no Hindu, there is no Mussalman.'" (Trans. Singh, Khushwant, *A History of the Sikhs*, vol. I p. 32 & 33)

The inhabitants of Sultanpur pondered over these strange words and wondered if perhaps Nanak had lost his reason. It was only later that their deep significance was understood and they came to be looked upon as the proclamation of a new faith. According to Macauliffe, the *Mool Mantra*, the opening of the *Japji*, was delivered by Nanak at this time.

Much later, Nanak spoke about his strange experience. While he had been swimming in the river he had heard a faraway voice with a strange dream-like quality to it. The voice had been so soft that at first he had not been able to understand the import of the words. Then he had understood that the voice was telling him to go from village to village and from town to town to deliver his message and teachings.

There was great rejoicing among Nanak's disciples at their teacher's safe return. The Nawab, too, was happy that everything had ended well. He was sure that in a little while, things would settle down, calm would be restored, and Nanak would resume his duties. As things turned out, calm was never restored and Nanak never returned to his duties.

The first words that Nanak had uttered "There is one God. There is no Hindu, there is no Mussalman", were quoted far and wide. They finally reached the ears of the *qazi* of Sultanpur who was livid with anger. He had heard that some Muslims too attended Nanak's meetings. The blasphemous teachings of this upstart were already beginning to disrupt the lives of devout Muslims. If this was not nipped in the bud Allah alone knew what further effect they could have on the faithful. So the *qazi* asked for, and was granted, audience with the Nawab.

"My lord, Nanak is getting out of control. His teachings are sacrilegious! Have you heard what he is saying now? 'There is no Hindu, there is no Mussalman'. People have lapped this up as if it is some kind of catch phrase and it is doing untold damage in Sultanpur and the surrounding areas."

The Nawab was beginning to enjoy this. "He includes the Hindus in this seemingly heretical statement—it has not caused them any alarm."

"Oh, them!" the *qazi* uttered contemptuously. "They are such cowards. Nothing better can be expected of them. But *we*, the faithful, cannot sit by and let him get away with this."

Daulat Khan realised that even though he himself was amused at the whole situation, the *qazi's* anger was not something to be taken lightly. Unless something was done to placate him, he would turn rabid in his denunciation of Nanak during *namaz*, and he would have a highly explosive situation on his hands. "What do you suggest we do, O *Qazi*?" he asked. He thought it best to follow the *qazi's* advice, knowing his propensity to conveniently disassociate himself from uncomfortable situations.

The *qazi* recommended that Nanak be sent for and confronted with his blasphemous teaching. The Nawab duly sent for Nanak. "The *qazi* is perturbed by one of your remarks, Nanak. Tell us what you mean when you say 'there is no Hindu, there is no Mussalman'. Are not the *qazi* and I followers of the Prophet?"

"There is no Hindu, there is no Mussalman," Nanak repeated. "There is only the true follower of God."

Nanak's reply incensed the *qazi*. "And what are you?" he asked, his voice loud and harsh with rage.

Nanak only smiled and in his soft, gentle voice said, "I am neither a Mussalman nor a Hindu. I try first and foremost to live as a man of God. In my eyes, the Hindus and the Mussalmans are equal; their faith, and their religion is equal."

It was time for the Friday prayer and the *qazi* saw his chance to trap Nanak. "It is time for the Friday prayer. Do join us in offering this prayer in the mosque."

So the Nawab, the *qazi*, and Nanak set off for the mosque. The *qazi* took his place at the head of the congregation. During the *namaz*, when all the other worshippers knelt in prayer, Nanak remained standing. When the *namaz* had been completed the *qazi* turned to the Nawab. "My lord, this man is a liar! He said that for him all religions are equal but he did not join us in the *namaz*. And he has the temerity to say that there is no Mussalman. This is sacrilege of the worst order and he must be punished."

"Tell me, my friend," the Nawab said to Nanak, "what explanation do you have to offer?"

Nanak did not reply directly to the Nawab's question. Turning instead to the *qazi* with a twinkle in his eyes he said, "You are a man of God, in the house of God, and you have just led a congregation of a thousand men in prayer. I know that you will speak nothing but the truth. Tell me, what was on your mind while you led the prayers?"

The *qazi* hesitated. He was cornered but knew he had to speak the truth. "I was thinking of my mare." He spoke softly but the silence around was so complete that he could be heard clearly by everyone. "My mare had a foal last night. It was a difficult birth but all went well. There is an open well next to the stable and I was worried that the foal would fall into it and I would lose him."

"So tell me, learned one," Nanak asked, "does prayer consist only in kneeling and bowing and reciting a few words?"

"No," said the *qazi*. "True prayer comes from a focussed mind so that when you praise God, you think only of Him and of nothing else. You are right, Nanak. While my body was bowing to God, my mind was full of other things."

"And do you become a Mussalman by merely reciting the *namaz* five times a day?"

The *qazi* pondered over this and then replied in carefully chosen words. "No. We must be firm in our faith, our hearts must be clean, and we must not have any greed or pride. We must accept the will of God. We must be unselfish and kind to all. Only then can we call ourselves true Mussalmans."

"And are you all these things?" Nanak asked in a kind, compassionate voice.

"No. I am not all these things." The *qazi*'s voice was firm. He had at last understood the import of Nanak's words.

"If you, the spiritual head of all the Mussalmans in Sultanpur, are not a true Mussalman, how can you impart any religious knowledge to your congregation?" Nanak finished gently.

Guru Nanak was now ready to go out beyond Sultanpur and spread his message to all the people who cared to listen to him. Daulat Khan requested Nanak not to leave Sultanpur. After the incident with the *qazi*, the Nawab was convinced that Sultanpur needed a teacher like Nanak. Jai Ram and Nanki too begged Nanak not to leave them and Sulakhni pleaded with him to consider the plight of their two little boys who would be deprived of a father's love. But Nanak had made up his mind and was beyond all inducements and coercion. So in 1496, Nanak, with Mardana as his sole companion, set out on his missionary journey.

FIRST UDASI

Nanak went on his way, preaching the truth as he had perceived it, and showing mankind the path to salvation. He eventually spent twenty-three years on the road and travelled not only in India but also to Tibet, Ceylon and the central Asian countries of Arabia, Iraq and Iran. Today, with all the modern means of transport available to us, we cannot help but marvel at the distances that Nanak covered when the fastest means of transport available were horses or animal-driven carts. We marvel, too, at the remote and isolated places that Nanak managed to reach: he travelled through barren deserts and across high mountain ranges, along lush fertile valleys and through vast, endless plains. He passed through remote little hamlets and through splendid, majestic towns and cities. During his travels he met many kinds of people, rich and poor, simple village folk, learned scholars and saints. He visited many famous temples, mosques, and places of pilgrimage. He saw people celebrating various festivals and was exposed to different traditions and customs. And everywhere he went, people found peace in his words of love and in his gentle smiling face. In the evening, he sang hymns in praise of God and people came to listen to his songs and to hear his sermons. They learnt lessons of kindness and love, and experienced a desire to walk the path towards spiritual awakening.

Nanak was accompanied on all his travels by Mardana, his childhood friend who did a commendable job in serving as his companion and proved to be an invaluable asset in making people familiar with Nanak's hymns. In the innumerable sessions of *kirtan* that were conducted on the journey it was Mardana's musical accompaniment that made it easier for the listeners to retain the essence of the hymns. Three of Mardana's own compositions find place in the *Guru Granth Sahib*. "He (Mardana) has a special place in the Sikh ethos and is the only Sikh disciple to be permitted to use Guru Nanak's name in his hymns. Barring this exception, this was a privilege solely reserved for the Gurus." (Singh, Roopinder, *Guru Nanak: His Life and Teachings,* p. 59)

Having stated so categorically that "there is no Hindu, there is no Mussalman" at the moment of his spiritual awakening, Nanak ensured that he would not be mistaken for a follower of either religion. He dressed in clothes that set him apart from any known sect and thus emphasised his non-adherence to any one faith. He wore the long, loose *choga* that is worn by Muslim dervishes, but it was of the reddish ochre colour favoured by holy men and ascetics professing the Hindu faith. He wore a white cloth belt around his waist, which echoed the dress of the *fakirs*. On his head he wore the cap that *kalandars* wear, partially covered by a turban, which made him look like the follower of one of the Sufi sects. On his feet he wore the wooden sandals favoured by all religious men. Through his dress he sought to emphasise the universality of his message.

Historians and scholars have done a great deal of research to establish Guru Nanak's long travels or udasis on each of his extended forays from Sultanpur. The source materials they have drawn upon are the janamsakhis and the earliest accounts of Guru Nanak's travels written by Bhai Gurdas. They have also studied the common trade routes of the early sixteenth century and the locations of the gurdwaras constructed to commemorate Guru Nanak's visits to various places.

Traditionally, most scholars divide Nanak's travels into four journeys: the first to the east till Jagannath Puri, the second southwards to Ceylon, the third northwards to Kashmir, Ladakh, Tibet, Nepal and Sikkim, and the last one westwards to Multan, and then on to Jeddah, Mecca, Baghdad and Iran. According to the *Mehrban Janamsakhi*, Nanak carried on southwards to Ceylon from Jagannath Puri without returning to Sultanpur. Hence this version records only three udasis. Modern scholars like Kirpal Singh and Kharak Singh also tend to combine the first and second journey on the grounds that it was more logical for Nanak, if he intended to go to Ceylon, to travel southwards from Puri than to return to Talwandi and set out again, especially when Jagannath Puri was well-linked to the south at that time. Even the *Puratan Janamsakhi,* which is the source of the popularly held belief that Nanak made four distinct journeys, states that Nanak returned to Talwandi from his first journey after a gap of twelve years. It would have taken him this length of time only if Ceylon too had been included in his first itinerary. There is, of course, a lot to be said for this point of view. But the present account follows the popularly held view of the *Puratan Janamsakhi*, that there were not three but four udasis.

The first udasi or spiritual mission began in the year 1496. It commenced from Sultanpur, where Nanak had experienced the spiritual awakening that compelled him to spread the divine message far and wide and motivated him to embark on his marathon journeys. It is said that no sooner had they set off on their journey than Mardana complained of hunger, as he so often did throughout their travels together. Nanak sat down in the shade of a tree and pointed to a village a mile away. It was a prosperous looking village and the freshly painted white walls gleamed even under the overcast sky. "Go, Mardana. The people in that village will surely have some food to spare," Nanak said.

The village belonged to the prosperous Uppals and they were indeed happy to meet Nanak's companion. They had heard of Nanak and the story of his strange disappearance and subsequent enlightenment. They fed Mardana all kinds of delicious food till he thought his stomach would burst. They also plied him with rich clothes and gifts that they thought would be of use to the two travellers on their journey.

Nanak was amused to see his friend struggling back along the road, burdened with gifts. "What is all this?" he asked. "I didn't think the Uppals would expect you to carry such a heavy burden to show your appreciation for their generosity. Where are you supposed to deliver this?"

Mardana dropped the bundles at Nanak's feet and wiped the sweat from his brow. "No, no. These are the clothes and gifts that the Uppals have given us to make our journey comfortable."

Nanak laughed at this. "You have walked just one mile with these bundles. Did you find the walk pleasant?"

Mardana shook his head. "It was quite easily the longest and most difficult mile of my life," he admitted.

"Then how will all these things make our journey comfortable? We cannot clutter up our lives, now or ever. We must travel light, live simply, and not worry about tomorrow, secure in the knowledge that God will always provide—perhaps through the generosity of people like the good Uppals."

Mardana was loath to leave all the valuable gifts behind. "What will happen to them?" he asked, indicating the bundles.

"This is a public thoroughfare. Someone is sure to find them. May they bring happiness and pleasure to the one who finds them. But do not worry about these things. Desire for material possessions never brings true happiness."

Nanak and Mardana crossed the Beas and came to the area where Amritsar now stands. It was the month of *Sawan*, when the monsoon is at its strongest. Dark clouds covered the sky and the winds that blew were cool and refreshing. Myriad birds chirped their joy at the pleasant change of season. Nanak felt his heart fill with pleasure at the abundant beauty of nature.

"Mardana, do you hear the call of the birds?"

"Yes, Master, it is more beautiful than any music that man can make."

"Then let us rest for a while and savour the beauty of this music and this place."

There was a large pond with a thick grove of trees on its bank. Nanak rested under one of these trees. Mardana sat beside him, strumming his *rabab* and Nanak sang a hymn in praise of God who had created this beautiful world. Years later, when Guru Arjun Dev, the fifth Guru, looked for a suitable site to build the Harmandir Sahib, the holiest of Sikh shrines, it was this site that he chose. The tree, under which Nanak rested still stands in the compound of the temple, gnarled and shrivelled, but still very much alive, venerated by all who visit the shrine.

Nanak went on to Lahore and after a short stay carried on to Talwandi. His mother was delighted to see him again and would not let him out of her sight. Kalo realised Nanak had changed. He was ill at ease with the idea that he had given up his work with the Lodhi to become some kind of a Guru, preaching a strange new way of life. He was not sure that any good would come from the path that Nanak had chosen to follow. He felt uncomfortable in his son's company and quickly left to inform Rai Bular of Nanak's arrival.

Rai Bular had been seized by a strange sickness and had sought treatment from many quarters without success. He had bouts of fever that left him so weak and emaciated that those who loved him worried for his life. A treatment prescribed by the physician Hardas cured him of the fever, but he never fully recovered his health. He was no longer able to eat a full meal or enjoy a good night's rest. When Kalo informed him of Nanak's arrival, his face lit up with joy. Forgetting his weakness he hurried to Kalo's house. He arrived flushed and breathless. "Oh, Nanak," he said, drawing Nanak into a warm embrace. "I despaired of ever seeing you again. Through all the long months of my illness my only wish was to look once upon your face before my Maker called me." His love and admiration for the young man was there for all the world to see. Nanak, in turn, looked closely at his mentor and was alarmed to see the ravages wrought by the malady.

"I often thought of you, Rai Sahib," he said, as he helped him to a *divan* and propped him up with cushions.

"You have changed, Nanak," Rai Bular said. "I can see a divine radiance in your face; a radiance that comes only when one has been touched by God."

"Yes, Rai Sahib, I feel that I have been touched by a divine spirit, a spirit that tells me I must go forth and teach my perception of truth and the right path to as many people as possible."

"And what is this perception of truth? The right path?"

Nanak pondered for a moment and then answered, "There are four stages on the path to salvation. The first three—discipline or *dharma kand*, knowledge or *gyan kand*, and action or *karam kand*—lead to the fourth stage of blissful merger in God or *sach kand*." Their discussion continued late into the night and Rai Bular found great peace in Nanak's words.

In the few days that he stayed in Talwandi, Nanak held prayer meetings in which he showed the congregation a new path to salvation. On listening to him Rai Bular knew that Nanak had realised his quest and he accepted him as his Guru. Kalo, too, was moved by Nanak's words, and felt that this was perhaps the path divined for his son by God.

Mardana, of course, made the most of his short stay in Talwandi. He indulged to his heart's content in all the delicious food that had been denied to him during his travel. He enjoyed the open-mouthed wonder and admiration of his listeners when he told them exaggerated stories of the splendour of Sultanpur, the richness of the Nawab's palace and court, and of the Lodhi's special affection for Nanak and himself.

After a few days, Nanak announced that it was time for him to move on. All those who had heard him preach were convinced that his sermons were inspired. Tripta too believed that the call for him to go forth and share his message with the world was a divine call and she did not stop him from leaving.

From Talwandi, Nanak and Mardana travelled northwest for about sixty miles and came to the town of Saidpur Sandiali. Some years later this town was to make history of sorts when it was captured by Babar.

Shortly before he reached Saidpur, Babar had gone hungry for a few days and his life had been saved by Emina, the wife of a *bhishti* or waterman, who gave him some roasted grain to eat. When he later captured Saidpur, he renamed it Eminabad to honour the woman who had saved his life. But when Nanak came to Saidpur, Babar's invasion was still very much an event of the future.

As Nanak reached the outskirts of the town, he stopped a passer-by and asked, "Tell me, my friend, who is the poorest man in your town?"

The stranger laughed at Nanak's question. "That is indeed a strange question! If it is the poorest person you seek, it is undoubtedly Lalo, the carpenter. But let me warn you that he will not have anything more than a stale crust to offer you, if even that. And if you need to rest for the night the only bed he will be able to offer you is a tattered *chattai* on the floor."

Nanak smiled indulgently. "You have been most helpful. Now would you be kind enough to guide us to Lalo's hut?"

The stranger was intrigued. In spite of his warnings this strange *fakir* seemed determined to go to the poor carpenter's house. He shrugged and led the way to Lalo's hut.

It was indeed a ramshackle place—a small room, with a thatched roof which had given way in some places, and a mud wall enclosing a small courtyard. The door of the courtyard was wide open, hanging loose on its hinges.

"Lalo!" Nanak's escort called through the open doorway. "You have a visitor; in fact, two. They are determined to draw upon your generous hospitality for the night." He sniggered and hurried away to share this juicy gossip with his friends. These were strange times indeed—a stranger, so obviously from a high caste, choosing to stay in the lowly carpenter's home!

Lalo was about forty-five, with an open, cheerful face and his body was lean and wiry from long hours of physical labour. He looked closely at the two men standing at his door. From the radiance on Nanak's face and from his appearance he knew he was in the presence of a holy man. He bent down and touched Nanak's feet.

"You honour me with your presence, *Swamiji*. What can I do for you?"

"As you can see, we are travellers who have walked many, many miles today and we are tired and hungry. We would be grateful if you could give us food and shelter for the night."

Lalo was dumbstruck at this request. "Everything I have is at your command, *Swamiji*. But I am a low-born carpenter. Will you not lose caste if you share my food and my home?"

Nanak remembered the aborted *janeu* ceremony and a sad smile came to his face. "I have no caste to lose. For me there is only one caste, the caste of humanity."

"Then you are most welcome," Lalo beamed and led them into his house. He looked around uncertainly for something to seat his guests. There was a rope cot placed upright against the courtyard wall. Lalo straightened it out and they saw that the ropes had frayed and given way in many places.

"Don't worry," Nanak said. "I believe you have a *chattai*—just spread it out and we'll be happy to use it."

When Lalo unrolled the *chattai*, Nanak saw that it was indeed as worn out as the stranger had warned them it would be. Lalo brought them some water so they could wash off the dust of their journey. He busied himself with a wooden stove at the far end of his courtyard that served as his kitchen. Soon, he had placed before them two *thalis* containing small portions of food.

"You must forgive me, *Swamiji*, for such poor and meagre fare—this is indeed all that I have."

"Do not apologise, my son; it is God who provides. Besides, what greater generosity can there be than giving away all that one has?" Nanak made the carpenter sit beside him and eat from his *thali*, and Lalo was overwhelmed by the stranger's kindness and affection. He wondered what sect this holy man belonged to. Whatever his particular faith, it was undoubtedly a compassionate one, Lalo thought.

After the evening meal was done, the three sat together and Nanak spoke to him at length about the mission that he had embarked upon. Then Nanak and Mardana sang a few devotional songs and Lalo joined in as best he could. He did not understand all that Nanak preached but he did understand that if people practised these teachings the world would be a far better place to live in, especially for people like him.

"O holy one, then are all men really equal, the rich and the poor, the Brahmin and the Shudra?" Lalo asked.

"Yes, Bhai Lalo. Even when a man is so rich that his pots and pans are made of gold, it is of little value in the eyes of God. What really matters is not how rich you are or which caste you belong to—what matters is that you should be absorbed in the True word and all your

74

thoughts and actions should arise from the depths of Truth." After a pause the Guru recited a verse:

"There are ignoble among the noblest
and pure among the despised.
The former shall though avoid
And be the dust under the foot of the other."
(Trans. Singh, Khushwant, *Japjee–Sikh Morning Prayer*, p. 24)

At last the lateness of the hour caught up with the two travellers as did their weariness. Lalo lay awake on the floor of the courtyard, marvelling at this strange and wondrous experience that had come his way. Next morning, when the travellers prepared to set out on their way again, Lalo threw himself at Nanak's feet. "I have never before received such love and respect from anyone and my spirit has never experienced such peace. I beg you, *Swamiji*, do me the honour of staying a few days in my humble abode. It will be blessed forevermore."

Nanak looked into the carpenter's face and knew that the plea came from the bottom of his heart. "All right then, Lalo," he said, putting down his bundle of spare clothes. "I will stay with you for a few days."

Lalo was beside himself with joy. He went about in a trance, oblivious to the world, his mind focussed only on Nanak's words and on the beauty of the hymns that were sung in his little house every evening. Saidpur was soon abuzz with rumours and gossip regarding the strange, high-born *sadhu* who had chosen to take shelter in the home of a low-caste carpenter. Grist was added to the rumour mill when his strange and oft-repeated words "there is no Hindu, there is no Mussalman" were bruited about the town. There were those who dismissed him out of hand; it was not unusual to find fake *sadhus* and *fakirs*. Nanak was probably just another charlatan out to trick simple-minded people and deserved to be treated with contempt. Besides, it was he who was losing caste by hobnobbing with a low-caste carpenter.

But there were others whose curiosity was aroused. Who was this strange man who had chosen to live with the impoverished Lalo when he could have found comfortable lodgings? What was this peculiar doctrine that he was preaching—what exactly did it mean? Curiosity, once sufficiently whetted, will not deny itself satisfaction and so the curious thronged Lalo's house in large numbers. Nanak's discourses and hymns were captivating and gradually the congregation began to grow.

There was much that was new and strange in Nanak's teaching but it struck an immediate chord in their hearts. They came every evening, bringing along friends and family, to listen to his message of universal brotherhood. Soon the congregation overflowed out of the poor carpenter's courtyard.

The Muslim Rai of Saidpur was a man who was not particularly adept at or interested in governance and administration. He left this entirely to his Hindu *diwan* or chief administrator, Malik Bhago, who ruled with an iron hand. He was ruthless in exacting the taxes due to the Rai and in exploiting the poor and the downtrodden. Stories of his ruthlessness were legion and it was said that he was a man without an iota of compassion or humanity. As a result of this exploitation, Bhago had become an exceedingly wealthy man. He had built a huge sprawling *haveli* which rivalled that of the Rai in its splendour. He and his family dressed in richly embroidered robes and wore the most magnificent jewellery. His wealth and position brought him immense power and the people of Saidpur bowed and scraped before him.

Bhago's only weakness was his son. After years of waiting a son had been born to him and Bhago doted on the boy. He was handsome, intelligent and surprisingly polite and well-behaved, considering all the attention that was lavished upon him. Bhago said a thousand prayers daily in gratitude to God for this wonderful gift. Every year on the boy's birthday Bhago would organise a *brahm bhoj* for the holy men of the area. His messengers would go far and wide, scour the countryside for men of religious or spiritual leanings, and extend their master's invitation. The *bhoj* was always well-attended, not merely because the feast was extravagant and everyone came away laden with presents but also because no one dared to risk annoying Bhago.

Like all devout Hindus, Bhago believed that much was to be attained by feeding holy men. Not only would he receive their blessings, he would also earn merit in the eyes of God. By arranging the *brahm bhoj* on such a large scale he sought long life, health, and prosperity not only for his son but also for himself.

On the appointed day there was such a great conclave of holy men assembled in Bhago's courtyard that it could have overshadowed a gathering at the pilgrimage centre of Hardwar. From early morning till late night ascetics, *fakirs*, *sadhus*, and *tantriks* thronged Bhago's *haveli*. After partaking of the lavish feast, they showered their blessings on Bhago and his son and went their way laden with presents. Bhago personally supervised the meal to ensure that all his guests were well looked after.

That year, the *brahm bhoj* took place during Nanak's sojourn in Saidpur. Late in the evening, when the stream of holy men had shrunk to a trickle and then dried up altogether, Bhago turned to his retainers. "Are you sure that every mendicant you invited was present here?"

"Yes, my lord," they answered. "All the holy men we had invited on your behalf were here."

Bhago was pleased; he had done his best to ensure that his son had been sufficiently blessed for the coming year. As he turned to retire to his personal chambers, one of his retainers spoke up, "There is one holy man who did not come."

"Did not come? Was he not invited? Who failed to invite him?" There was anger in Bhago's voice. A hush descended on the crowd of retainers and they all hung their heads, afraid to look their master in the eye.

"I invited him myself, Sahib," the retainer said nervously. "I told him what a great feast it was and how all the holy men of the area would be present."

"And yet he did not come?" There was surprise and perplexity in Bhago's voice. That someone could turn down an invitation from him was beyond his comprehension. "Perhaps he is unwell," Bhago said. "Go and inquire after him and if he needs medical attention, ensure that he gets the best. If the illness is of serious consequence, bring him to the *haveli* so that he can be cared for."

The retainer hurried to Lalo's hut. Illness was the only reasonable explanation for Nanak's absence at the *brahm bhoj*. But when he reached there he was surprised to find him busy preaching to the usual throng of disciples in Lalo's little courtyard. He could not believe his eyes. The man obviously had no idea of the *Malik*'s anger and was not aware of the consequences of his insolence. He returned to the *haveli* and stood before his master, head down, unable to find words to convey his news without inviting his master's wrath.

"What is it? Is the *sadhu* dead?" Bhago growled.

The retainer remained silent and Bhago strode impatiently towards him. "Speak up! Have you lost your tongue?"

"No, Sahib. He is not dead," the messenger replied in a low voice, his eyes still fixed on the ground.

"Perhaps he is extremely ill and you have lost hope of his recovery?" Bhago suggested.

The servant knew there was no help for it; the truth had to be told. "No, Sahib. He is well and is, at the moment, preaching to a group of people."

"What?" Bhago expostulated, unable to believe the implication of the messenger's statement. "You mean he deliberately chose to ignore my invitation? He chose to ignore an invitation from Malik Bhago?" His voice rose with anger. Servants and family members peered into the courtyard, cringing in fear at the thought of what lay ahead.

"You! Bijlee Pehlwan!" Malik Bhago called the huge wrestler who was the captain of his guard. "Take twelve of your men and bring this ... this ... *sadhu* to me."

"Be at peace, Sahib. It will not take twelve men to bring the *sadhu* to you."

As it happened, Nanak had finished his discourse by the time the *pehlwan* arrived. He willingly followed him to Malik Bhago's *haveli*.

As Nanak stood before him Bhago was a little awed by the supernatural radiance on his face. No one had ever dared to look back at him with such an unflinching gaze and Bhago felt his confidence waver.

"Have you not heard of the richness of my *brahm bhoj*? Holy men wait impatiently for this annual feast and trudge long distances to attend it. But you, who were specially invited, chose to share a stale crust of bread with a lowly carpenter instead." In spite of himself Bhago found that his anger had been tempered by the *sadhu*'s presence. He could not bring himself to use the bitter, abusive words that he had rehearsed in his mind before the *sadhu*'s arrival. Nanak greeted the *diwan*'s words with a sweet, gentle smile, and Bhago found that all anger left him to be replaced by incredulousness. "What manner of man are you?" His voice was now little more than a whisper.

Nanak took a step forward and put his hand on Bhago's shoulder. "A right thinking man, my lord. What you say is true. I preferred the stale crust of bread to the lavish feast and rich presents of the mighty *diwan*. I request you for a moment, only a moment, to look into your heart. Lift the veils of pretence and hypocrisy and look at your true self."

A hush had fallen on the crowd. Bhago was speechless as Nanak continued, "Where does the great wealth that you are so proud of come from? If you are honest you will admit that it comes from the cruel exploitation of the poor and the downtrodden, causing untold misery and suffering. Lalo's wealth—the little there is of it—comes from hard labour and the sweat of his brow." Nanak paused for breath and those who crowded around looked at their master's face for signs of his legendary anger. But there were none. Bhago stood patiently, waiting for Nanak to go on. "The amount you spent on this feast was but a drop in the ocean of your wealth; it made no difference to you. As for Lalo, he had only that crust of stale bread. Yet he happily gave it to a stranger and went hungry himself."

Bhago's hardened, brutal heart began to soften and the inescapable truth of Nanak's words dawned on him.

"And last of all, you had a selfish motive, a desire for a return. You fed thousands of holy men so that you could earn their gratitude and blessings for your son. Lalo gave with no motive. His only desire was to feed a hungry stranger at his door. His crust of bread, stale as it was, was leavened with the milk of human kindness, while your feast was seasoned with the tears of the poor and oppressed."

Bhago looked penitent and there was a look of humility on his face. "Come, Nanak," he said, "take me to Bhai Lalo's hut so that I may know the taste of bread that has been leavened with the milk of human kindness."

Nanak stayed in Saidpur for many days and when he left, Bhai Lalo took it upon himself to conduct the daily meetings and to preach the lessons that Nanak had taught him. Malik Bhago became Bhai Lalo's most ardent disciple. Guru Nanak was to meet Lalo several times in the years to come.

Nanak and Mardana crossed the Punjab through Harappa and came to Tulamba. Close to the entrance to the town stood the *serai* of Sheikh Sajjan, a man who professed to be above the distinctions of caste and religion. He dressed in flowing robes of spotless white. On his forehead he wore a *tilak* of sandal wood paste, the mark of a pious Hindu, and around his neck he wore a rosary, the symbol of a devout Muslim. He welcomed all travellers to his *serai* and spent his days attending to their needs. His hospitality to travellers was widely known and Sheikh Sajjan became something of a legend. People spoke of his selfless generosity and looked upon him as a man of God.

But there was a secret side to Sheikh Sajjan's personality. Once in a while he would identify a truly wealthy traveller and treat him with his usual kindness and generosity, making him believe that his host was truly a man of God. But in the silence of the night, Sajjan would creep into his room and, with an efficiency born of long planning and experience, kill the unsuspecting traveller. He would dispose of the body and take the traveller's money and possessions. When questioned about the strange disappearance of his guest he would claim that the guest had left very early in the morning and his henchmen would bear witness to the fact that they had seen him safely on his way.

By the time Nanak came to Sajjan's *serai* there had been a sufficient number of "disappearances" to give rise to rumours which pointed the finger of suspicion firmly at Sajjan. But his standing in society and his reputation were such that no one dared to openly accuse him of murder.

If Nanak and Mardana had heard of these rumours, it did not keep them from stopping at Sajjan's *serai*. Sajjan greeted them with his usual warmth, gave them hot water to bathe and good wholesome food to eat. He escorted them to their room and bade them good night with a great show of goodwill and kindness. But in his heart he harboured evil. From the moment he had set his eyes upon Nanak he had marked him out as his next victim. He was convinced that the radiance on Nanak's face came from a lifetime of comfortable and rich living. He was sure that Nanak wore the strange garb to make people believe that he was a poor *fakir*. A true *fakir* would have been easily distinguishable as a Hindu or a Muslim. The traveller had obviously exercised abundant caution in choosing this garb to hide his wealth but it was this very disguise which gave him away. Well, this was the last night that he would ever need a disguise!

Sajjan waited for the early hours of the morning. The hot bath, the sumptuous meal, and the weariness of their journey would have had their effect and his victim would be fast asleep. But when he stole quietly towards Nanak's room, Sajjan was surprised to find light streaming through the open door and to hear soft music echoing through the corridor. The music was so beautiful that it drew him like a magnet even though he knew that his quarry was still awake. He paused at the door and listened to the song. The melody and the poignant music stirred his heart. He was moved to tears by the beauty of the hymn. In those few moments he was given a glimpse of divinity and, in the radiance of that light, a deep awareness of his own sinful life. He knew at once that this was a defining moment. After experiencing such spiritual ecstasy he could never be the same again, never go back to his evil ways.

The music filled his senses and Nanak's hymn reverberated in his mind:

"Bright & brilliant is the bronze
But the moment it is rubbed its blackness appears.
This cannot be removed even if washed a hundred times."
(*Raga Suhi*, Trans. Duggal, K. S., *Sikh Gurus*, p. 17)

Now there was no turning back for Sajjan. He rushed into the room and fell at Nanak's feet. He confessed his evil deeds and begged forgiveness.

"By making a full and honest confession of your evil deeds you have taken the first step on the path of redemption. If the rest of your life is spent living the right way, complete redemption will be yours." In the days that followed, Nanak preached to him the path of right living.

Sajjan gave away everything he had and spent the rest of his life in true and selfless service of others and in spreading Nanak's word. They say that in the town of Makhdumpur in Pakistan there is, to this day, a much revered tomb that is said to be that of Sheikh Sajjan.

From Tulamba, Nanak and Mardana visited Pak Pattan. This town was originally named Ayodhan but the name had been changed when Sheikh Farid settled here. Nanak spent a few fruitful days in discussion with Sheikh Farid's successor Ibrahim, who was so learned and devout that he was often referred to as a second Sheikh Farid. This visit gave Nanak an opportunity to collect many hymns and spiritual songs composed by Sheikh Farid. In the years to come these songs became such an integral part of Nanak's teachings that when Guru Arjun Dev compiled the Adi Granth, he gave pride of place to these compositions.

From Pak Pattan, Nanak went to Karra and Pehowa, arriving at the holy town of Kurukshetra on the eve of a solar eclipse. The eclipse had become the occasion for a religious fair, attracting thousands of pilgrims including *sadhus* and religious leaders. Nanak found himself drawn into a discussion on the subject of eating meat. One of the learned leaders vehemently condemned this practice, stating that it had to be banned, especially in Kurukshetra, as it defiled the sanctity of the holy town. Nanak gently pointed out that abolishing meat-eating would not sanctify a place. It was only when the inhabitants of a town followed the path that led to spiritual progress that the place became sacred.

The Guru is said to have composed a hymn on the occasion, which finds a place in the Adi Granth on page 1289:

> "Those who abjure meat and sit holding their noses
> Eat men at night;
> They make a show of hypocrisy for others
> But have no true knowledge of God."
> (*Var Malhar*, Trans. Sarna, Navtej, *The Book of Nanak*, p. 58).

From Kurukshetra, Nanak came to Panipat where he met Abu Ali Qalandar, the successor to the Sufi saint Sheikh Sharaf. The saint was impressed by Nanak's learning and understanding of Sufi beliefs and by his high level of spiritual attainment. He could see that Nanak had come face to face with divinity.

Nanak and Mardana finally arrived at Delhi. By now Nanak's teachings were widely known and he was greeted by a group of people, comprising both Hindus and Muslims, who were already his followers. There was a heated discussion among them as everyone wanted the honour of hosting the Guru during his sojourn in Delhi. Nanak listened to the discussion, a soft smile playing at the corner of his lips. He cast his eye over each member of the group and saw a thin, frail man standing a little away from the others. He appeared to be a Muslim *fakir* and was obviously the poorest member of the group.

Nanak held up his hand and silence descended upon the group as he called out to the *fakir*. "O holy one, I do not hear you arguing with your friends—am I to believe that you do not wish to have me in your home?" The *fakir* looked at Nanak and shook his head.

"He is a *fakir*," one of the more prosperous of the group clarified. "How can he offer you hospitality, O Guru, when he himself is dependent on the charity of others?"

"I, too, am dependent upon the charity of others. I am sure the *fakir* and I will get on well. What is your name, O holy one? Or have you abjured even that?"

It turned out that the *fakir* was named Majnu and lived in a flimsy little hut built on a mound, which afterwards came to be called Majnu-Ka-Tilka. Nanak stayed there for a few days. He and Mardana encouraged their small congregation to learn their hymns and every evening Nanak preached to those who came to listen to him. Years later, Guru Tegh Bahadur, the ninth Guru, also stopped at this site and today there is a very impressive gurdwara which marks these visits.

From Delhi, Nanak and Mardana travelled towards the hills and came to the holy city of Hardwar, an important pilgrimage town for the

Hindus. It was early morning when the two entered the town. They were greeted with the sounds of prayers being chanted and hymns being sung to the accompaniment of temple bells and conch shells. Thousands of pilgrims bathed in the cold water in the belief that the holy waters would wash away all their sins. As the sun rose in the eastern sky, the pilgrims offered water to it. Nanak went up to a young man and asked, "Why are you throwing water towards the sun, my friend?"

"You must be the most illiterate and ill-informed Hindu in the world," the young man laughed at Nanak. "I am offering water to the sun to quench the thirst of my ancestors."

Nanak stepped into the river, bathed, and turning his back to the sun, began to toss water towards the west. The pilgrims nearby stopped in their act of quenching the thirst of their ancestors and stared at this strange man, amazed at his eccentric behaviour. An elderly gentleman called out to him. "What are you doing, my good man? Have you gone mad? Why are you offering water in the wrong direction?"

"It is not the wrong direction. My land is near Lahore which, as you know, is towards the west. There has been a dry spell in that area and my crops are in danger of being ruined. I am throwing water in that direction to irrigate my land."

All those who heard him burst into loud laughter. Nanak pretended to be angry and hurt.

"Why are you laughing at me?" he asked.

"You are truly mad," one of the young men said. "How can the water reach your fields near Lahore?"

"How far away is the land of your ancestors?" Nanak countered calmly.

"It is 49½ *crore kos* away," a learned pandit replied.

"Well, if the water you throw can reach a spot which is 49½ *crore kos* away, surely the water I throw can reach my farm which is only 250 *kos* away?"

The pandits and the worshippers exchanged glances but none had the courage to abandon their ancient practice. One by one, they drifted away. Nanak knew that his words had found their mark.

Nanak and Mardana now left the plains and went on to Kotdwara and then to Srinagar in Pauri Garhwal. From here they travelled to Joshimath, following the well-travelled but difficult pilgrim route that passed through the ancient pilgrim centres of Kedarnath and Badrinath. When he visited these *dhams* Nanak thought of his father's visit to these places all those long years ago, when he had come seeking the boon of a child. He smiled wryly to himself—he himself came seeking nothing, wanting only to spread his message of Truth.

He crossed the Antra and Leplu La passes and followed the Kali River to Almora. People there were still given to making human sacrifices to appease their gods and Nanak spent considerable time convincing them to abandon this cruel practice. By the time he left he had won over all the local priests to his way of thinking and this horrible custom died a well-deserved death.

The Guru now followed the pilgrim route down from the hills and reached a centre of *nath yogis*, about thirty miles east of Haldwani. There is a *reetha* (soap nut) tree here, which, tradition claims, was sweetened by the divine presence of the Guru. The place is now called Reetha Sahib and there is a gurdwara to commemorate his stay here. From Reetha Sahib, Nanak came into the Terai area and followed the Deoha stream, arriving at a place called Gorakhmath, named after Gorakhnath who founded the sect of *nath yogis*. Nanak entered into a discussion with the *siddha yogis* on religion and metaphysics. Nanak's summing up of these discussions takes the form of a discourse that has been included as the *Siddhagosht* in the *Guru Granth Sahib*. It is said that the *siddha yogis* were so impressed by Nanak that their leader insisted he join their order.

Nanak replied:

> "The lotus in the water is not wet,
> Nor the waterfowl in the stream,
> If a man would live, but by the world untouched,
> Meditate and repeat the name of the Lord Supreme."

(*Siddhagosht*, Trans. Singh, Khuswant, *A History of the Sikhs*, vol. I p. 42)

Years later, Gorakhmath was renamed Nanakmath in honour of Nanak's visit here and his influence on the *siddha yogis*. There are many followers of Nanak living in this area who go by the name of *nanakpanthis*.

From Gorakhmath, Nanak turned south and came to the town of Tanda Vanjara, a trading centre situated in the present day district of Rampur. After a short sojourn here Nanak went on to Gola, a town sacred to the Hindus, situated on the bank of the river Sarda, about twenty miles from the present day town of Lakhimpur. He crossed the river Ghajjra and reached Ayodhya, a very old pilgrim centre, believed to be the birthplace of Lord Rama, and went on to Prayag and Benaras. In all three cities Nanak taught that renunciation of the world was not essential for spiritual attainment and that this goal could be achieved even while living in the world of men. He preached that ritual bathing in holy waters did not cleanse the impurities of the heart and soul. This purity could be achieved only by following the right path in life and by praying for the grace of God.

> "Truth, self-discipline, right action are the lines to draw.
> Contemplation of His Name is the holy bath."
> (*Raga Suhi*, Trans. Sarna, Navtej, *The Book of Nanak*, p. 62)

Nanak encountered men of religion who were hostile, not only towards the followers of other religions but also towards those within their own faith who followed a different mode of worship. To them he preached that a true man of God would show tolerance for all beliefs and forms of worship.

Nanak's teaching was often met with hostility and resentment. But there were some who were enthralled not only by his beautiful hymns but also by the practical and rational approach of his teachings. Wherever he went, Nanak left groups of devoted followers who built gurdwaras to mark the places where their Guru had stayed.

At Benaras, where he had a fairly long halt, the Guru struck up an acquaintance with Pandit Chatur Das who was famed for his piety and learning. Their discussions centred mainly on the subject of idol worship. The Guru preached that the worship of idols was a waste of time because it did not lead to salvation. The short period allotted to us on this earth would be more fruitfully spent taking the Almighty's name and cultivating inner virtues.

> "Oh Brahmin,
> You worship and propitiate the stone god.
> Why irrigate land that is waste?
> Why plaster a weak, falling wall?
> — Build a raft of the Lord's name
> — and pray He shall ferry you across."
> (*Raga Basant Hindol*, Trans. Sarna, Navtej, *The Book of Nanak*, p. 27)

The Guru stayed in the Kamekha area, close to the present day railway station, and there is an ancient gurdwara marking the place of his residence.

From Benaras, Nanak and Mardana travelled to Gaya on the banks of the river Phalgu. Gaya was the place where Lord Buddha attained enlightenment and was one of the most important pilgrim centres for the Buddhists. But at the time of Nanak's visit Gaya had become an important pilgrim centre for the Hindus too. Nanak reached here during the period of *sharad* when most Hindus fast, and offer rice cakes and light lamps to ensure that their ancestors reach heaven. Nanak preached the futility of such rituals. The only way one could reach heaven after death was to perform good deeds in this life. There is an old gurdwara in Gaya too that marks Nanak's visit.

From Gaya, on his way to Hajipur, Nanak passed the ruins of the ancient city of Pataliputra, where the city of Patna was to spring up in the coming years. Patna was to become a big centre of pilgrimage for the Sikhs because the tenth Guru, Guru Gobind Singh, was born here. But during Nanak's time there were only the desolate ruins of the once splendid city of Pataliputra. The *kachcha* path brought Nanak to the town of Hajipur, situated at the confluence of the Ganga and the Gandak. Here Nanak won a disciple in Salis Rai, who, in addition to being a merchant, was a scholar of great repute.

The next important place that Nanak visited was Malda, situated at the confluence of the Ganga and the Mahananda. Malda was at that time a very important centre of Sufi learning. Nanak spent a few days here in fruitful discussion with Sufi saints and scholars. From Malda, Nanak travelled north to Assam. At the time of Nanak's visit, Assam was divided into two broad regions, with the river Barna marking the boundary between them. The region west of the Barna was called Kamrup while the region east of the river was called Asa Desh, peopled mainly by the Ahoms. Asa Desh was then ruled by Raja Swarag Narain (1497-1593).

Nanak camped at Dhubri, which is the main town of the Goalpara district of Assam. It was here that he met the famous Vaishnavite sage Shankardev. When Guru Tegh Bahadur followed the path of Nanak's first udasi, he raised a monument at the site where Nanak had stayed in Dhubri.

Nanak then travelled along the Brahmaputra to the Kamrup area and came to a place near modern day Guwahati. It was pleasant weather and on the first evening Nanak decided to camp out in the open under a banyan tree.

"I am starving," Mardana declared. "I think I'll die if I don't get something to eat soon."

Nanak smiled but refrained from reminding Mardana that he was perpetually hungry. "This place seems prosperous enough. I am sure you will find someone kind-hearted enough to give you some food."

So Mardana went forth. The first person he saw was an attractive young lady, beautifully dressed and wearing exquisite jewellery. "You seem a stranger to our town, Sir," she said coyly. "Is there anything I can do for you?"

"Young lady, I have travelled a long way today and not only am I weary and exhausted but I am truly famished. I would be grateful if you could give me something to eat."

"Is that all?" the young lady said with a laugh. "Come with me to my mistress' house. She is known for her hospitality and generosity to strangers."

Mardana allowed himself to be led to a house which was, in fact, a palace. He stopped at the gate. "Who is your mistress? She appears to be an exceedingly wealthy woman."

"You have seen but the gate; wait till you see the inside. My mistress is Nurshah and she is the chieftain of this region. Do not be surprised—in our land we follow the matriarchal system and it is the daughter who inherits from the parents."

Mardana followed her into the splendid palace and was led into the presence of Nurshah. Mardana had thought the servant was beautiful, but her beauty now paled into insignificance in the presence of her mistress. Nurshah was truly the most beautiful woman Mardana had ever seen. She rose to greet her guest and led him to the seat beside her. She plied him with questions about his home and the purpose of his visit. Gradually Mardana succumbed to the charms of Nurshah. Her perfume enveloped his senses. He forgot Talwandi and Sultanpur, he forgot his family, and he even forgot Nanak. His only desire now was to be with this beautiful woman.

After he had been fed, Nurshah led him to a luxurious bed and while one of her maids lulled him to sleep with a soft lullaby, another maid gently pressed his tired legs. And all the while, Nurshah sat on the bed beside him. It was only when he had drifted into a deep sleep that she clapped her hands and all her servants laughed with glee.

The smitten Mardana was unaware that Nurshah made a habit of casting her spell on unwary strangers and enslaving them. In fact, the palace was swarming with men who had fallen for her charm and had become her slaves. It was because of this that Nurshah was regarded as a sorceress.

When Mardana did not return, Nanak was worried and spent the entire night praying for the safety of his beloved companion. In the early hours of the morning he set out to look for Mardana, asking passers-by for information about his whereabouts. One of them smiled and replied, "Nurshah must have made a captive of him in her palace," and he went on to give details of what his chieftain was wont to do with unsuspecting strangers. "But take care," he cautioned, "that you yourself do not fall prey to her charms." Nanak only smiled at this and, thanking the stranger, asked to be shown the way to Nurshah's palace.

Though it was early in the morning Nurshah was up and bedecked, almost as if she was waiting for Nanak. She tried every trick in her book to seduce Nanak but to no avail. Recognising that her worldly charm stood no chance against Nanak's spiritual strength, she threw herself at his feet. "Who are you, O holy one? And where do you get the strength to resist enticements that no man has been able to resist?"

In the discussion that followed Nanak made her realise that the power she exercised over her captives was futile and totally devoid of meaning or substance. It is said that she was so moved by Nanak's words that she forever abjured her evil ways. She released all her captives from bondage and became a follower of Nanak.

Other places that Nanak visited on this, the first of his four travels, were Golaghat, Shillong, Sylhet, Chittagong, and Dhaka. From Dhaka he proceeded to what are now the cities of Calcutta and Cuttack. At that time, Calcutta was little more than a village that had come up around the old temple of Kali.

From Cuttack, Nanak followed the well-established pilgrim route to the town of Puri with its famous temple to Lord Jagannath. Nanak and Mardana set up camp a little way from the temple but their evening session of devotional songs and Nanak's preaching soon began to draw a small crowd. Many people, on their way to the temple, stopped instead to listen to Nanak. Pandit Krishnalal, the head priest, heard about the crowds following Nanak and was curious to meet this strange *fakir*. One day, he inconspicuously joined the crowd and he was so impressed that he insisted Nanak attend the *aarti* at the temple the next evening.

The *aarti* was an extremely elaborate and moving ceremony and all who saw it could not but be touched by its beauty. Dozens of small terracotta oil lamps were lit and placed on silver salvers studded with precious stones. Rose petals were scattered all around the temple, their perfume intermingling with the heady smell of incense. The sound of conches and bells resounded in the temple. Against this background of light, perfume, and sound, the congregation sang the hymns designated for the ceremony with devotion.

Nanak explained to the crowd that the *aarti* performed by Nature for its Maker was so much grander and more beautiful than any that man performed in the temple. He composed a hymn on this occasion which is recorded on the thirteenth page of the *Guru Granth Sahib*:

> "The sky the salver, the sun and moon the lamps,
> The stars studding the heavens are the pearls
> The fragrance of sandal is the incense
> Fanned by the winds all for Thee
> The great forests are the flowers.
> What a beautiful aarti is being performed
> For you, O Destroyer of fear."
> (*Raga Dhanasri*, Trans. Sarna, Navtej, *The Book of Nanak*, p. 73)

Nanak also met the famous saint Chaitanya Mahaprabhu at Puri. Ishwar Das, in his biography of the saint, describes how Nanak and Chaitanya sat together for many days, deep in discussion, and even performed *kirtan* together.

It was at this point of the udasi that Mardana showed signs of weariness. He would sit quietly for hours, not responding to anything around him, and when he no longer showed any interest in food, Nanak knew that there was something seriously wrong. It did not take long for him to draw Mardana out and make him reveal the cause of his despondency.

"Oh Master, I miss my home and my children. We have been through so much and we still have such a long way to go. I wonder if I will live long enough to set eyes upon my children again." He paused and added wistfully, "They must have grown up now. I wonder whether I will even recognise them."

Nanak decided to return to Talwandi. They travelled through the densely wooded forests of Central India, which were inhabited not only by fierce animals but also by man-eating tribes. The janamsakhis tell us that Nanak reformed one of these cannibal tribes by converting its chieftain Kauda to peaceful ways.

They travelled through the deserts of Rajasthan, crossed the river Sutlej, and came to Pak Pattan. They again spent time with Sheikh Ibrahim before returning to Talwandi. Nanak completed his first udasi in 1509.

Great was the joy of the inhabitants of Talwandi when they heard that Nanak and Mardana had returned. They crowded around the two to hear stories of their experiences during their travels. In the evenings they turned out in full force to join the *kirtan* and to listen to Nanak's sermons. Rai Bular was overjoyed to know that his faith in Nanak had been vindicated. Mehta Kalo and Tripta, who had despaired of ever seeing their son again, rejoiced to see him looking so well, exercising a benevolent influence on the minds of men. Mardana's family, too, was deliriously happy, and hung on to every word that he uttered. They were amazed at the mastery that he had achieved on the *rabab* and at his rich repertoire of hymns.

Having completed his first udasi, Nanak too was content to be back in Talwandi.

6

SECOND UDASI

For a while everyone in Talwandi believed that Nanak had come back for good but he soon declared his intention of embarking on his second udasi. His parents tried their best to make him change his mind. "We are old, my son, and we may be gone before you return."

"It is God's will," Nanak said, and from the quiet conviction in his voice Tripta and Mehta Kalo knew that his resolve was implacable. They had also comprehended the larger purpose for which their son was destined, and putting aside their objections, they blessed him with all their hearts.

However, before embarking on his second udasi, Nanak returned to Sultanpur to meet his family. He spent almost a year there and a quiet humdrum pattern of everyday life was established. Nanak took on his duties as a householder with seeming enthusiasm but it was clear to everyone that he would soon set out on his next missionary journey. Sulakhni realised it too and was saddened but she put up a brave front. She asked to be allowed to visit her parents in Pakhoke, near Batala, while Nanak was away. They were old and infirm now, and they longed to see their daughter. So it was decided that Sri Chand, the elder boy, would stay in Sultanpur with Nanki, and Lakhmi Das, the younger child, would go with his mother to Batala. Having made the arrangements, Nanak set out on his second udasi.

On this second journey, which began in 1510, Nanak crossed the Sutlej, close to the present day town of Goindwal, and then went on to Bhatinda. There is a touching and poignant story pertaining to this part of Nanak's journey. It is said that late one evening, while searching for a place to rest, Nanak came to a solitary little hut, built well away from all other human habitation. The hut was in darkness and when Nanak called, a figure emerged, who, from his clothes and his general appearance, appeared to be a *fakir*. He stood patiently at a respectful distance, waiting for Nanak to speak. "O holy one," Nanak said, "forgive me for this intrusion. I know that you have chosen to live in this isolated wilderness so that you can be alone. My companion and I are tired and weary and can go no further. Give us the comfort of your roof for just this one night and I assure you that we will be gone long before the break of day."

Even in the gathering gloom Nanak could clearly see the look of incredulous amazement on the *fakir's* face. "Forgive me," he said, "I am no *fakir* and have no pretension to holiness. I do not shun human company from choice—I am compelled to." He held out his hands, swathed in dirty bandages. "I suffer from leprosy and have been driven out of the town. If I come even within shouting distance they pelt me with stones, so afraid are they of contagion. So, good sir, I would advise you to resume your journey at once so that the shadow of one as cursed as I will not fall on you and bring you misfortune."

Nanak took a step forward and holding the leper's bandaged hands in his own, raised them to his forehead. "When you stand before your Maker you will not be judged by the scars on your body but by the scars of sin on your soul. This affliction is not of your making. Be not ashamed of it; one should only be ashamed if one chooses evil over good."

The leper fell at Nanak's feet and wept. It is probable that Nanak stayed with the leper and nursed his affected limbs because the janamsakhis claim that at the time of Nanak's departure the leper was cured of his affliction.

Stories of Nanak's piety and humanity spread far and wide. More and more people came to understand the beauty of Nanak's simple message to the leper—it was not the ugliness or the disfiguration of the body that was a matter of shame but it was the ugliness of the soul, of the evil deeds that men performed, that was shameful.

Nanak moved on to Bhatinda and from there to Sirsa, a well-established centre of Sufi scholarship. Evidence from the diary of a wandering minstrel of the time suggests that Nanak spent well over four months in this place. While in Sirsa Nanak stayed with a Muslim *fakir* outside the town. A wall of the *fakir's* abode, with an inscription testifying to Nanak's stay here, has been recently discovered. Nanak then moved on to Mathura, another very important pilgrimage centre for the Hindus, replete as it is with references to the life of Lord Krishna. The Chinese traveller Huien Tsang, visiting Mathura in the first half of the seventh century, describes it as a Buddhist centre with twenty monasteries and a population of over two thousand Buddhist monks and nuns. But by the time Nanak came to Mathura, all traces of Buddhism had been effaced, and the town was a major centre of the worship of Radha-Krishna. Nanak saw many temples in various states of ruin, some reduced to piles of rubble by the imperial forces of Sikandar Lodhi, the ruler of Delhi. Nanak was saddened by this senseless destruction and the plight of the citizens under such a ruthless, intolerant ruler.

From Mathura, Nanak came to Ajmer, a pilgrimage centre important to both Hindus and Muslims. The Hindus revered Ajmer because of the sacred Pushkar Lake while the Muslims looked upon it with respect because the *dargah* of the revered saint Moin-ud-din Chisti was located there. Nanak reached Ajmer during the Pushkar fair when thousands of pilgrims throng the city. He had the opportunity to preach to large gatherings and his message was carried by them to faraway places.

Nanak's next stop was the holy city of Ujjain. Even at that time the city was old and every nook and corner was replete with history. He then travelled via Deogiri, Daulatabad, and Baroach on to Nanded, which is regarded as one of the most important centres of the Sikh religion. It has a strong association with Guru Gobind Singh and also with Banda Bahadur. What most people overlook is that it has an association with Nanak too and there is an old gurdwara called Gurdwara Mal Tehri which commemorates his visit to the town. Nanak passed through Bidar, which was at that time the capital of one of the five kingdoms which resulted from the break up of the Bahmani Empire.

From Bidar, Nanak moved on to Palam-Kattayam, a small hamlet situated halfway between the towns of Palam and Kattayam and thus taking its name from both. When he set up camp for the night, he was visited by a group of *siddhas*. Nanak was preaching to a small group of people, explaining the concept of sharing everything one has with others, no matter how little. The *siddhas*, arrogant in their spiritual strength, and contemptuous of this little-known *fakir* who dared to talk about spiritual matters in their presence, decided to show Nanak up as a charlatan. At the end of Nanak's sermon, one of the *siddhas* came up to him with a single grain of wheat.

"Tell us, O learned one, if we have only one grain of wheat to our name, how is it possible to share it with anyone?"

Nanak smiled, not losing his equanimity for a moment. He took the proffered seed and beckoning Mardana, whispered something in his ear.

Mardana went away and the congregation waited impatiently to see what this strange *fakir* would do. Perhaps he would use a magic spell and have the seed multiply, the superstitious among the crowd whispered to each other. But the sceptics were pleased because they thought the falseness of the *fakir*'s preaching would be revealed. As the moments ticked away, restlessness crept over the crowd.

Just then Mardana returned with a bowl of water. Very carefully, he measured a small amount into the cupped hands of each member of the congregation, who, regarding it as some form of *prasad,* drank it reverently. When all had been served there was still some left in the bowl.

"My friend Mardana ground the grain of wheat into flour and mixed it with water so that we could all share it. If one puts one's mind to the task there is always a way of sharing, no matter how little one has."

There were loud murmurs of approval as the congregation broke up and Nanak gained many new disciples that day.

Nanak passed through Trivandrum and came finally to Rameshwaram. Here too there is an old gurdwara called Nanak Udasi Math Gurdwara, commemorating Nanak's visit. From Rameshwaram, Nanak sailed across to Ceylon, on the way passing Setbandh, the bridge that the Hindus believe was constructed by Lord Rama when he invaded Lanka to free his wife Sita from the custody of King Ravana.

Nanak probably landed at Trincomalee which is near the port of Mattiakulam, also known as Batticaloa. Most of the Guru's time in Ceylon was spent in the area around Trincomalee, though he did also visit Mannar, Anuradhapura, and Sitawaka, which was reputed to be the place where Ravana had imprisoned Sita. All these towns were part of a kingdom ruled by the Shaivite king, Raja Shivnabh.

Legend has it that there was a jewel merchant by the name of Changa Batra who conducted his business in Sitawaka. Various legends ascribe various names to this merchant. Some suggest that it was Mansukh, the merchant of Lahore who had become Nanak's follower after the marriage of Mardana's daughter. A few suggest that he may even have been Bhagirath. This merchant had travelled far and wide in India to obtain goods that would cater to the tastes of his clients. During his travels to North India he had been influenced by Nanak's teachings and followed them faithfully. He performed no Hindu rituals, did not observe fasts, and did not worship idols. He would begin his day with the recitation of Nanak's *Mool Mantra* and when he returned home, tired and exhausted after the day's business, he rejuvenated his spirit by singing his Guru's hymns.

King Shivnabh heard of this merchant and of his strange religious practices. He summoned Changa Batra to his palace and spent long hours asking him questions about his Master and his beliefs. He was both intrigued and impressed by the simplicity of Nanak's teachings. They did not enjoin one to practise any severe austerities nor did they lay down complicated rituals. The king longed to meet this unique teacher. Part of this longing came from a deep malaise of the heart, a result of his childless state. Nothing in his own religious practice could help him come to terms with his situation and he felt intuitively that Nanak alone could help him find peace of mind. After he had listened to Changa Batra explain some of his Guru's basic teachings, the king would ask, "Tell me, O merchant, will I meet your learned Master?"

And the merchant would smile at the longing in the king's voice and reply, "Who knows, Your Majesty? They say that faith can move mountains. If you pray with all your heart, God will bring about such a meeting." So when the king was particularly despondent, he would pray that God grant him a meeting with the great teacher from the north. He would listen to Nanak's *bani* with greater attention and he would invariably find solace and comfort. It was as if the Guru, living thousands of miles away, knew of his sadness and had spoken the words just for him.

The years slipped by. Shivnabh and his queen had now come to terms with the fact that they would have no child. One day the queen sent for him while he was attending to his official duties. The moment he entered her chamber, he knew that it was a matter of great urgency. Her face was flushed and she spoke in a voice tremulous with excitement. "I have just received news, my lord, that there is a holy man camping in a garden outside the city gates. He says he is neither a Hindu, nor a Mussalman, nor a Buddhist. He does not practice any traditional rituals and recites his own prayers. In the evenings, he sings devotional songs accompanied by a remarkable *rabab* player, and encourages people to join in. From what I hear, his teachings echo the philosophy of Changa Batra's teacher." Shivnabh's heart skipped a beat; was his wish finally about to come true?

The king and the queen put aside their rich clothing, and adopting the garb of simple village folk, they made their way on foot to the Guru's camp. They bowed before him and found places for themselves among

95

the group of followers who sat cross-legged on the grass. As they listened to Nanak's hymns, their hearts were uplifted with divine joy and they saw that others around them shared their rapture. The words of the song were simple and soon the king and queen were joining in the refrain. They knew that they had been transformed by being part of this experience and that nothing would ever be the same again.

It was obvious that Changa Batra was one of Nanak's foremost disciples because he played a leading part in the organisation of the meetings. He recognised the royal couple but made no attempt to introduce them to the Master. On their fourth or fifth visit, Nanak signalled to them to come and sit beside him.

"You have become regular members of my congregation. I feel we need to know each other," said Nanak. The king and queen looked at each other uncomfortably. "You need not be embarrassed. Even if my friend Changa Batra had not told me who you were, I would have gathered as much from the dignity of your bearing. I see sadness on your faces and I wonder if there is anything I can do to lighten your burden."

The king spoke to the Guru and told him of their sadness at being childless.

"You must be patient," said Nanak, and went on to tell them the story of his own father and all that he had suffered when it seemed that he would remain childless. "You must bow your head before the will of God," he said. The king and queen were silent, still haunted by unhappy thoughts. Looking at them with deep compassion, Nanak continued, "It is a common human condition to look only at unfulfilled desires in our lives. We never count our blessings. If God fulfils our lives in ninety-five ways and does not fulfil them in five, we take the ninety-five for granted and feel unhappy that He has not deemed fit to grant us the five missing boons. You are a gifted and benevolent king, your subjects love and admire you, and your rivals fear your strength. You have a beautiful and devoted wife. There is only one blessing that God has not given you and therefore you cease to find joy in everything else that He has granted you."

The king and queen had many meetings with Nanak. Though they did not abandon their own faith, they found comfort in Nanak's words and followed his teachings in their own way. Nanak stayed in Ceylon for two years and during this period a son was born to the royal couple. Both husband and wife were convinced that the divine blessing had come to them through Nanak's grace. To show their gratitude, the queen stitched him a cotton robe with her own hands. Together, husband and wife went to thank the Guru and distribute sweets among the congregation after the evening prayers.

Even today, in a place called Kurukal Mandal, twelve miles south of Batticaloa, there exists a shrine to the memory of "Siddha Baba" who visited the place about 450 years ago. Recently an inscription of a dialogue between one "Jnanakacharya" and the then king of Kottee has been discovered. From the views propounded by the *acharya* regarding the nature of God and his antipathy to idol worship and the caste system, it is believed that he was none other than Nanak.

After two years Nanak believed that his mission in Ceylon was complete and decided to return home. He followed the axis of the Western Ghats and passed through Nasik, Baroda, Junagarh, Dwarka, and Bhuj. Then he crossed through Rajasthan to the Punjab and finally came to Multan.

Multan was known for its *pirs* and saints, including the descendants of Sheikh Baha-ud-din Zakaria. Each of them had their own following and had learned to live in a kind of uneasy peace with the others. They now heard of Nanak having set up camp just outside the city. They had, of course, heard of this Guru and his revolutionary teachings. A few of the eminent holy men met to discuss the arrival of this *pir*.

"We have our differences," one of them said, "both in our beliefs and in our personal lives. These differences often culminate in heated argument but in our hearts we know that we are one. We believe in Allah and follow the teachings of Prophet Mohammad. We cannot let an apostate like Nanak come into our midst and upset the even routine of our lives by preaching blasphemous credos like 'there is no Hindu and no Mussalman'."

The others nodded their heads in agreement. "But how do we keep him out?" Another senior religious leader added, "He is, in his own way, a man of God. An open confrontation with him will not do us any good, especially if it is reduced to an attempt to physically restrain him from entering Multan."

There was a long silence as the holy men mulled over this difficult problem. At last, the youngest of the group spoke up. "I have had the opportunity of meeting Nanak before. He is a very intelligent man. Let us send him gifts among which will be a bowl filled to the brim with milk. I am sure he will understand the symbolism of this present—that Multan is already filled to the brim with assorted holy men and there is no place for any more."

This suggestion was greatly appreciated and a group of messengers was sent to Nanak's camp, bearing the gifts from the *pirs* including the bowl of milk. Nanak at once understood the import of this gift and smiled. Then he reached out and plucked a flower from the jasmine tree beside him. He took a single petal and lowered it gently onto the milk. Then he smiled again at the messenger. "Give my thanks to the *pirs*," he said softly. "Tell them I am truly blessed in receiving their gifts. Bear this bowl carefully back to them."

The *pirs* understood at once what Nanak was trying to tell them: his presence in Multan would be like the presence of the petal in the bowl of milk. Just as the petal did not displace even a drop of milk, he would not displace a single *pir*. He would float gently along with all the other holy men and cause no turmoil or disruption in their lives or in their following. Though some of them still harboured reservations about Nanak's presence in their midst, they could not help being impressed by the subtlety and clarity of his answer.

In the days that followed, Nanak did indeed prove that he was like the petal of the jasmine flower. He won the admiration and respect of all the *pirs* by his gentleness, humility, and deep understanding of Islam.

He returned finally to Talwandi to the great joy of his old parents and the frail Rai Bular, now completely confined to bed. Nanak spent many days by Rai Bular's bedside, in silent communion with the gracious old man who had been such an important part of his life. Rai Bular finally breathed his last, his head in Nanak's lap, happy and content that he had lived to see Pandit Hardayal's prophecy come true.

Mehta Kalo basked in his son's fame. As Nanak's teaching had spread all over the Punjab and beyond, Talwandi had become famous. Visitors from far off places had already begun to visit Nanak's birthplace in increasing numbers. Tripta and Kalo would feel their hearts swell with pride and Kalo accepted that he had been wrong to doubt his son. Although Tripta was happy to have Nanak home at last, she rarely had the opportunity to spend time alone with him. He was kept engaged with all his visitors and she, having taken charge of the daily *langar*, found herself busier than ever. After a few months Nanak went back to Sultanpur. On the way he passed once again through Lahore and came into contact with Duni Chand, a wealthy merchant, who was also the *Amil* of Lahore and who became Nanak's devoted disciple.

Nanak finally arrived at Sultanpur. This second udasi had lasted five years.

THIRD UDASI

N anak stayed in Sultanpur for almost two years before he was seized by the desire to undertake another missionary journey. His old employer Daulat Khan was now the Governor of Lahore and had become so powerful that he had virtually declared himself the independent ruler of Punjab. In spite of his enormous power, Daulat Khan remained a great admirer of Nanak's. Hearing that the Guru intended to set out again on his travels, he came to Sultanpur and tried to persuade him to change his mind.

"You are needed here, Nanak," he said gently. "Be done with your travelling and guide your own people by bringing the true message to them."

"My disciples have set up centres in many places and are doing wonderful work in propagating my message. I need to go further afield and preach to those who otherwise would not know the true way."

Nanki and Jai Ram joined in Daulat Khan's pleas. "Think of us, my brother," Nanki said. "We are getting on in years and who knows if we will be here when you return."

"If that is God's will, then so be it. I hear an inner voice telling me to go and I must obey. I cannot rest until my mission has been accomplished."

And so, in 1517, Nanak embarked on his third udasi. He went first to Pakhoke, near Batala, where his wife Sulakhni and his sons were staying. The elder boy, Sri Chand, was now twenty-three while Lakhmi Das was twenty-one. Sri Chand, like his father, was given to staying away from home for long stretches of time in the company of ascetics and holy men. He spent the major part of the year going on various pilgrimages and came home only for short durations of time. Lakhmi Das was now married and living the life of a householder. Nanak stayed in Pakhoke for a few days and then moved on. But before he moved northwards towards the mountains, which was the direction this third journey would take, he paused for a while in the area between the Ravi and the Beas. He was attracted to one particularly peaceful spot. He lingered there longer than usual and some of his disciples began to wonder if perhaps the Guru was tired of continuous travel and was making this third journey reluctantly. But after the morning prayers, he said, "This is a wonderful place. I feel the peace and serenity here seep into me and draw me closer to God than ever before. When my travels are over I would like to set up a *dera* here and make it my home."

Among the disciples who heard Nanak express this desire was one Ajit Randhawa, a wealthy agriculturist from Pakhoke. Ajit wasted no time in buying up the land and gifting it to his Guru. Nanak advised those of his followers who would not be able to make the difficult journey with him to the mountains to set up home here and wait for his return. In the years to come the Sikh community in Kartarpur grew as more and more people came to live here.

The third and perhaps most arduous of the Guru's udasis began from Kartarpur in September 1517. Nanak crossed the Sutlej at the point where it flows down from the Siwaliks and flows gently over the plains. It is at this place that the seventh Guru, Guru Hargobind, founded the settlement of Kiratpur. At the time of Nanak's visit the spot was marked by the camp of a venerated *pir*, Budhan Shah. It is quite possible that Nanak spent a few days in Budhan Shah's camp.

From the *mukham* of Budhan Shah, Nanak moved into the mountain and came first to Mandi, a small town of great importance because it was the meeting point of several hill routes that connected the various kingdoms and principalities of the hills. About ten miles from Mandi was the sacred and famous *kund* of Skand Dhara around which the pilgrim town of Riwalsar had sprung up. Nanak visited Riwalsar and also Jwalamukhi, a Hindu pilgrim centre now situated in the Gopipur *tehsil* of Kangra district. He then moved on to Kangra and from there, to Baijnath, at one time a powerful state that had established its supremacy over the neighbouring hill states. But at the time of Nanak's visit its power had declined considerably and the ruler of Baijnath paid tribute to the king of Kangra. For this udasi, in deference to the cold and mountainous terrain that he was going to pass through, Nanak made a modification in the dress which had by now become his hallmark. He wore leather, and sometimes felt, on his feet, and woollen headgear. His robe, too, was made of homespun wool, to protect him not only from the severe cold but also from the violent winds that are so frequent in these northern mountains.

From Baijnath there is a route leading through the Dulchi pass to Kulu and Nanak probably followed this route. While in this region Nanak visited the settlement of Manikaran, beside Parbati, the turbulent mountain stream. There are hot sulphur springs in Manikaran and it is said that Mardana, hungry as ever, was delighted to be here, because on the Guru's advice he found an easy way to cook his food. All he had to do was tie his food up in a bundle and dip the cloth in the boiling water of the spring. In the gurdwara that has come up to commemorate the Guru's visit to this place, the food for the *langar* is stilled cooked in this way and tourists and pilgrims find great delight in cooking small quantities of rice and *dal* in exactly the way Mardana did.

From here Nanak crossed over the Chandrakhani pass to come to the village of Mallana. This village is inhabited by a people who belong to a distinct ethnic race. Tradition has it that they are the descendants of Greeks who chose to stay back in India after Alexander's invasion and who have zealously guarded the purity of their race. Even today, they regard visitors with suspicion and hostility. Nanak, with his gentle, peaceful ways, won the confidence of the local people and stayed here for some time. Some sacred relics of the Guru are still preserved and worshipped here. (Singh, Kirpal, *Janamsakhi Parampara*, p. 104)

Nanak now moved on to Spiti, which borders western Tibet. It was a difficult trek through this stark and barren stretch of land but he was moved by the dramatic beauty of the landscape around him. Nanak entered Tibet by crossing the Shipki pass. He then travelled towards the Lipu Lekh pass and traversed the Gangotri and Kedar Kshetra regions. He followed the ancient pilgrim route to finally arrive at the sacred lake Mansarovar, the source of the river Sutlej. He was overawed by the majesty of the holy mountain Sumer or Kailash, which is 22,000 ft. It was in this region, resonating with spiritual vibrations, that Nanak had his famous encounter with the eighty-four *siddhas* who had attained a state of enlightenment. A detailed account of his discussions with them has been recorded by Nanak in *Siddhagosht*. Bhai Gurdas also records Nanak's visit to Mount Kailash in his *vars*.

The *siddhas* were holy men who had renounced the world and retreated to the isolation of caves and shelters high up in the mountains to meditate and lead a pure life, unfettered by human desires, human hopes, and human despair. By living this life they hoped to attain the highly desired state of *moksha* or freedom from the eternal cycle of birth and death. *Moksha* was the highest form of spiritual bliss that a human being could aspire to. Some of the *siddhas* had been living in these remote mountains for well over forty years without any contact with the world of men. When they crossed Nanak's camp on their way to Rakas Tal, they were both incredulous at his presence there and intrigued by his strange dress; perhaps he too was seeking to escape the material world by venturing so far into the remote mountains. Their curiosity got the better of them and forgetting their resolve to abjure the company of men, they stopped at Nanak's camp and addressed a host of enquires to him.

"Who are you and what are you doing here, so far away from the world of men?"

"My name is Nanak," he answered, "and I travel now to Tibet and Nepal."

"Are you a Hindu or a Mussalman?"

The question brought a smile to Nanak's face. "There is no Hindu or Mussalman, and so I can be neither. I worship the one and only Eternal Lord."

The *siddhas* were intrigued by this strange answer but did not immediately press the *fakir* for an explanation. "Where do you come from?" they asked.

"I was born in the village of Talwandi but I come from the town of Sultanpur, close to Lahore."

The *siddhas* crowded around Nanak, their curiosity about the world they had abandoned aroused by Nanak's presence. They plied him with questions about the social, economic, and political conditions in the Punjab.

"The state of the world is bad. There is darkness all around. Corruption and sin have taken over the reins of authority. Goodness and honesty have been pushed into the shadows. The world cries for justice."

The *siddhas* clicked their tongues in righteous indignation. "It is good that we have abandoned that evil world to live a pure and simple life in a world untainted by corruption."

"Yes," Nanak agreed. "By escaping into these high mountains you have indeed been able to safeguard and protect your values. But tell me, if all the good and pure people escape into remote caves, who will restore virtue and goodness?"

The *siddhas* looked at each other, unable to answer Nanak's question.

"As men of God are we not also expected to lead others to the path of virtue?"

One of the *siddhas* spoke up. "Even the most virtuous cannot remain untainted in the material world. It is not possible to follow the path to spiritual salvation while living in the midst of so much evil and corruption."

"Then should all men take *sanyas* and come up into the mountains like you? If this is the only way to protect and nourish goodness in the present times then who will perform all the various activities that keep the world going?" Nanak questioned.

Once again the *siddhas* were at a loss for an answer and Nanak pressed home his point. "Those among us who have seen the light should serve as a beacon to others. Through our own example we must show that they too can achieve great spiritual progress. We can inspire goodness among men and restore the balance in favour of virtue by living in the world of men. Our lives must be like the lotus, which lives and blooms in the murky, smelly marsh and yet remains unstained and unblemished."

Though Nanak did not succeed in converting the *siddhas* to his beliefs, he did leave them with the conviction that there was a path to salvation other than the one they had chosen to follow.

Nanak travelled extensively through Tibet and records maintained by lamas attest to the fact that he spent time in monasteries, studying and discussing Buddhist philosophy. He was regarded with reverence as Rimpoche Nanak and looked upon as a reincarnation of Padmasambhava.

From Tibet, Nanak moved on to Sikkim and Nepal. He participated in the religious fair at Brahmkund, where he interacted with the learned *sadhus* and *swamis* who had congregated there. In the evening people flocked to his *kirtan* and listened to him preach his concept of the worship of one God. The predominantly Hindu population looked upon Nanak as a holy man of great sagacity and referred to him as Nanak Rishi. Nanak arrived at the capital Kathmandu and camped at a site on the banks of the Bhagmati, close to the ancient and sacred temple of Lord Pashupatinath. Though people did not understand, or subscribe to, many of his doctrines, they were captivated by the *kirtan* and collected in large numbers to listen to his divine music.

The fame of these daily sessions spread far and wide and it was not long before the royal family heard of them too. Intrigued by the stories about Nanak, the king of Nepal himself came down to the banks of the Bhagmati to listen to him. He was fascinated by what he heard and, at the end of the session, asked if he could do anything for the holy man. Nanak smiled. "I thank you for your consideration and kindness. My needs are few and I am well looked after by my followers here." The king was impressed by Nanak's reply and knew that he was in the presence of a truly great man. Even today, there is a gurdwara in Kathmandu to commemorate Nanak's visit to that city. There are relics of Nanak's scattered all over this region—at the village of Chung Thang, situated above the confluence of the Teesta and Lachung Chu rivers in Sikkim; at the Lachen Monastery on the way to Gurudongma lake; and in Kathmandu. There is a gurdwara called Nanak Lama Sahib in the area close to the Lachen Monastery.

Nanak passed through Gartok and Rudok and crossing the Chashul pass, entered Ladakh. He came first to Upashi and then moved on to Karunagar, twenty miles away. If one were to visit the villages around Karunagar one would find that a remarkable legacy of Nanak's visit is the fact that in many of these villages the people worship Nanak and Nanak alone. (Singh, Kirpal & Singh, Kharak, *History of the Sikhs and Their Religion*, vol. I p. 46)

Nanak then trekked on to the monastery of Hemis or Hemis Gompa, as it is popularly known. He rested there for a while and the monastery still preserves the stone on which he sat. Nanak passed through Leh and then followed the Indus till he came to Skardu in Baltistan. There is a gurdwara here in memory of the visit. From Skardu he followed the old route to Kargil, through Dras, across the Zojila Pass to Baltal.

Nanak came down into the beautiful and picturesque Liddar Valley at Pahalgam in Kashmir. Pahalgam is the place from where thousands of pilgrims begin their annual pilgrimage to the sacred cave of Amarnath during the months of July and August. Nanak came to Pahalgam when the little town was swarming with pilgrims. Some eagerly awaited their turn to make the difficult trek up to the cave. Others rested awhile on their way home, exhausted but joyful at having successfully completed the pilgrimage. Nanak used the opportunity to introduce them to his views on faith and religion and to the beauty of his *kirtan*.

From Pahalgam Nanak moved towards Srinagar. He came to the town of Mattan, the site of the ruins of the historical Hindu temple of Martand, forty miles to the east of Srinagar. Here he met Brahm Das, a learned Kashmiri pandit of Bij Bihara, who was greatly respected by the local community. Though possessed of a sharp, analytical mind, and profound learning and wisdom, there was one virtue that Brahm Das sadly lacked, and that was humility. He was arrogant and rude, given to belittling and ridiculing others. When he heard that a wise and learned *rishi* had camped in Mattan, he could not resist the temptation of going forth and showing his superiority. He came to Nanak's camp and began to make fun of Nanak's strange dress.

"You are a man of learning, O Pandit," Nanak said in his calm, gentle voice. "You should know that it is of little importance how we dress our body."

> "Religion lieth not in the patched coat the yogi wears,
> Not in the ashes on his body.
> Religion lieth not in rings in the ears
> Not in a shaven head,
> Nor in the blowing of the conch-shell
> If thou must the path of true religion see
> Among the world's impurities, be of impurities free."

(*Raga Suhi*, Trans. Singh, Khuswant, *A History of the Sikhs*, vol. I p. 42)

Gradually, Brahm Das was drawn towards Nanak. He participated in the singing of devotional songs and listened to Nanak when he preached.

"What is it you seek in this world, learned one?" asked Nanak, rhetorically. "You seek fame and greatness. You desire to be known for your learning. Wherever you go you carry cart-loads of Sanskrit texts to show the world how well-read you are. What you desire and seek is ephemeral, an illusion coveted only by men of the world. If you are truly a wise man on a sincere quest, your desire would be to merely be a humble instrument of God. Though you despise and look down upon men of the world, like them, you too worship *maya*. The followers of this Guru can never hope to attain salvation."

Nanak had a profound impact on Brahm Das and he strove hard to become a true instrument of God. In Mattan, as in nearby Anantnag, a gurdwara marks the spot where Nanak stayed.

Nanak visited Srinagar and then followed the Jhelum River to Baramullah. From Baramullah, he made his way to Hasan Abdal, also known as Panja Sahib, where too there is a gurdwara commemorating his visit.

At this point, Nanak felt a deep and intuitive urge to return to Sultanpur and this time Mardana did not need to prod him to turn back. On his way he came to Tila Bal Gudai, a major centre of the *siddha naths*. Here Nanak met a conclave of these hermits and had a long religious discourse with them, very much along the lines of his discourse with the eighty-four *siddhas* on the bank of the Rakas Tal. He resumed his journey, crossed the rivers Jhelum and Chenab, and came to Sialkot where the Gurdwara Bir Sahib marks the site of his camp. He passed through places like Parser and Saidpur where he met his old disciple Lalo, now a teacher of Nanak's precepts with a large congregation attending his meetings.

Nanak came at last to Talwandi and crowds of people welcomed him home. Kalo and Tripta were overcome with emotion. There could be no doubt now that Nanak had become a truly great man who was respected and revered wherever he went. After staying long enough in Talwandi to spend time with his parents and ensure that they were well-cared for, Nanak moved on to his beloved Sultanpur.

Great was the joy in Sultanpur on Nanak's return. Nanki and Jai Ram hung on to every word that he spoke, their faces suffused with happiness. Nawab Daulat Khan came down from Lahore to meet Nanak as soon as he heard of his arrival.

Nanak's decision to return home was to prove tragically intuitive. A few days after his return, Nanki fell prey to a mysterious illness and within a few hours it was clear that the end was near. Nanak sat on her cot, her head in his lap, and as he caressed her hair, all the memories of a lifetime flashed through his mind. He felt his heart lift with gratitude for the unstinting and adoring love that he had always received from his sister. He prayed silently that God would spare her pain and suffering.

He could feel her drifting away and his heart was heavy with sorrow. Just when the end seemed near, Nanki opened her eyes and smiled wanly at her brother. "You knew ... that is why you came home." She struggled to continue, "You have brought me great happiness and joy. You are close to God; can you intercede on my behalf and ensure that I am born again as your sister in the next birth?"

Nanak held her close and replied, "Your great and selfless love gave me the strength to be what I am. I will pray to the Almighty that he makes you my sister in the next birth too."

Nanki turned her head towards Jai Ram, who reached forward and held her hand in both his. Tears sprang to her eyes as she looked lovingly at him. Then she heaved a long sigh and closed her eyes.

Neither Nanak nor Jai Ram gave way to grief. They busied themselves with the funeral. When they returned from immersing the ashes, Jai Ram lay down on his cot and wrapped himself in his quilt. Nanak thought at first that he wished to be left alone with his grief and did not disturb him. But when the hours stretched on, Nanak went into his room, only to find that he was suffering from a raging fever. The *vaid* was sent for but it was clear that Jai Ram had lost the will to live. Nanki and Jai Ram had been a devoted couple and without her, Jai Ram was a mere shadow of his former self. Three days later, he too had passed away.

There was nothing to hold Nanak back in Sultanpur any more. He bid a sad farewell to his old employer Daulat Khan and both knew that this was their final goodbye. They would never meet again.

LAST UDASI

Before proceeding on his last udasi, Nanak stopped for a few days in Kartarpur to see how the place had developed. Through the untiring efforts of Ajit Randhawa and Duni Chand, a veritable township had been set up as more and more of the Guru's disciples flocked to Kartarpur and made it their home. Nanak stayed for a while in the house that his disciples had built for him and sent for Tripta and Kalo from Talwandi and for Sulakhni and his sons from Pakhoke. The family was together at last, even though briefly. People travelled long distances to come to Kartarpur to seek solace in the Guru's teachings. They asked him questions, listened to his hymns, and their pain and anxiety soothed, returned home. Although Kartarpur had become an important centre for his followers, Nanak felt the old restlessness come upon him again. With Mardana by his side, he set out on his last udasi, this time towards the west.

Nanak went first to Pak Pattan to re-establish contact with Sheikh Ibrahim Farid. The two men had great respect and admiration for each other and had always found pleasure in each other's company. He then proceeded to Multan, passing through Tulamba where he again met his disciple Sajjan, who was now a devout Sikh disseminating his Guru's teachings to the people of this area. Multan is an ancient town of the Punjab, which finds mention in contemporary Greek accounts of Alexander's invasion and also in the journal that Huien Tsang, the Chinese Buddhist pilgrim, maintained of his visit to India. Nanak spent a few days here in discussion with Sheikh Baha-ud-din, the leader of the Suhrawardy Sufi tradition. Nanak also visited Uch, formerly known as Deogarh, a great centre of spiritual and religious learning. The *pirs* of Uch were well-known all over the Punjab. So greatly were they venerated that, years later, Guru Gobind Singh was to disguise himself as one to escape from the forest of Machiwara.

From here, Nanak went on to the town of Sukkur on the western bank of the Indus, and crossing the river Habb, entered the region which is now known as Baluchistan. In a remote fold of the inaccessible mountains is the famous pilgrim centre of Hinglaj, revered both by the Hindus and the Muslims. Here he encountered a group of Vaishnavites whose curiosity was aroused by his strange garb. They crowded around him and plied him with questions and Nanak once again had an opportunity to talk about his perception and understanding of the concept of God and religion.

> "Not by thought alone
> Can He be known,
> Though one think a hundred thousand times
> Not in solemn silence,
> Nor in deep meditation.
> Though fasting yields an abundance of virtue,
> No, by none of these
> Nor by a hundred thousand other devices
> Can God be reached.
> How then shall truth be known?
> How the veil of bare illusion torn?
> O Nanak, thus runneth the writ divine:
> The righteous path, let it be thine."
>
> (*Mool Mantra*, Trans. Singh, Khushwant,
> *Japjee–Sikh Morning Prayer*, p. 17)

From Hinglaj, Nanak descended to the sea shore at Kuriana and visited the famous and venerable temples of Koteshwar and Narayan Swami. There is, even today, a sacred tank in Kuriana named after Nanak, built in memory of his visit. Similarly there is a Nanak Dharamshala close to the port of Sonmiani, or Miani, from where he took a ship to the Arab port of Al Aswad on the Red Sea, near the holy city of Mecca. He joined a group of pilgrims who were performing the *Haj*, the sacred pilgrimage which all devout Muslims are enjoined upon to undertake at least once in their lifetimes. He dressed like a *Haji* and carried a staff, a prayer mat, the holy book, and a pot to carry water for the ablutions that are a mandatory requirement before prayer.

Mecca was a convenient halting point on the caravan route and was an important town even before it became a holy Islamic city. It is referred to in the Qur'an as "a permanent resort of the caravans during

109

summers as well as winters" (Sura 106. Singh, Kirpal & Singh, Kharak, *History of the Sikhs and Their Religion*, vol. I p. 48).

It was dusk when they reached the outskirts of Mecca and Nanak preferred to spend the night outside the city at a quiet, wayside mosque. It was dark by the time they finished their spartan meal and said their prayers. Exhausted, they lay down in the corridor, and drifted quickly into deep and untroubled sleep. Next morning, the attendant who swept and cleaned the mosque before worship, was up and about at his usual early hour. He was used to finding weary travellers who often sought shelter in the mosque. But that day the sight of the two pilgrims horrified him. Nanak was fast asleep, his feet pointing towards the Ka'aba! The attendant was shocked at this terrible act of sacrilege and ran up the flight of stairs to inform the *maulvi*.

Maulvi Rukn-ud-din was beside himself with anger. He was a highly learned and respected religious head and in all his long years as a priest had never come across such an act of sacrilege. He hurried after the attendant and saw that the *fakir* did indeed have his feet pointing in the direction of the holiest of the holy. Without a moment's hesitation, he struck Nanak hard across the chest with his staff. Nanak woke up with a start.

"You sinner!" the *maulvi* shouted. "You have slept with your feet pointing towards the house of God. You must rub your face in dust and beg Him to forgive you."

"You are right, O holy one," Nanak replied in his usual calm manner. "I have indeed committed an act of sacrilege and I will have to atone for it. But before I begin to do that I must ensure that I never sin again. Will you help me by pointing my feet in the direction where God does not dwell, so that I do not make the same mistake again?"

The *maulvi*, touched by Nanak's humility and genuine repentance, turned to the attendant for help and together they lifted Nanak's legs and turned them around so that they were not pointing in the direction of the Ka'aba.

"There you are," he said.

"Are you sure that God does not dwell in this direction?" Nanak asked with a twinkle in his eye.

The *maulvi* was perplexed. He turned to look in the direction in which he had placed Nanak's feet. What he saw, in the early morning light, was a vista so beautiful that it could only have been created by an all-pervading divine spirit. He looked back at Nanak and realisation

110

dawned. His religion preached the omnipresence of God and despite being a custodian of that religion, he had confined Him within the walls of religious buildings. He realised too, that he was in the presence of a great soul.

Nanak stayed on with Maulvi Rukn-ud-din for a few days and they spent a lot of time sharing views on various matters. The more he listened to Nanak the more he was impressed by the depth of Nanak's learning, knowledge, and understanding of matters pertaining to the spiritual and the religious, of his analysis of all religions and by what he was attempting to achieve through his preaching.

Word of this wisdom and learning spread through Mecca like wildfire and the religious leaders of Mecca joined the growing group at Nanak's evening prayer session, questioning him about the relative merits of Hinduism and Islam. Nanak was impressed by their lack of bigotry and their desire to learn about a religion of which they knew so little. Bhai Gurdas in his *var* summarises the essence of Nanak's replies to these questions. The Guru explained how both religions had been designed as paths to salvation to attain the blissful state of nearness to God. Both religions preached that in following this path what was of the utmost importance was the performance of good deeds. But somewhere along the way the followers of both religions had forgotten this. They had begun to emphasise tradition and ritual and had forgotten the essence of these religions. Without righteous action, all the trappings of religion—the dress one wore, the prayers one said, the religious rituals one performed and the pilgrimages that one undertook—were meaningless, external trappings like the colour of the Kasumbha flower which is washed away by the rain.

From Mecca, Nanak and Mardana moved on to Medina where the Prophet Mohammad had lived for many years before his death. His tomb there attracts millions of pilgrims every year. Nanak's fame as a wise and learned man had preceded him and when he reached Medina it was to find a large crowd waiting at the city gates to welcome him. Nanak and his teachings made as great an impact in Medina as they had in Mecca.

After spending a respectable length of time in Medina, Nanak decided to return to India, following the overland route which passed through Baghdad. This route had first been charted by Khalifa Harun-ul-Rashid's wife, Zubeda Begum. It was also the route that the fourteenth century traveller Ibn Batuta had followed on his journey from Baghdad to Mecca. Though it was a shorter and more convenient route than the one passing through Palestine and Syria, there was a stretch between Faid and Baghdad which was extremely difficult and discouraged travellers. But by now, Nanak and Mardana were experienced enough and were easily able to overcome the hardships of this difficult terrain.

Baghdad was a beautiful, historic city, which gained importance through the centuries as a thriving centre of trade. Due to the resultant prosperity, it also became politically powerful. In Islam, politics and religion are inseparable, and it was inevitable that this great town, with its tremendous economic and political importance, should also become a great religious centre. It was, at the time of Nanak's visit, under the rule of the Safavi dynasty of Iran. Nanak's visit to Baghdad finds mention in the writings of both Bhai Gurdas and Bhai Mani Singh. Bhai Gurdas also says that Nanak "fixed up his place of stay outside (the town)". Archaeological evidence is provided by the discovery of an old Turkish inscription outside Baghdad. The widely accepted translation of this inscription reads: "See how the most glorious Lord God fulfilled the wish that for Baba Nanak new structure be built. Seven saints helped (therein). Its date (worked out to be that): the fortunate disciple made to flow new (well or spring) of water in the land 927." (Singh, Kirpal, & Singh, Kharak, *History of the Sikhs and Their Religion*, vol. I p. 49)

In Baghdad, as in Mecca and Medina, Nanak earned a place for himself in the hearts and minds of lay people as well as the learned and the holy. So much so that the leading *pirs* and *maulvis* attended his discourses and were deeply impressed by what they heard. Nanak stayed in Baghdad for four months and a small circle of devoted disciples grew around him. The best known of these disciples and also perhaps best loved by the Guru, were Bahlol and his son. Bahlol was a *pir* who was well-respected and revered in Baghdad. He had long discourses with Nanak and found that the Guru was able to give him answers and explanations for many of the questions that had troubled and perplexed him over the years.

Outside Baghdad there is an edifice popularly called Bahlol's tomb, which stands silent testimony to Nanak's visit and his association with Bahlol. In the early years of the twentieth century a wandering Hindu poet-saint by the name of Swami Ananda Acharya visited this site. He found an inscription here dated 912 *Hijra* which has since been lost. When loosely translated this inscription read: "Here spoke Nanak to

Faqir Bahlol, and for these sixty summers since the Guru left the soul of Bahlol has rested on the Master's word like a bee poised on a dawn-lit honey rose" (Singh, Kirpal, *Janamsakhi Parampara*, p.132). Inspired by this inscription Swami Ananda Acharya composed his long, well-known poem *Snow Birds* in which he describes the devotion Bahlol had for Nanak and the bond that existed between them.

From Baghdad, Nanak set out on the well-established caravan and pilgrim route through Kermanshah and on to Teheran. On the way he passed through Isfahan and Meshad. The name Meshad means "place of martyrdom" and is thus named in memory of Khalifa Harun-ul-Rashid, his son, and son-in-law who were martyred there in the early ninth century. In Meshad, as in Tehran and Isfahan, Nanak held discussions with the religious and spiritual leaders of the Shia faith.

There is an interesting story pertaining to this part of Nanak's journey. One evening Nanak camped in a small, abandoned mosque on the outskirts of a town. He and Mardana ate of the simple food that they were carrying with them and then commenced their evening *kirtan*. Hearing the sound of their singing, people began to gather to find out what was going on in the mosque. Some of the more orthodox were shocked by the profanity of song and music within the premises of the mosque, activities that Islam expressly prohibited in all places of worship. Word was immediately sent to the *maulvi*. Informed of the sacrilege that was being committed by Nanak and Mardana, the *maulvi* collected other religious leaders and called upon the local *darogah* to arrest this *kafir* who seemed determined to disturb the peace and quiet of their little town. The irate mob, led by the *maulvi* and the *darogah*, rushed towards the mosque. But as they came within hearing distance, they heard the recitation of *suras* from the Qur'an rendered in the most beautiful and melodious manner they had ever heard, each Arabic syllable enunciated clearly and with a perfect accent.

They stopped in their tracks, dumbfounded. Their anger dissolved completely when, after the recital, they heard Nanak embark upon a commentary on each of the *suras*. His erudition would have satisfied the most exacting theologian or scholar of the Qur'an. The stones they had carried to pelt the *kafir* with fell from their hands and they knelt, one by one, to listen to this strange *fakir* who was such an authority on their sacred book. In the days that followed it became obvious to them that Nanak did not belong to any one religion—he preached a path which was open to all men to follow. Thereafter, Nanak was treated with great deference and respect.

Nanak and Mardana went along the Amu Darya to Bokhara. They crossed into Afghanistan and, still following the old trade route, visited Balkh, Kabul, Kandahar, and Mazar-i-Sharif. Kabul, the present capital of Afghanistan, was the seat of Babar's government at the time of Nanak's visit. A gurdwara was built in the old city to commemorate Nanak's visit and it became the centre of the biggest Sikh congregation outside the Punjab. Some Sikhs remained in Kabul to preach Nanak's teachings and Bhai Gurdas also served for some time as a priest at a gurdwara there. The gurdwara was in existence till the nineteen forties, when it sadly fell victim to the Afghan government's efforts to expand and reconstruct the old quarter of its capital city.

From Kabul, Nanak and Mardana crossed the Khyber Pass and came to Peshawar. They passed through various other towns till they reached Lahore and finally Saidpur. Nanak was in Saidpur when Babar mounted his third invasion of the Punjab in 1520. The Lodhi court in Delhi was torn by factional intrigues and no effort was made to protect the kingdom or its people from the savage brutality of the invaders. The emperor, Ibrahim Lodhi, was not a strong king and this encouraged his rivals to eye his throne and plot his downfall. His uncle, Alam Khan Lodhi, was in secret contact with Babar, seeking his help to overthrow the emperor and seize power. Daulat Khan Lodhi, Nanak's old employer and the governor of Lahore, cherished the ambition to become the independent ruler of the Punjab. It served the interests of both these powerful men not to interfere with Babar's forays into Ibrahim Lodhi's kingdom. In fact, four years later, the two were to actually invite Babar to invade India.

Against this background Babar's soldiers had an easy time invading the Punjab. His army crossed the Chenab and attacked the town of Sialkot. The defenders offered only token resistance and the town was taken without a fight. Though the local population had to bear the ravages of rape and plunder, the people, by and large, were spared death and the town itself escaped any major damage. The invading army turned east to Saidpur where Nanak had arrived on his way home to Kartarpur. Saidpur put up a stiff resistance and many of Babar's soldiers were killed in the battle. An angry Babar gave orders to inflict the severest penalty on the town and its inhabitants. Entire quarters were put to the sword; streets flowed with blood and the stench of decaying bodies filled the air. Scores of buildings were destroyed and for days the fires of destruction burned with total impunity, consuming what had once been a prosperous and happy town.

Profoundly moved by the pain and suffering of the people of Saidpur, Nanak composed a beautiful and moving hymn called the *Babar Vani* which is part of the *Guru Granth Sahib*.

Nanak and Mardana were among the thousands of men and women who were imprisoned but they did not deviate from the daily practice of *kirtan* and prayers. The other prisoners derived hope and strength from Nanak's preaching and his beautiful rendition of *shabads*. The warden of the prison, who subscribed in large measure to Sufi beliefs, could not help but notice the change that Nanak had wrought in the prison. The all-pervading atmosphere of gloom and despair had given way to an air of cheer and optimism. The prisoners had gained confidence and self-respect and busied themselves in useful and productive work.

The warden was convinced that the Guru was a saint. He sought an audience with Babar and pleaded for Nanak's release. "The longer we keep him in shackles, O Master, the greater will be the burden of sin that we will carry when we come face to face with our Maker."

Intrigued by the warden's unusual plea for the release of one of his prisoners, Babar came to the prison to visit Nanak. He noticed the radiance on Nanak's face and the reverence and respect with which the other prisoners regarded him. After engaging Nanak in discussion, he too was convinced of Nanak's saintliness. The warden was right—it was a sin to imprison so holy a man. He offered Nanak and Mardana immediate freedom and showered them with presents.

"This is but a small token of my repentance. I will know that you have forgiven me if you accept these presents."

"I have already forgiven you," Nanak said, "but it is the forgiveness of Allah that you should seek. The only way for you to show true repentance is by releasing all the inhabitants of Saidpur and restoring their property to them."

So great was Babar's admiration for the Guru that he immediately did what Nanak asked of him. Having brought some measure of relief to the suffering population of Saidpur, Nanak at last made his way to his *dera* in Kartarpur.

KARTARPUR

I
t was the time of day called dusk in English, and *godhuli* in Hindi. The birds chattered incessantly as they settled down for the night and cattle lowed as they were herded homewards, the dust from their hooves clouding the air. Smoke from a hundred cooking fires curled up slowly into the purple sky. Men returned from work, tired and hungry, eager for a meal and the comforting warmth of home. It was the hour of longing and home-coming.

Sulakhni waited, she knew not why. It was winter; darkness set in early and there was a nip in the air; she huddled closer to the fire. After serving Kalo and Tripta their dinner, she had prepared their nightcap of warm, sweetened buffalo milk. She had eaten her meal, washed the utensils and put them away. And yet she waited beside the dying fire. Her husband was away on his fourth *udasi* and though news had trickled in that he was now wending his way homeward, she did not know when he would reach Kartarpur. He would probably make numerous detours and though he was close to home, it could be months before he finally arrived. No, she said to herself with a sharp stab of pain, she did not wait for him.

Her sons, too, were away. Sri Chand was on a pilgrimage to the city of Benaras and like his father, there was no knowing when he would return. Lakhmi Das, who enjoyed the good life, now chose to spend more and more time with his wealthy in-laws. Her thoughts turned again to Nanak. She wondered how he was. He was getting on in years and she worried that the present journey would have exacted a toll on his health. As the sharp pain of longing shot through her again, she knew she ached for a glimpse, no matter how brief, of her husband. She smiled wryly and admitted to herself that she waited for her husband, just as she had done every evening of her life.

Night had fallen and a deep stillness had descended upon the world. Nanak's humble, three-room house stood at the very end of a narrow, cobbled street and this isolation added to the quiet of the night. The main street of Kartarpur, bustling with life till late evening, was too far away for the sounds to carry to Nanak's house. Sulakhni sighed, wishing that the silence would be broken by the sound of wooden clogs approaching home.

Her thoughts turned again to her sons—they were both her children and yet they were so different from each other. Sri Chand was twenty-six and, like his father, had turned to spiritual and religious matters early in life. Looking back at his childhood, it was evident that it was Nanki's influence that had propelled him in this direction. Nanki had adored her brother and when she took custody of his son, she did her best to cast him in his father's mould. She encouraged him to study the holy texts and after he had mastered them sufficiently, she urged him to discuss the finer points with learned men. She had watched with pride as he was drawn deeper into his spiritual quest and had often said with great satisfaction that the son was growing up to be the spitting image of his father.

Sulakhni shook her head sadly. Though father and son had chosen the same path, Sri Chand did not have his father's humility. In spite of his great wisdom and his huge following, Nanak had always remained simple and modest. Despite frequent disagreements with men of different faiths, he was never known to lose his temper. He retained his calm and equanimity, always speaking in a soft, gentle voice. On the other hand, the more learned Sri Chand became the more proud and arrogant was his behaviour. He was contemptuous of anyone whose ideas differed from his. Sulakhni had often seen him lose his temper and use impolite language with anyone who disagreed with him. Nanki had not lived long enough to see how wrong she had been when she had proclaimed that Sri Chand was like his father.

Her thoughts turned to Lakhmi Das, the apple of her eye. When he was a child, she could not bear to let him out of her sight. She had guarded him jealously but she admitted now that she had failed him. Every time he had shown any interest in matters connected with religion or had even suggested meeting a holy man, her heart had filled with fear. She had been afraid that he would take after his father and she would lose him too. So she did everything in her power to keep his mind on worldly things. Her parents helped by showering him with presents—clothes, toys, and all kinds of goodies. But she had paid a heavy price for this upbringing. Her son had turned out to be a completely selfish and self-centred young man, who showed no consideration for others. In spite of all her careful ministering, she had, in the end, lost him.

Her thoughts turned to her in-laws, old Kalo and Tripta. What a gift Nanak had given her by bringing them to Kartarpur! Caring for them comforted her in his absence. They never took her for granted and were grateful for every little thing she did for them. They appreciated her patience over the long periods that she had had to wait for her husband to return.

Sulakhni had never once complained, or suggested by word or deed that she had been deprived or neglected. She always spoke of Nanak and of the great work he was doing, with quiet pride. She recited selections from his *bani* and sang some of the hymns he had taught her during his brief periods at home. Kalo and Tripta found strength in listening to the *bani* and *kirtan*. It was as if Nanak spoke to them through Sulakhni's words and they did not miss him as much as they had done before. They blessed her with every breath of their being and Sulakhni, in turn, prayed that God would give them a long life, for without them she would not have known how to cope with her loneliness.

The fire had almost burnt itself out and she inched closer to steal its last remaining warmth. As she warmed her hands, she listened for a sound in the all-pervading silence. It came to her then, the faint sound of distant footsteps. Her heart skipped a beat, it could not be! The sound became louder and clearer as the footsteps approached the house. It seemed so familiar, the sound of wooden clogs, clip-clopping on the cobbled street. No, she told herself, it couldn't be. So many times she had run to open the door only to find the fierce, howling wind mocking her. Now as the sound of footsteps came closer, her heart began to sing. There could be no mistaking that sound—he was home!

She got to her feet and ran to the door. There he was in his strange *fakir* dress, which hung loosely on a skeletal frame. His face was gaunt and thin with the weariness of long years of travel. She felt a twist in her heart when she saw that his beard had turned almost completely grey. They looked at each other for a long moment. Then he smiled and she fell at his feet, weeping.

"Sulakhni?" Tripta's voice called out to her across the courtyard. "Sulakhni *puttar*, who is it? Who has come?" The weak and tired voice, normally little more than a whisper, now rang out loud and clear with strength that hope alone can bring. And Sulakhni knew that she had not been the only one listening to the silence of the night, waiting for the sound of those familiar footsteps. Nanak drew Sulakhni to her feet and together they went in to his parents.

It was a joyous homecoming. The news of Nanak's return spread like wildfire and thousands of followers from far and near thronged Kartarpur to catch a glimpse of their beloved Guru and to hear his words once more. One of the first things that Nanak did was to put aside the strange garb that had been his hallmark all these years. He dressed like any householder and set himself a routine that he was to follow for the remaining years of his life. He would begin the day with a bath and then the congregation would meet, *kirtan* would be sung, and prayers recited. A convention was established of reciting the *Japji* and the *Asa Di Var* in the mornings, with Mardana playing the *rabab* for the *kirtan*.

Mardana had also brought his family from Talwandi to Kartarpur. His son, Shehzada, had a passion for music and often joined his father in playing the *rabab* and singing the sacred and beautiful *shabads*. It gave Nanak great happiness to see the son following so willingly in the footsteps of his father and the bond between the two, even after years of living apart. After the prayers Nanak would go to work in the fields. These fields were part of the area that Ajit Randhawa had gifted to Nanak. As more and more people had settled in Kartarpur, the area around the *dera* had become flourishing farm land. At about ten in the morning Nanak would eat a simple meal, rest for a while, and complete the tasks that he had allotted himself for the day. Evenings were spent in prayer and the singing of hymns. The Guru's compositions of *Sodar* and *Aarti* would be sung. At night, Nanak would partake of the *langar* and return home.

Nanak had spent almost a quarter of a century travelling far and wide and meeting people from many faiths. He had preached the concept of one God and denounced idol worship. He had defined a faith that emphasised the concepts of love, compassion, and equality. He had tried to free people from the shackles of meaningless ritual and superstition. He had insisted that one did not have to renounce the world to achieve salvation. Now, by casting aside his ascetic's robe and leading the life of a householder, he was giving practical shape to his teachings. He was no longer merely preaching but living the life that he advocated.

Soon Sri Chand and Lakhmi Das heard of their father's return to Kartarpur and came home. After the initial awkwardness born of long years of separation, a cordial relationship was established between the father and the sons. But both the boys were so different from their father, so different in their beliefs and values, that in spite of the best efforts on both sides, no real bond of paternal affection was forged between them. Nanak knew he was more to blame for this than either of the boys and was consequently more gentle and indulgent with them than he would otherwise have been.

Kartarpur soon became a flourishing community. Ajit Randhawa and Duni Chand, the *Amil* of Lahore, continued to send in generous contributions for the infrastructure that was necessary to accommodate the increasing population. Some of Nanak's followers had abandoned their property and their homes to stay permanently with the Guru in Kartarpur. For them, the community provided land, material, and labour for the construction of their homes. There were others who flocked to Kartarpur only as pilgrims. They were usually provided accommodation by the people of Kartarpur. But as the years went by, the number of pilgrims swelled and it became impossible to accommodate them, especially during religious festivals. There was a pressing need for an alternative arrangement.

Nanak's *kirtan* and prayer sessions were held in large open grounds. But during spells of inclement weather, these meetings had to be cancelled. Nanak asked for a huge hall to be built to accommodate the entire congregation and prevent disruption of prayers by the unreliable weather. To comfortably lodge the vast multitude of pilgrims, a *dharamshala* was also proposed. Word of the project spread, and by the time the master builder had finalised his design, cartloads of building material had already been brought to Kartarpur by Nanak's devoted disciples. Neat piles of bricks, lime, and wooden beams could be seen all over the site. Soon, an army of men with all the necessary building tools had descended upon Kartarpur, ready to contribute their labour to their Guru's project. This was the beginning of the tradition of *kar sewa*, which has, over the centuries, underpinned all construction activity in gurdwaras. At the end of eighteen months, both the *dharamshala* and the assembly hall had been completed.

From the very early days, an essential component of Nanak's *satsangs* was the community meal, of which all members of the congregation were expected to partake. At first, it was seen as little more than a gesture of hospitality that Nanak was extending to guests who had come to his home. But as the years went by, and the practice continued even when Nanak conducted his meetings away from home, people realised that he had introduced this practice deliberately to emphasise two essential features of his teachings. When people sat down together and shared a meal they put aside all reservations about caste and creed. A Hindu broke bread with a Muslim, a Jat and a Shudra often ate from the same plate. By doing so, the concept of the equality of man was put into practice. The community meal brought the rich and the poor together. The rich made generous contributions to the *langar* in cash or in kind and the poor were fed. By practising charity and expressing concern and compassion for the poor, the rich were practising essential elements of Nanak's philosophy. The number of pilgrims in Kartarpur who partook of the *langar* steadily increased and soon Nanak added a community kitchen and dining area to the *dera*. This complex of *dharamshala*, prayer hall, and the *langar* became the prototype for all Sikh centres established thereafter.

Nanak's life in Kartarpur had become so settled that people were now convinced that he had come home to stay. By putting aside his *fakir's* garb and putting on that of the householder, he had made a categorical statement of his intention. The days took on a placid tone and time flew by gently and effortlessly. "Participation in religious and other activity on equal community terms was a vital feature of the style of live evolving in Kartarpur" (Singh, Harbans, *Guru Nanak & Origins of the Sikh Faith*, pp. 180–181). This period of Nanak's life "combined a life of disciplined devotion with worldly activities set in the context of normal family and regular *satsang*" (McLeod, W. H., *Guru Nanak and the Sikh Religion*, [Oxford 1960] p. 228).

"In the trackless world of that time the old father of his people travelled on foot. The Afghan and the Baloch, the Turk and the Tartar, the Sufi and the Brahmin, the fair and the dark races mingled in his great heart. The disciples, both men and women, came from all directions and took part freely in the songs of the Guru." (Singh, Puran, *The Book of the Ten Masters*, pp. 25–26)

One day, while Nanak was ploughing his fields, he paused to wipe the sweat from his brow and through the morning haze, saw a figure in flowing robes running towards him. He recognised his elder son Sri Chand. "Come, Father," he said gently. "Mother wants you to come home."

Instinctively Nanak knew why Sri Chand had come to call him. "Is it your grandfather?"

Sri Chand did not look at his father but nodded his head in the affirmative.

"Does he still breathe?" he asked.

"Yes, but only barely."

Nanak untied his oxen and letting them loose in a grove nearby, he hurried home. Kalo was lying with his head in Tripta's lap. Sulakhni sat to the side, fanning him. His body shook with the effort of drawing each breath, but his eyes lit up when he saw Nanak. He stretched out a frail hand and Nanak clasped it warmly. Utterly at peace now, Kalo breathed his last.

Tripta did not cry. Very tenderly, she closed her husband's eyes and began to recite a hymn that her son had composed. Seeing her mother-in-law's composure, Sulakhni too suppressed her sobs. The next few days were taken up by the funeral ceremonies and through all the prayers and rituals, Tripta sat in peaceful composure. When people offered their condolences, she accepted them in silence but she remained detached from all that was happening around her. She prayed continuously, without weeping or making a sound, eating only when she was forced to. By the third day everyone was worried.

"What is it Mother?" Nanak asked.

"I must pray," she replied, her voice clear and strong. "I must prepare myself; I have to embark on a long journey to join your father."

The day after the obsequies were over, Tripta passed away in her sleep. Tripta and Kalo had lived to a ripe old age and passed away in peace, having seen their son achieve the greatness that had been foretold for him.

Nanak did not venture forth on any more *udasis* but he did travel to nearby places. He would go to preach at a fair or to meet an old disciple who was too sick or infirm to come to him in Kartarpur. Wherever he went he was treated with the greatest respect and deference. On one of these trips to a village now known as Kathunangal, Nanak met a young boy. He had stopped to rest under a tree and had seen the boy grazing his cattle. He could sense the boy's curiosity and was amused by it. He closed his eyes pretending to be asleep and soon, he became aware that the boy had crept up to him. He opened his eyes and smiled reassuringly at the boy who had brought him a bowl of fresh milk. Nanak took the proffered bowl and drank the milk.

"I needed that," he said, wiping his mouth. "And I am indeed obliged to you for this gift, Bhai—what is your name?"

"My name is Bura. I belong to a family of Randhawa Jats," the boy answered.

"And how old are you Bhai Bura?" Nanak asked.

"I am twelve years old, O holy one," Bura answered.

"And are you always so kind to all men?" Nanak asked.

"I try to be—especially to holy men, whose company I always seek."

"And what do you want to gain from such company?"

"I seek freedom from the cycle of birth and death."

Nanak was surprised by the boy's answer. Something so profound was usually sought by those who had experienced suffering, or by sages who had dwelt on the illusory nature of life. The young boy should have been seeking boons more appropriate to his age, maybe riches, or a long life for his parents, or marriage to a beautiful girl. "What you seek is unusual. What has turned your mind to such thoughts?"

The boy was quiet for a while, his brow puckered in a serious frown as he marshalled his thoughts. "When Babar invaded the Punjab, his soldiers camped in this forest. They came to the village and took whatever they could lay their hands on. When they were ready to march on, they cut down all the corn in our fields while we watched in helpless anger. I stood there too and I saw how they did not discriminate between the ripe corn and the green corn. They cut it all down together. As I watched them I realised that death makes no distinction between the young and the old. It strikes the young and strong as suddenly as the old and the infirm. Why then should I wait for old age to seek salvation?"

Nanak was impressed by such deep wisdom in one so young. "Bhai Bura, you have been wrongly named by your parents. You should be called 'Baba Budha'—the one with the wisdom of an old man."

In the years to come, Bura became Nanak's devoted disciple and made Kartarpur his home. Everyone referred to him by the name that had been given to him by the Guru and Baba Budha lived up to his name. In spite of having sought *moksha* at the age of twelve, he lived to be a truly venerable old man: he lived to the ripe old age of 125. He performed the installation ceremony of five Gurus and saw the construction of the Harmandir Sahib. He witnessed the compilation of the *Guru Granth Sahib* and its installation at the Harmandir Sahib. Because of the respect and regard he commanded in the community, Guru Arjun Dev appointed him as the first *granthi* of the Harmandir Sahib. He finally passed away when Guru Hargobind was the Guru.

Through his teachings and his own example Nanak instilled the philosophy of *sewa* into his disciples. The highest merit in life could be earned through selfless service to others. If labour had to benefit one's soul, it had to be directed towards helping others and the community at large. This philosophy was practised by all who came to Kartarpur. Those who were farmers, like Nanak, tilled the land, and shared the produce. Those with special skills, like potters, weavers, carpenters, and masons, used them in the service of the *sangat*. The complex in Kartarpur had been built entirely through such service. The women contributed to *sewa* by cooking for the *langar* while the men served the meals and washed the utensils. Those who had medical skills treated the sick and the injured without charging a fee, those who were learned explained Nanak's *bani* to others while those who were musically inclined contributed to the *kirtan*. Everyone in Kartarpur served the community in some way or the other.

Nanak gathered a group of disciples who were to become famous in their own right. Among these was a disciple named Moola Keer who gained the love and admiration of his Guru. He had been a devoted follower of the Guru and recited the *bani* and always tried to live by the Guru's precepts. He worked hard during the day, lived a simple life, ate frugally, and gave his savings away to charity. He was honest and kind and did everything he could to help others.

One day, a Sikh pilgrim on his way to Kartarpur stopped at his door and sought shelter for the night. Moola Keer welcomed him with open arms and made him comfortable. The Sikh, who was well-versed in the Guru's *bani*, joined Moola Keer in his evening prayers and Moola was impressed by his guest's familiarity with the Nanak *bani*.

That night, while Moola and his family were fast asleep, their guest ransacked the house and stuffed all the valuables that he could lay his hands on into his bag. In the morning, the Sikh joined Moola Keer in the recitation of the *Japji* and then, after a simple breakfast, sought permission to leave. As he escorted him to the door, the visitor's bag slipped from his hand and fell to the ground. The jewellery and other valuables spilled out. The guest looked at his host in alarm, but Moola merely picked up all the valuables and stuffed them into the visitor's bag. Handing it to him with a quiet smile, he gently said, "God be with you and may you receive the Guru's blessings!"

All through his journey to Kartarpur, the enormity of what he had done haunted the pilgrim. His guilt was magnified a hundredfold in the face of the extreme magnanimity and graciousness of his host.

He came at last to Kartarpur and into the Guru's presence. The Guru, noticing his preoccupation and discomfort, sent for him when he was alone. "Bhai Sikha," the Guru said, "there is something troubling you. Tell me if there is anything that I can do to lighten your burden."

"I have done something terrible and sinful. I carry a heavy burden of guilt and I must carry it alone. No, my Guru, there is nothing that you can do to lighten it, except perhaps ask God to forgive me."

"My son," Nanak said gently, "tell me about it. The mere telling of our troubles to others lightens the burden for us."

After a moment's hesitation the Sikh told his Guru of his sin and of the saintly mien of the man whom he had wronged.

"No matter how grave the sin, a confession earns you the right to forgiveness. Moola Keer appears to be a saint and if he is indeed my disciple, I would like to meet him."

Moola Keer was sent for and when he reached Kartarpur, he was ushered into the Guru's presence. Nanak came straight to the Sikh's strange story.

"Why did you give the valuables back to this thief? You should have handed him over to the *kotwal*."

"He is a Sikh, O Master," Moola replied "and I know that he would not steal unless he was in dire straits. I realised that his need was greater than mine and I gladly handed over to him what he so desperately wanted."

The Guru looked with affection at the man who would sacrifice so much to protect the honour of his faith. But there was one more question that he needed to ask.

"On his return from Kartarpur to his hometown, this Sikh will need to stop for the night in your village once again. Will you welcome him into your house and treat him with the same honour and kindness?"

"Of course I will," Moola answered. "You have taught us that one of the best ways to worship the Almighty is serving others without cause or motive, not seeking any reward."

The Guru rose to his feet and drew Moola into a warm embrace. "Bhai Moola, you are a true Sikh. You have understood my teachings by practising them every day of your life." Moola was soon to move permanently to Kartarpur and assume great responsibility in the management of the community.

Another famous and favourite disciple of Nanak was a young man by the name of Lehna, who lived in the small town of Khadur. Lehna would wake at five and meditate under the tamarind tree in his courtyard. This had been his habit for so long that his wife Khivi no longer knew when he stole out of bed. Usually he was so lost in prayer that he did not notice when the birds began to twitter. But on that fateful day he was not able to concentrate and was fully aware of the break of day and of the sound of the birds. He was possessed by a strange restlessness. This had begun to happen quite frequently in the recent past. He was an ardent devotee of the goddess Durga and during the *Navratras* he went on a pilgrimage to Jwalamukhi. He had always felt a deep happiness and peace in the presence of the goddess. But on his last visit he had experienced only restlessness, a feeling that persisted to this day. Then, from the neighbour's courtyard, he heard a soft, clear voice deep in prayer. It was a strange hymn, but the cadence was beautiful and when the worshipper finished his recitation, Lehna's restlessness had vanished.

Lehna's father, Pheru, was a rich and powerful trader and Lehna spent all morning helping him. But his mind kept going back to the beautiful hymn and he wondered who had composed it. By mid-morning he could not bear the suspense anymore. He excused himself from his work and made his way to his neighbour's house.

"Tell me the name of the hymn you recited this morning, Jodha, and the name of the one who composed it."

"It is the *Mool Mantra*," Jodha said, with a smile. "It is written by my Guru, Guru Nanak of Kartarpur."

Lehna was to leave for Jwalamukhi with a group of pilgrims the following day. Eager to meet this Guru, he tried to persuade them to consider a stop at Kartarpur. But they did not agree. So the next day, all the pilgrims tied bells to their wrists and ankles and set out on their way to the Devi, singing and dancing as they went. But each time Lehna sang *Jai Mata Di*, he heard Jodha's soft, sweet voice reciting *Ek Onkar, Sat Naam, Karta Purkh*. Even in the presence of the goddess, it was Jodha's voice that kept humming in his ears.

It was a strange, emaciated Lehna who returned to Khadur. The other pilgrims reported that he had eaten very little and kept to himself. For two days and two nights Lehna stayed in Khadur. Then, while everyone was asleep, he mounted his horse and rode to Kartarpur. He came to the Guru's *dera* just before dawn. This was his favourite time of the day. It was also the favourite time of the day for Guru Nanak, who called it the *amrit vela*. As Lehna rode into the *dera* he noticed that everything was still and quiet. He got off his horse and tied a cloth around the horse's hooves so that their sound would not break the silence. As he came to the centre of the *dera* he heard a strong, beautiful voice break into the same hymn that Jodha had recited: *Ek onkar, sat naam, karta purkh.*

He was overcome by the beauty of the voice and the hymn. He let go the horse's bridle and fell on his knees. He lowered his forehead to the ground and wept, and knew that this was what he had been searching for; he knew that he had at last come home.

After the morning prayers, Lehna went up to a Sikh disciple who seemed to be some kind of a leader.

"I am Lehna from Khadur," he introduced himself. "I have come for the *darshan* of the Guru and to serve him."

"You are more than welcome, Lehna of Khadur. I am Bura Singh but people call me Baba Budha." He smiled as he said this and Lehna smiled too. "You must be tired. Let me show you where you can stay and where you may stable your horse."

Within a few days it was as if Lehna had always been in Kartarpur. Wherever there was work to be done, Lehna was the first to reach out and attempt to do it. No task was too lowly for him. He was in the fields at the break of dawn. When any construction work was to be done, he laboured from morning till night. In the summer he would fan the people who ate in the *langar* and after the evening meal Lehna toiled on in the *langar*, washing and stacking the utensils. And all the while, his mind was on the Guru's words, the words he had heard during the prayer services. He tried to live by these words, content to sit quietly on the fringes and take in the beauty of his Guru's teaching. He had no desire to seek his Guru out or to be noticed by him.

But with Lehna's unstinting and devoted service, it was only a matter of time before the Guru noticed him. Lehna had always been very fond of children and he loved to spend an hour or two every evening with the children of his village. They were drawn to him, begging him to tell them stories and to teach them new games. Lehna was always ready to oblige. In Kartarpur, too, he would join the children in their play before evening prayers and the whole *dera* would echo with their laughter. People would smile and exclaim, "What a child this stranger is!"

The Guru had noticed the stranger and the dedication with which he applied himself to every task. One evening, as he left his home to go out for the evening prayers, he was greeted by the loud, joyous laughter of a group of children. It made him smile.

"Bhai Budha, what is it that makes our children so happy?"

"Master, they have found a new playmate," Bhai Budha replied, pointing to Lehna. The Guru approached Lehna, who bowed low, waiting for him to pass. But the Guru did not pass him by. He stood before Lehna and put his hand on Lehna's head.

"Who are you?" he asked in a gentle voice. "And where do you come from?"

For a moment Lehna stood there, overwhelmed and speechless. The Guru had put his hand on his head, the Guru had addressed him. He felt such a deep joy that he was afraid to speak and break the spell. But the Guru waited for his answer.

"I come from Khadur," he said, his voice so low it could hardly be heard. "My name is Lehna."

"Lehna," the Guru said, running the name softly off his tongue. "Whose Lehna?"

Lehna did not understand.

The Guru said, "Your *lehna*, your debt, was here with me and that is why God has brought you to Kartarpur."

The years went by and Lehna worked hard to repay his debt to his Guru by working with tireless devotion in the service of the *sangat*. Each night he went to bed happy in the knowledge that he had done his best. He sought no reward, no special mark of affection from the Guru. Soon, everyone in the community knew of his extraordinary service to the Guru who also showed a marked regard for his devoted follower.

In 1530, Nanak made a short journey across the Ravi to Achal, a village in Batala district, where there was an old and famous temple dedicated to Kartikeya, the son of Lord Shiva. Every year, a fair was organised on the occasion of Shivratri, Lord Shiva's birthday. Like all village fairs, it was an extremely colourful occasion, with the singing of hymns in praise of Lord Shiva, the consumption of *bhang*, and the subsequent joy and merriment. It was also an occasion when holy men of various sects came together and spent long hours in discussion. It was to participate in these debates and to preach his precepts that Nanak, accompanied by Lehna, who was now his constant companion, came to Achal.

It was late evening when they reached the village. Nanak, by now, was acknowledged as a great teacher and as news of his arrival spread, people rushed to welcome him, abandoning the lectures they had been listening to. Some came because they had heard that his blessings brought peace, others for advice because he was reputed to be learned and wise. The mass exodus from the *pandals* made many of the *sadhus* jealous of the Guru and they looked for an opportunity to belittle him. Bhangar Nath, the leader of a group of *siddhas*, looked at Nanak and his lip curled in scorn. "You call yourself a holy man and come here to engage in discussion on matters pertaining to the spirit and the soul. But look at you; you wear the clothes of men who engage in the petty business of earning and spending money, who fritter away their mental and emotional strength on the mundane problems of their families. We have heard that you actually work in the fields every morning. You are nothing more than an ordinary farmer and yet you dare to discuss spiritual matters with us *siddhas*, who have renounced the world to seek enlightenment."

Nanak merely smiled, not offering a rejoinder.

Another *siddha* said, "Actually, he is worse than a farmer, he is an apostate. For twenty-three years he wore the clothes of a *fakir*, renounced the world, and travelled from one pilgrim centre to another seeking salvation. Much was made of him by the people he met. Look at him now. He has discarded the clothes of a *fakir* and resumed life in the material world. Men evolve from the world of the flesh to the world of the spirit. He is the only one I have heard of who has regressed from the world of the spirit to the world of the flesh."

Again Nanak merely smiled and held his peace. The listeners sat wondering when the Guru would respond.

"You earned much merit, when you had renounced the world. People spoke of you with veneration and holy men looked upon you as an enlightened soul. Your life had become pure and white, like milk. By going back to the life of the householder, that milk has soured and curdled," Bhangar Nath said dismissively.

At the end of this tirade, Nanak finally spoke. "Perhaps what you say is true, O learned ones. But are you sure that the life of the householder and everything connected with it is unclean and impure?"

"Yes, of course," Bhangar said impatiently. "How can you even ask such a question?"

Nanak paused, looking carefully at the gathering of *sadhus* and at the crowd that had now closed in upon them. "You are ascetics. Don't you depend on alms for sustenance?"

129

The *siddhas* looked at each other impatiently. Nanak had lost his mind to ask such ridiculous questions.

"Who gives you this food?" Nanak asked. At last, the purport of his questions dawned on his listeners. "It is the householders," Nanak continued. "And if everything about the householder and his life is, as you say, sheer dross, why do you accept alms from him?"

There were smiles on the faces of people in the gathering. The Guru had spoken in favour of the ordinary man and put the arrogant *siddhas* firmly in their place. Nanak and Lehna returned to Kartarpur a few days later.

During this period Nanak organised his hymns and discourses according to subject and set them down on paper. The hymns based on his discussions with *siddhas* on numerous occasions—in the forest outside Talwandi, at Gorakhmath, at Sumer (Kailash) and at Achal— were now collated into a single, long hymn called *Siddhagosht*, which Guru Arjun Dev included in the *Guru Granth Sahib*.

Old age and illness had finally caught up with Mardana, Nanak's companion of forty-seven years. He was now seventy-six years old. Many famous *hakims* and *vaids* came to treat him but to no avail. Nanak was always by his bedside, comforting him as he drifted in and out of uneasy sleep. Memories flashed through his mind and he remembered the plump young man who had accompanied him on his first udasi. Nanak smiled as he remembered that Mardana had always had a hearty appetite. Mardana had travelled with him through sun and rain and snow accompanying him to regions that were strange and unfamiliar. He had looked after Nanak devotedly, finding joy in that service. He had played his *rabab* with such feeling that those who listened were moved by the music. He had been with the Guru for so many years that he had become a part of the Guru's way of life and a part of the Guru himself. All these memories came chasing one another through Nanak's mind as he looked at this sleeping companion.

"God," he prayed silently, "be merciful to my friend. He is a good man."

Though the illness continued to weaken him day by day, Mardana seemed to be at peace with himself and his approaching death. Early one morning, he opened his eyes and saw the Guru still sitting by his side, exactly where he had been when Mardana had fallen sleep.

"Master," he said, without fear, "my time has come."

"So be it, my dearest friend," Nanak said, "I will build a shrine to your memory so that the world shall forever remember Nanak's companion, Mardana."

"No, Master," Mardana said, with a small smile. "My spirit is attempting to find release from this cage of flesh and bones. Do not seek to hold it in a prison made of stone." He paused for breath. "In years to come, whenever people talk of you, as they will, my name will be mentioned too. I only wish to be remembered as a true disciple of Nanak."

Nanak caught his friend's hand in both his and squeezed it gently. In Mardana, he had found the respect and devotion of a disciple, the love of a friend, the support and affection of a brother, and the joy of a companion. They had been together for so long and been through so much that their souls were bound together in a way that the world had rarely seen, a bond that even death could not break.

"Go, Master, it is time for the morning prayer." His eyes fixed on his Master's face, Mardana left this world. Nanak gently closed Mardana's eyes and drew the sheet over his face. Someone in the room began to sob and Nanak saw that it was Shehzada. He drew him into an embrace and consoled him. Then he went quickly to bathe so that he could be in time for the morning prayers.

Nanak began his discourse. When it was time for *kirtan*, he looked, as always, towards the spot where Mardana sat. He saw Shehzada, sitting in his father's place ready to start playing on his *rabab*. Nanak smiled and began his song.

Nanak now came to depend more on Lehna, who was eager to devote his life to his Guru and stay on in Kartarpur. But Nanak reminded him of his obligation to his father Pheru and to his wife Khivi. The Guru encouraged him to keep in touch with them and to visit Khadur as often as he could. "If you cut yourself off from your family, Lehna, and always stay by my side, you will be no better than the ascetics who renounce the world in the hope of achieving salvation." Sometimes Pheru and Khivi accompanied Jodha on his visits to Kartarpur and spent a few days there. They listened to the *kirtan* and to Nanak's discourses and understood why Lehna had chosen to be with the Master. Khivi would have liked to stay permanently in Kartarpur but Pheru needed to be looked after and was too old to move to a new place.

One day, on his way back from Khadur, Lehna was delayed and reached Kartarpur in the late evening. There had been a sudden heavy downpour and he had taken shelter in a village, impatient at this delay in meeting his Guru. The moment the rain stopped he rode out again, spurring his horse to greater speed to make up for lost time. He arrived at last in Kartarpur, to find that the Guru was still out in the fields with his son Lakhmi Das. He stabled his horse and ran to the fields. As he went to touch the Guru's feet, the Guru drew him into a silent embrace.

There were three bundles of freshly cut fodder that still lay in the field, waiting to be carried home. "I'll send a servant to carry this as soon as I get home," Lakhmi Das said. But without a word, Lehna lifted the bundles onto his head, one upon the other, and made his way back through the fields. The fodder was wet and the muddy water dripped down his neck, covering his shirt with smudges. It was a beautiful shirt made of a soft, expensive Chinese silk that Khivi had bought from a trader who had passed through the village. No one in the village had a shirt like this and she was proud that she had given her husband something so beautiful. He, who cared nothing for worldly things, had teased her about it. "When will I ever need to wear something so grand?" he had asked her. "When you go to meet your Guru" she had replied. So on the day of his return he had worn this special shirt. And here it was now, sticking to his back, soiled and dirty. But he did not notice this. He was happy to be performing a service for his Guru. It was Sulakhni who noticed it the moment she saw him with the load of fodder on his head. She took Guru Nanak aside.

"How could you do this?" she asked. "How could you allow Lehna to carry this load and dirty his clothes with mud?"

"When the mud comes from such willing and selfless service, it does not remain mud—it becomes saffron. And when the load of fodder is carried by Lehna it is no longer a load but the halo of God's blessing."

Sulakhni looked at Lehna, so humble and meek, and then at her proud and arrogant son and she knew the truth of Guru Nanak's statement.

One day a report was brought to the Guru that one of the newly built walls in the *dharamshala* had given way and the Guru hurried to see the extent of the damage. Part of a wall had indeed crumbled as a result of incessant rains. If not attended to immediately, there was danger of the entire wall coming down and the roof caving in.

"Son," he said addressing Lakhmi Das, "this must be attended to immediately."

"Yes, Father," Lakhmi Das said, stifling a yawn because it was late and he was sleepy. "I will send for the mason and have it attended to first thing in the morning."

The Guru did not say anything more and returned home. Lehna slipped away into the darkness and brought two labourers back with him. The mason was away on a visit to a neighbouring village and would not be back till the next morning. Lehna organised all the material—bricks, lime, and sand for the mortar. He struggled through the night, rebuilding the wall as best as he could.

By the time the Guru stopped at the site on his way to morning prayers, the wall had been sufficiently rebuilt to avert any more danger to the building. The Guru lauded Lehna's selfless service and word of this incident spread through the community. It was soon clear to everyone that Lehna would be the next Guru although there were some who felt that Sri Chand, Nanak's elder son, who was a very pious man, ought to succeed his father.

One morning, Nanak addressed Lehna. "Bhai Lehna," he said, in his beautiful voice, "you have shown over these long years that you are flesh of my flesh and blood of my blood. You are my 'Angad', part of my *ang*, my body." Lehna caught Baba Budha's eye and Baba Budha smiled. "Because you are my Angad," Guru Nanak continued, "you must continue the work that I have begun. Come Bhai Budha, come forward and apply saffron paste to Angad's forehead." Then he put five copper coins and a coconut at Lehna's feet and bowed to him. Lehna was ordained as the second Guru of the Sikhs—Guru Angad Dev. The Guru had appointed his successor during his lifetime to make sure that there would be no opposition later. To avoid any trouble between Guru Angad and his son, Guru Nanak decided that Guru Angad should go back to Khadur. Without his physical presence the opposition to Guru Angad would slowly melt away and there would be no conflict with Sri Chand. As always, Guru Angad bowed to his Master's wishes and returned to Khadur.

By choosing Angad as his successor, Nanak made two points clear to his community. The succession would not pass automatically to the Guru's son: kinship would never play any part in the choice of a successor. The successor would be one who was closest in spirit to the Guru and who had, in his own life, practised all the Guru's teachings. By not choosing Sri Chand as his successor Nanak made it clear that the Sikhs would never be led by an ascetic. The Guru was the role model for all Sikhs and if an ascetic became the Guru, all Sikhs would aspire to be ascetics too. Nanak had preached that one should aspire to spiritual salvation while living the life of a householder and to ensure that all Sikhs believed and practised this, it was imperative that their Guru too be a householder.

In later years, Sri Chand founded the Udasi sect which is still popular in Northern India and has many *deras*. Lakhmi Das set up a *gadi* at Dera Baba Nanak which was handed over to his direct descendants. The current scion of the family is Baba Sarabjot Singh Bedi, who lives in Una in Himachal Pradesh.

The months rolled by and though Nanak missed Angad sorely he was happy that he was doing well in Khadur. He preached all that he had learnt from Nanak. When people heard him they said that they heard Nanak's voice and it was as if the spirit of Nanak was now in Angad. More and more disciples flocked to Khadur and it became another important centre of the Sikh religion with a prayer hall, a *langar* and a *dharamshala*. Angad worked zealously to spread his Guru's message but his heart ached with the longing to be with his Master again. Sometimes the desire to abandon everything and rush to Kartarpur would come upon him, but he knew that Nanak wished him to pursue the work that he had started without a break in its continuity.

One day he got word that the Master wished to see him. His heart leapt with joy. He paused just long enough to give a few instructions to ensure the efficient running of the *dera* in his absence and then hurried to Kartarpur. As he entered the city he realised that there was something drastically wrong. He met Baba Budha outside Nanak's house. "Tell me, Baba Budha, what is wrong?"

Baba Budha bowed and said in a grave, quiet voice, "It is the Master. The end is near."

When Angad entered the house he saw Nanak sitting on a cot in the courtyard, looking frail and weak. But he rose to his feet as Angad entered the courtyard and bowed to the second guru. "It is good of you to come, Guru Angad, for my end is near. You must take charge of my legacy to the world and help me prepare for the end."

He handed Angad the manuscripts of all his writings and then, accompanied by Guru Angad, Sulakhni, Sri Chand, Lakhmi Das, Baba Budha, and Moola Keer, and followed by thousands of his disciples, made his way to the bank of the Ravi. Here he chose an old acacia tree and sat patiently under it, waiting for the end. Angad and the other disciples waited with him. Word of the approaching end spread quickly and his disciples hurried to the site for one last darshan of their Guru.

The hours passed slowly by and evening descended upon the world. Some followers had provided earthen oil lamps and they were now lit and placed before the Master. The light from these lamps illuminated the Guru's face so that he could be seen from afar. Night descended upon the gathering and a cold wind began to blow. "I am tired," Nanak said, softly. "I must rest. Sing the *Kirtan Sohila* for me and so lull me to sleep." He lay down and a few of his disciples began to sing the hymn they had so often sung with Nanak in the evenings, and as they sang, the despair and sadness left them, and their voices rang out loud and clear. The hymn was taken up by people sitting further and further away from the Guru until a thousand voices sang together and ascended to heaven in prayer for their beloved Guru. Listening to this powerful rendition of his immortal composition, Nanak drifted off into eternal sleep. It was September 22, 1539.

TEACHINGS

I t is commonly believed that in an age when a Ravana is born, a
Rama is sure to take birth. It is said that without the extreme
poverty in which millions in Calcutta live, there would be no
Mother Teresa. In other words, it is only when the world is in dire need
of solace and succour that a saviour is born; it is only when society is
riddled with corruption and distortion that a reformer arises. Nanak was
born in a period of political and social turmoil, brought about by a
combination of ignorance, corruption, and oppressive rule.

The common man had been subjected to myriad forms of
oppression. The religious conflict and hostility between the conqueror
and the local population had led to intense suffering. The rulers sought
to convert all Hindus to Islam either by brute force or by the imposition
of heavy taxes. The rigid caste system had already led to the exploitation
of the lower caste Hindus.

Corruption had made in-roads into every segment of society.
Those in power were busy amassing wealth with impunity while others
sought to make their lives more comfortable in any manner they could.
The practise of religion too had been corrupted and had lost its true
significance. The mushrooming of various sects in Hinduism had
strengthened the concept of the reality of God, resulting in a divide
between the followers of different sects. Islam, which preached the
oneness of God and the equality of man, had been transformed in its
practice in India. The sheikhs and sayyads gained importance as
intermediaries between man and God. As a result, they were
considered superior to other muslims and the caste system spread its
tentacles within Islam too. *Pirs* and *shaheeds*, saints and martyrs, were
worshipped and their shrines or *dargahs* became places of pilgrimage.
People credited them with miraculous powers, praying at their *dargahs*
and seeking favours. Superstition had crept into the practice of Islam
in India.

Riddled with ignorance, people had lost sight of the eternal truth and religion was reduced to the practice of empty rituals. Weary of the superficiality of life, some fell back upon the Vedas and the Qur'an for comfort, hoping to hear the voice of God in their words. Others sought escape by renouncing the world, believing that asceticism was the only path to salvation.

Even as a young boy, Nanak was extremely sensitive to the world around him. This sentiment led him to ponder on the ills that beset society and the world at large, and to seek a possible cure. Through the long years of introspection, and interaction with people subscribing to a wide spectrum of religious and spiritual beliefs, he was motivated to discover a path to salvation that ordinary men could follow. Such a path would help man break the shackles of ignorance that bound him, even as he continued living in the material world.

One quality that marked Nanak out from other spiritual seekers was his ability to fearlessly criticise the evils that he found around him and to denounce those, in both the temporal and the spiritual realms, who perpetuated these evils. The nature of his criticism was unique—it was usually laced with humour though it could, on occasion, be biting.

Nanak's philosophy, based on equality, appealed to the world at large. The spiritual path that he prescribed could be followed by all men, irrespective of the faith or caste they belonged to. His first words on attaining enlightenment "there is no Hindu, there is no Mussalman" are the premise of his teachings.

All through his missionary journeys, he took care to ensure that he would not be identified with any one religion. Bhai Gurdas, writing in the early seventeenth century says: "The qazis and the mullahs gathered and began questioning him on religious matters ... Opening their books, they asked which the greater religion is—the Hindu or the Muslim?" Baba (Nanak) answered the pilgrims:

"Without good deeds both lead only to suffering,
Neither Hindu nor Muslim finds refuge in (God's Court)."
(Var 1:33, Trans. McLeod, W. H., Exploring Sikhism, p. 43)

Nanak was a zealous missionary but he remained gentle and tolerant, highlighting the kindness and compassion that forms the basis of all religions. His path was a unique combination of belief, thought, and action. He reinforced what he taught in myriad ways. His life embodied his teachings; his followers were drawn from diverse faiths, castes, and nationalities; he was open to debate, discussing philosophies at length with wise and learned men; and he composed and sang the beautiful hymns which form his *bani*, the basis for all Sikh spiritual and religious practices.

Nanak's *bani is* made up of long philosophical poems which he composed from time to time during his life. These poems owed their inspiration to a whole range of thoughts and emotions. They express his delight at the elements so skilfully painted by the Creator on His vast canvas of Creation as well as his anguish at the plight of the people who had been oppressed for centuries.

Because he preached to the common man, it was appropriate that the hymns be in the language that he understood. Sanskrit and Arabic, the languages of the holy books, had long since passed out of common usage. Pandits and mullahs alone understood these languages and had become the custodians and interpreters of religion. They alone presided over the important rituals performed at birth, marriage, and death. As a result they wielded undue power over the people and exploited their ignorance. Through his simple language Nanak broke the hold of the mullahs and the pandits. But he was not rigid and did not hesitate to use Persian, Arabic, or Sanskrit. His *bani* incorporated the terminology of the Upanishads, the Sufis, and the *siddhas*. This amalgam enriched the Punjabi that he used without in any way removing it from the ken of his followers.

Nanak's *bani* induced a spirit of self-respect, dignity of labour, brotherhood of man and belief in one Supreme Lord. There are 974 hymns composed in nineteen *ragas* by Nanak which are included in the *Guru Granth Sahib*. Among the more popular are the *Japji, Asa Di Var, Siddhagosht, Sodar (Rehras), Babar Vani* and *Alahniyan*.

JAPJI

It is said that Nanak composed the *Japji Sahib* at the time of revelation in Sultanpur. The hymn consists of thirty-eight stanzas of varying length, and addresses not only deep spiritual issues like human salvation but also emphasises the theology, ethics, philosophy, and practice of the Sikh religion. Unlike most of the other compositions in the holy Granth, the *Japji Sahib* was not set to music, and was perhaps not meant to be sung but to serve as the basis for serious meditation and reflection. The *Japji*, by tradition, has became a morning prayer and all true Sikhs recite the poem in the early hours when the mind is ready to absorb contemplative thought. Recitation of the *Japji* forms the basis for enlightened action during the remainder of the day.

> There is One God.
> He is the supreme truth.
> He, the creator,
> is without fear and without hate.
> He, the Omnipresent,
> pervades the Universe
> He is not born,
> nor does He die to be born again.
> By His grace shalt thou worship Him.
>
> Before time itself
> There was truth.
> When time began to run its course
> He was the truth.
> Even now, He is the truth
> And evermore shall truth prevail.
> (Trans. Singh, Khushwant, *Japjee–Sikh Morning Prayer*, p. 47)

~

> As hands or feet besmirched with slime,
> Water washes white;
> As garments dark with grime,
> Rinsed with soap are made light;
> So when sin soils the soul
> The Name alone shall make it whole.
>
> Words do not the saint or sinner make.
> Action alone is written in the book of fate.
> What we sow that alone we take;
> O Nanak, be saved or forever transmigrate.
> (Trans. Singh, Khushwant, *A History of the Sikhs*, vol. I p. 44)

~

> Those who are sold to lust for wealth,
> Talking to them or listening

Is like blowing of the wind.
They who meditate on the Lord God
They alone earn His grace and falsehood rescind.
   (Trans. Duggal, K.S., *Sri Guru Granth Sahib*, vol. I p. 51)

        ∾

Reflection, even a millionfold
Will not reveal Him
Silence, deep in His love
Will not bring peace
The hungry do not lose their hunger for Him
With all the world's valuables
Not one of man's thousand wisdoms
Will serve him in the Lord's court.
How then can one be true?
How to tear the screen of untruth?
O Nanak, by obeying His pre-ordained will.
   (Trans. Sarna, Navtej, *The Book of Nanak*, pp. 133–134)

SIDDHAGOSHT

Nanak had lengthy discussions with the *siddhas* on at least two occasions—at the sacred Mount Kailash and at the Shivaratri fair in Achal. The *Siddhagosht*, which takes the form of a dialogue, is a summation of those discussions. Two yogis participating in this dialogue—Charpat and Loharipa—were the leaders of two important sects of *yogis*. Charpat believed that it was possible to prepare an elixir from mercury which would enhance life and ensure longevity. Loharipa had a great impact on people and converted many people to the path of the *yogis*.

They raise two sets of questions. The first is of a personal nature regarding Nanak's origins and his appearance. Nanak answers these in a cursory manner. The second set of questions is philosophical in nature and concerns the origin of the universe, the nature and role of the Guru, etc. Nanak answers in detail and enlightens the *yogis*. At first, the *siddhas* address Nanak as "balabh" or boy but at the end of the dialogue they refer to him as "Anadha Nanak", "Swami", and "Purakha" as a mark of their respect for him.

The *Siddhagosht* is composed in the *raga* Ramkali and consists of seventy-three verses of six lines each. Nanak's replies are steeped in humility and show his great respect for all spiritual practices. He does not condemn the practice of yoga as a path towards spiritual enlightenment. Without any antagonism or hostility, he attempts to strip it of ritualism and superstition. As against the Hatha Yoga practised by the *siddhas*, Nanak recommends the simpler practice of Sahaj Yoga. The use of an entire range of yogic terminology and vocabulary reveals the extent of Nanak's study and understanding of yogic practices. The *Siddhagosht* is regarded as one of Nanak's most profound and philosophical compositions and is noted for the richness of the symbolism that it employs.

> The Lotus in the water is not wet
> Nor the water-fowl in the stream.
> If a man would live, but by the world untouched
> Meditate and repeat the name of the Lord Supreme.
> (Trans. Singh, Khushwant, *A History of the Sikhs* vol. I, p. 42)

~

> Where does He dwell,
> He who cruises across the turbulent ocean?
> The out breath is said to travel ten fingers,
> How does it spell?
> How does one who speaks and sports, steady one's mind?
> How does man see the Unseen kind?
> Says Nanak:
> Listen O Yogi, Nanak tells nothing but the truth.
> You must discipline your mind.
> The devotee must meditate on the Word Divine.
> It is His grace which brings about the union.
> He understands, he also sees.
> Good deeds help one merge into Divination.
> (Trans. Duggal K.S., *Sri Guru Granth Sahib*, vol. III p. 2133)

~

> "By the Master's teachings
> Is the ocean of existence crossed,
> And the teacher realises the
> The Lord in all spots to abide."
>
> (Trans. Singh, Kirpal & Singh, Kartar,
> *History of the Sikhs and Their Religion*, vol. I p. 76)

~

Say the Yogis:
What is the origin of life?
What faith predominates the time?
Who is thy Guru, whose disciple are you?
Uttering whose discourse do you remain unique?
Listen to what we say, O Nanak child.
Tell us of this discourse. How does the Lord ferry man across
    the terrible ocean?

Says Nanak:
The breath is the beginning; the True Lord hold's sway
The Lord my Guru, I his disciple love his meditation
The discourse of the Ineffable One makes me unique
O Nanak, the Cherisher of the world through the ages is my
    Guru.
Unique is the Lord and meditating on His discourse
His follower crosses the terrible ocean
And quenches the fire of his ego.
      (Trans. Sarna, Navtej, *The Book of Nanak*, pp. 144–145)

ASA DI VAR

This is another long composition by Nanak which is recited, like the *Japji*, in the morning. The form used is that of the *var*, which is a popular folk form of a heroic ballad. The *var* consists of twenty-four *pauris* or verses and fifty-nine *sloks* or couplets. Forty-four of the *sloks* were composed by Nanak while fifteen were composed by his successor Guru Angad Dev. The *sloks* precede, and serve as an introduction to, the *pauris*. This *var*, as all other compositions by Nanak, has invocations in praise of God. But its main theme is the social order of the day. He does not agree with the view that the world is illusory (*mithya*) and salvation lies only in renouncing it. He agrees that the world is transitory but insists that it is not unreal; it is the creation of the Lord. He believes that salvation can be achieved by using man's transitional period in this world for self-improvement and public good. The poem inspires man to cast off the shackles of ritualism, caste, and gender bias, which have rent the fabric of society.

When one's acts are righteous
Learning and knowledge follow.
When the five senses are mastered
Life becomes a pilgrimage.
When the heart is in tune
Then tinkle the dancer's ankle-bells.
What can Yama do
When I am in unison with You?
He who abandons desires.
He is the real sanyasi.
He who has mastered passions
Has become a true yogi.
He who has compassion
Is the true monk,
For he has killed his self without killing himself.
O Nanak, he who knows God's sportive ways
Knows God is One but has many disguises.
(Trans. Singh, Khuswant, *A History of the Sikhs*, vol. I pp. 348–349)

∼

Cymbals and bells of stray thinking play in the mind,
And the drums of worldly love are beaten and chime.
In the manner of the Kaliyuga Narad does dance
Where does the disciplined and virtuous have chance?
Nanak is sacrifice unto the Name of the Lord
The world is purblind,
the Master is the only enlightened Bard.
(Trans. Duggal K.S., *Sri Guru Granth Sahib*, vol. II p. 805)

The simal tree stands tall and straight
But if one comes to it with hope of gain
What will he get and whither turn?
Its fruit is tasteless
Its flowers have no fragrance
Its leaves are of no use.
O Nanak, it is the lowly that have goodness and true worth.
He that bows before all, before him all will bow,
It is the heavier in the balance that does lower go.
The wicked man bends double as does

143

The slayer of deer when shooting his dart.
What use is bending or bowing of head
When you bow not the heart?
(Trans. Singh, Khushwant, *A History of the Sikhs*, vol. I p. 349)

∽

Were you to knock at the door,
In His mansion the Master will listen.
He may receive, He may reject,
Either of these is exaltation.
Mark the light divine within, not the caste.
The caste hereafter has no consideration.
(Trans. Duggal K.S., *Sri Guru Granth Sahib*, p. 804)

∽

Within a woman conceived,
Of a woman born,
With a woman betrothed and married.
With a woman are sustained friendships
Through a woman, life goes on,
When a wife dies, one seeks another,
With woman man is bound,
Why call her bad then,
Who gives birth to Kings
From a woman is woman born,
Without her there is none.
Nanak, only the true Lord
Is beyond a woman.
(Trans. Sarna, Navtej, *The Book of Nanak*, p. 41)

ONKAR

Onkar is a summary of the discourses Nanak had with learned pandits and Brahmins. In this hymn comprising fifty-four stanzas Nanak defines the truly learned scholar. He is as humble as he is knowledgeable. He does not merely indulge in learned discussion but uses his knowledge to bring about moral regeneration in society. Nanak uses the words "panda" or "pandit" as a generic term for all members of the learned class.

From the Supreme Being, Sole and Unique got Brahma his
    existence.
Who in mind bore the Supreme Being, Sole and Unique.
From the Supreme Being, Sole and Unique, took birth
    mountains and yugas."

        (Trans. Singh, Kirpal, & Singh, Kharak,
      History of The Sikhs & Their Religion, vol. I p. 61)

       ~

All hesitation stands dispelled
The soul walks free of the veil of doubts
Irrelevant worldly reservation cease
And all doubts fade away.
Pure love is overwhelming
The mind is imbued with contentment
Merged in the Lord's love
The God oriented is liberated of all scepticism.
(Translation: Singh, Gajindar, *Guru Granth Sahib*, verse 12, p. 931)

BABAR VANI

This poem comprises four hymns, of which three are set to the *raga* Asa
and the fourth to the *raga* Tilang. The poem describes the suffering and
pain caused by Babar's invasion. The description is an eyewitness
account of the invasion and its effects, as observed by Nanak. It does not
remain a mere description of events but takes on a special hue as the
poet was not only an observer but also a sage. The poems are
outstanding in their spiritual and literary beauty.

He (Babar) has charged from Kabul
With the wedding party of sin
And demands gifts by force, O Lalo.

Modesty and righteousness
Are in hiding
Falsehood is in command, O Lalo.

The Qazis and Brahmins
Have had their day,
Satan reads the marriage vows, O Lalo.

Muslim women read the Quran
In suffering
Call on God, O Lalo.

O Nanak, paeans of blood are sung
And anointment is not by saffron
But blood, O Lalo.

Nanak sings the virtues of the Lord
In this city of corpses
And utters this truth:

The One who created men
And gave them joys
Behold them in His solitude.
He is True,
True His verdict
And true His justice
          (Trans. Sarna, Navtej, *The Book of Nanak*, pp. 147–148)

∼

They with the beautiful tresses
Sacred vermilion in their partings,
Their heads are now shorn with scissors
And dust chokes their throats
They who lived in palaces
No longer can even sit outside
Praise to thee O Lord, praise,
O Primal Lord, none knows your limits,
Endlessly, You behold Yourself in diverse forms.

When they were married,
Their bridegrooms handsome beside them,
They came seated in palanquins,
And adorned in ornaments of ivory,
Welcoming waters greeted them
And glittering fans comforted them from close,
Riches were gifted as they sat
And riches when they stood,

146

They ate coconuts and dates
And took pleasure on comfortable beds;
Ropes now are around their necks
Their pearl strings are broken.
The wealth and youthful beauty
That gave them joy, are now their enemy;
The soldiers have been ordered, and
Dishonouring them, they take them away.

(Trans. Sarna, Navtej, The Book of Nanak, pp. 148–149)

REHRAS (SODAR)

Bhai Gurdas records that the *Rehras*, or the evening prayer, which Sikhs recite around sunset, has been recited since Guru Nanak's time. "The like-minded met and together they chanted the *Sodar* every evening" (Trans. Anand, Reema & Singh, Khushwant, *Rehras Evensong*).

The *Rehras* also includes the compositions of Guru Amar Das, Guru Ram Das, Guru Arjun Dev and Guru Gobind Singh. It is a group of hymns in praise of the Almighty that lists the various attributes of God. It includes four short hymns by Nanak beginning with the *Sodar*, literally "the gateway to God". The Guru seeks to always remember God and praises the Almighty for his bounty to mankind. The path to salvation lies in meditating on *naam*, the name of God. In the *Sodar*, as the poet sings the praises of the Lord, all manner of celestial and mortal beings join in the praise, till the very elements are moved to participate too and sing God's praises. This hymn comprises nine stanzas of varying length and has been composed in the *raga* Asa.

As a beggar goes a-begging,
Bowl in one hand, staff in the other,
Rings in his ears, in ashes smothered,
So go thou forth in life.
With ear-rings made of contentment,
With modesty thy begging bowl,
Meditation the fabric of thy garment,
Knowledge of death thy cowl,
Let thy mind be chaste, virginal clean,
Faith the staff on which to lean.
Thou shalt then thy fancy humiliate,

With mind subdued, the world subjugate.
Hail! And to Thee be salutation.
Thou art primal, Thou art pure,
Without beginning, without termination,
In single form, forever endure.
(Trans. Singh, Khushwant, *A History of the Sikhs*, vol. I p. 337)

~

A whirlpool of boiling water is our abode
Our feet are clogged with the love of worldly things
We see people sink into those quicksands.

O my stupid heart yet know you not
If you forget the one God
All that is good in you will rot.

I am neither saintly, truthful nor erudite
I was born a fool and foolish I remain
Nanak pleads with you in earnest
Grant me refuge among those who you never forget.
(Trans. Anand, Reema, & Singh, Khushwant,
Rehras Evensong, the Sikh Evening Prayer, p. 53)

~

Were I given a hundred thousand tongues instead of one
And the hundred thousand multiplied twenty-fold,
A hundred thousand times would I say, and say again,
The Lord of all the worlds is One.
That is the path that leads
These the steps that mount,
Ascend thus to the Lord's mansion
And with Him be joined in unison.
The sound of the songs of Heaven thrills
The like of us who crawl, but desire to fly.
O Nanak, His grace alone it is that fulfils,
The rest mere prattle, and a lie.
(Trans. Singh, Khushwant, *A History of the Sikhs*, vol. I p. 338)

Nanak's *bani* sums up his perception of God, existence, and man's place and role in this world. Central to his teaching is his concept of God, about whose existence he harbours no doubts. He advocates strongly and clearly that there is one and only one God. The first word of the *Mool Mantra* of the *Japji Sahib*, and consequently of the *Guru Granth Sahib*, is the numerical one (1), which is used as a symbol to emphasise the unity of God, or as Nanak calls Him, the Supreme Reality. God is one and is indivisible and it is the same God that people all over the world worship. This concept is extremely important because the world has been broken up by followers of different religions who worship their own version of God and believe that their God is superior to any other. If people could understand this teaching, much of the hostility between practitioners of different religions would cease and violence in the name of religion would lessen.

Nanak preaches that God is formless, omnipotent, and omnipresent. Two important corollaries arise from this concept. If God is formless and omnipresent He resides in every aspect of creation; He even resides in man. We merely have to look within to realise His presence. We do not need to look for Him in temples, mosques and places of pilgrimage. Nanak preaches against all forms of idol worship because a formless and omnipresent God cannot be represented either in painting or in sculpture. The Supreme Reality is a force that can be realised but never seen. We can realise the *sargun* of the Lord by the reflection of His divine light in His creation. Nanak rejects the belief in the incarnation of the divine, as the Supreme Reality is omnipotent and has no need to assume human form to punish evil.

Nanak preaches that life is real and not *maya* or illusion as the ascetics would have us believe. In this concept, Nanak shows a spirit of affirmation which is the essence of all his teachings. He supports institutions like marriage and family, and encourages man to become a positive and productive member of society. He exhorts us to remember that the Supreme Reality that created this universe will not neglect His creation.

Nanak teaches that man can achieve salvation in this lifetime if his life is based on the principles of *sach* (truth), *dharam* (righteousness), *saram* (effort), *jnana* (knowledge) and *karm* (grace). In Nanak's teaching, *sat* is literally the Truth and is the first and most appropriate attribute of the One Absolute. "This denoted the ever-existent consciousness, the ultimate reality, the immutable nature of the omnipotent God" (Singh, Kirpal, *History of the Sikhs and Their Religion* p. 66).

Nanak elaborates on some prominent aspects of Truth. First of all, Truth opens the inner eye of higher consciousness which makes one feel the direct touch of the Supreme Truth as God. Secondly, when a man realises the Truth he goes beyond transmigration. The *atma* merges with the Supreme Reality and the cycle of birth and death comes to an end.

In the *Japji Sahib* Nanak explains that one who attains Truth is a *sachiar*. One of the pre-conditions of knowing the Truth is purging the heart of falsehood. *Dharam* is the path that man must follow to attain the state of *sachiar*. Nanak believes that one can attain salvation by performing noble deeds and mastering the five senses to overcome the misery caused by *kam* (lust), *krodh* (anger), *ahankar* (pride), *haumain* (ego), and *moh* (greed).

Saram is the effort to cultivate virtue, directed towards getting rid of passions, emotions, the sense of possession, and the ego. Through this effort the personality of the individual becomes a blend of all that is beautiful in human nature. Such a person rises above individual concerns and works for the good of mankind.

Karm or a state of grace is achieved when an individual has followed *dharam* and attained the Truth. He has realised the force that pervades all creation. In this state the grace of the Almighty is showered upon him and he becomes a true *bhagat* and gains *jnana* (knowledge) and achieves *ananda* (eternal bliss).

Nanak emphasises the role of the Guru in the individual's efforts to achieve salvation and the Guru finds frequent mention not only in his *bani* but in the entire range of Sikh scripture. When the individual embarks upon the path of *dharam*, he needs a Guru to guide him. The Guru could be God Himself or a human preceptor. It is the Guru who shows the individual the right path to salvation, and encourages him when the path becomes difficult. It is through the Guru's guidance that the *saram* bears fruit and man is transformed into an awakened person.

Though Nanak preaches that the world is real he also points out that life is transitory. Man lives in this world for only a short time, much like a traveller resting at an inn. Like the traveller who develops no attachment to fellow travellers, man too should remain detached in his relationships. This understanding helps him to follow the path of right conduct without being critical or judgemental of others.

Just as Nanak dwells upon the unity of God, he emphasises the oneness of mankind. The selection of hymns in the *Guru Granth Sahib* reflects this basic Sikh belief, for along with the hymns of the Sikh

Gurus are included those of Sheikh Farid (a Muslim saint), Namdev (a tailor), Kabir (a weaver), and Ravidas (a cobbler). Even though Guru Nanak belonged to a high caste, his constant and most faithful companion was Mardana who was not only a Muslim, but belonged to the low caste of *marasis*. He preferred the hospitality of Bhai Lalo, a low-born carpenter, to that of Malik Bhago, a rich and powerful official. Guru Nanak denounced all teachings which could not inspire respect and concern for other human beings.

Two of the most important institutions of the Sikh faith that Nanak established worked towards breaking down the walls that had divided men over the centuries. These were the institutions of *sangat* and *langar*. The *sangat* was the congregation of his followers where everybody came together on a common platform to meditate on the name of God. The *langar* was a community meal where all his followers ate together. He went a step further than other reformers and religious leaders of the time by regarding women as equal to men. He insisted that women be given the same status as men in society.

Nanak sought to re-interpret the conventional religious practices of the time. Both Hinduism and Islam had become religions of external authority and emphasis was laid more on rituals and ceremonies than on self-realisation. He laid emphasis firmly and exclusively on inner devotion.

> "Make mercy your mosque, faith your prayer mat
> and righteousness your Qur'an.
> Make humility your circumcision, uprightness your fasting and
> so you will be a true Muslim
> Make good work your Ka'aba
> Truth your pir and compassion your
> Creed and your prayer
> Make the performance of what pleases (God)
> Your books and,
> Nanak, he will uphold your favour"
>
> (*Var Majh, shlok* 1, *pauri* 7, Trans. McLeod,
> W. H., *Exploring Sikhism*, p. 5)

Nanak stressed that virtue is gained from action and not from abstract piety and theology. According to him the individual should ideally base his life on three precepts: *kirat karna*–to labour honestly, *naam japna*—to always remember Him and *vand chhakna*—to share with others whatever one has. *Naam japna* is the central precept as it involves a love of the Almighty, and *kirat karna* and *vand chhakna* are natural corollaries as they are based on love for others. If we truly love God, love of our fellow men will naturally follow. When we place God and our fellowmen before ourselves, our actions are directed towards *sewa*, or the selfless service of humanity. Service, love and devotion, according to Nanak, are the three pillars of the true faith. One who follows these precepts becomes *gurumukh* or God-oriented.

Nanak stressed the absolute sovereignty of God. Without His grace no amount of ritual, prayer, or study of holy books is of any avail. From his own early experience Nanak draws the following conclusion:

> "Several scriptures and books had he read
> But one (God) he had not found;
> Several Koran and Pooran had he read,
> But faith he could not put in any."
> (Trans. Cunningham, J. D., *The History of the Sikhs*, p. 39)

There are several passages in the *Guru Granth Sahib*, in the same tone. Man may read the Vedas and the Qur'an and attain temporary bliss, but without God salvation is unattainable. An expression of God's grace takes the form of *hukam* or the inner voice which spurs us along the path of righteousness. This inner voice is an expression of the Divine Will. Every true follower is exhorted by Nanak to happily accept the *hukam*. "Whosoever is obedient to the Lord's Will, accesses His treasures; the spurious do not find a place there and are cast among the defiled ones" (*Guru Granth Sahib, Raga Asa*, p. 421, Trans. Singh, Kirpal, *History of the Sikhs and Their Religion* p. 78). Whosoever learns to recognize *hukam*, according to Nanak, becomes a master in the art of living. He is able to suppress his ego and become a true *yogi*. Truth and truthful living are the greatest ideals of life and they can be achieved only by accepting *hukam*.

Nanak's teachings did not dwell only on spiritual and metaphysical issues. Tolerance and service are two important pillars of the faith he propounded. His concept of service was broader than the meaning commonly ascribed to it. *Sewa* involved the performance of altruistic moral deeds, including fighting for justice and human rights. "All created beings are Thine own, without service is no one's life fruitful"

(*Guru Granth Sahib, Raga Asa*, p. 354, Trans. Singh, Kirpal & Singh, Kharak, *History of the Sikhs and Their Religion*).

The ethical slant of Nanak's teachings was very strongly and clearly marked. According to him a *gurumukh* knows that though realisation of Truth is a high achievement, truthful living is an even higher achievement. He always works according to the *hukam*, observing the moral code laid down by the Guru. His life is characterised by contentment, truthful conduct, righteous effort, fearlessness, compassion, humility, and detachment.

By developing the concept of the Supreme Reality, Nanak also ensured that no divinity would ever attach to his person. He prevented his followers from being reduced to a sect that made Guru-worship their creed. He emphasised repeatedly that he was not gifted with any supernatural or miraculous powers. He claimed no divinity. He considered himself a teacher who, through his teachings, could lead people to the path of spiritual awakening. "Fight with no weapons save the word of God, a teacher hath no means save the purity of his doctrine."

Nanak's achievements as a teacher are best summed up by Bhai Gurdas when he describes the effect that his words have had upon the world:

> "The true Guru, Nanak, was then born
> The fog and mist evaporated
> And light shone on the earth.
> As the rising sun dispels the dark
> And outshines the stars
> As flee the herd of deer
> When the lion roars
> Without pause, without turning back for assurance
> So fled evil from the world.

(Trans. Singh, Khushwant, *A History of the Sikhs*, vol I. pp. 38–39)

THE JANAMSAKHIS

The janamsakhis were the first attempt to compile comprehensive biographies of Guru Nanak. An earlier attempt had been made by Bhai Gurdas, the nephew of the third Guru, Guru Amar Das, to record some biographical details of Nanak's life. It takes the form of a long poem with references and allusions to Nanak's times and teachings, giving us a brief sketch of his life. These references have the advantage of being more or less authenticated references.

The janamsakhis, interesting and fascinating as they are, do not carry the stamp of any such authenticity. They were written more than a hundred years after Nanak's death and were drawn, without exception, from oral tradition and were embellished by each generation. There are four janamsakhis that are extant and the authors, with the exception of Mehrban, remain unknown.

The most popular of the janamasakhis is the *Bhai Bala Janamsakhi*. For centuries it was believed that this set of janamsakhis had been authored by Bala and had been composed in the presence of the second Guru, Guru Angad Dev. In this janamsakhi, Bala claims to have accompanied Guru Nanak on all his travels and it was presented as an eyewitness account of a major part of the Guru's life. Recent research by scholars has shown that Bala did not accompany Nanak on his travels and as a result the veracity of these janamsakhis has become suspect. Even more, it has now been established that these janamsakhis are full of interpolations of dissenters who did not succeed in their claim to the guru-ship. The language used is colloquial and dates later than the language of the *Puratan Janamsakhi* and the *Mehrban Janamsakhi*. This janamsakhi was probably written in the second half of the seventeenth century.

The oldest of all the janamsakhis is the *Puratan Janamsakhi*. The first known manuscript of this janamsakhi was brought to England in 1815 by Henry Thomas Colebrooke and hence it was first called the *Vilayat Wali Janamsakhi*. This manuscript was preserved in the old

India Office Library. By the time the contents of the manuscript had been unravelled, a part of it had been destroyed by termites. A similar manuscript was discovered in Hafizabad and came to be known as the *Hafizabadi Janamsakhi*. The two manuscripts were collated and published by Bhai Vir Singh in 1976. The language of this janamsakhi is precise and similar to that of Nanak's hymns in the *Adi Granth*. This janamsakhi does not mention Bala.

A third janamsakhi was discovered in 1940. This is called the *Mehrban Janamsakhi* because the authorship is generally ascribed to Mehrban, the grandson of the fourth Guru, Guru Ram Das. Initially this janamsakhi was not taken very seriously because Mehrban's father, Prithi Chand, had not accepted Guru Arjun's succession to Guru Ram Das. But modern research has established the author of this janamsakhi as a man of great learning and knowledge, whose prose style is much appreciated. This janamsakhi contains the earliest explanation and commentary on the hymns of Guru Nanak. The *Mehrban Janamsakhi* also does not mention Bhai Bala. Unfortunately, research has shown that this set of janamsakhis also contains additions and modifications introduced by the Miras, another sect of dissenters.

The fourth janamsakhi is ascribed to Bhai Mani Singh, a highly respected follower of the last Guru, Guru Gobind Singh. It is said that scholars in Guru Gobind Singh's ministry, aware of the many unwelcome accretions to the other janamsakhis, asked Bhai Mani Singh to retell the story of Guru Nanak's life. In deference to the scholarship and literary merit of Bhai Gurdas, he at first demurred, stating that no better account of Guru Nanak's life could be written. The scholars then requested him to elaborate on the rather sketchy material in Bhai Gurdas' *var* and use this material as a basis for a full-fledged biography of Nanak. This janamsakhi does make mention of Bhai Bala but he is not central to the narrative. Modern scholars have cast grave doubt on the authorship of these janamsakhis and it is claimed that the story about Bhai Mani Singh was deliberately bruited about to give these janamsakhis a stamp of legitimacy and to make them more widely accepted than the others.

The janamsakhis must not be treated as historical records because they were not written by historians but by disciples of the Guru who wished to ensure that his legacy would be transmitted to future generations of Sikhs. After his travels in Arabia Nanak had assumed legendary status in the Punjabi mind and the origin of the janamsakhis lies in the myths that grew around him during his lifetime. Myths arouse awe and wonder among listeners and the janamsakhis too display this characteristic in abundant measure. They recount innumerable miracles that the Guru supposedly performed and the manifestations of his supernatural powers. These stories were written for a largely illiterate audience and the surest way to catch their attention was through fabulous tales of miracle and magic. As Khushwant Singh says: "The styles of these janamsakhis (with the exception of the biography of Mani Singh) show clearly that they were written by semi-literate scribes for the benefit of an wholly illiterate people. They abound with stories of miracles performed by the Guru; they contradict each other on material points; and some were obviously touched up to advance the claims of one or the other branches of the Guru's family which had been overlooked in the succession to the guru-ship." (*A History of the Sikhs*, vol I p. 299)

The janamsakhis are episodic in nature and do not adhere to any chronological pattern. The only janamsakhi which seems to have any systematic basis and structure is the *Mehrban Janamsakhi*. The other janamsakhis are ambiguous with regard to the time and location of the event being narrated. There are, among the different janamsakhis, major differences on many points. In spite of these obvious defects and weaknesses, the janamsakhis remain of the utmost importance in any study of Nanak.

When we speak of Nanak and his life, there are really two Nanaks that we are referring to. There is the Nanak of Faith and the Nanak of History. What we find in the janamsakhis is the Nanak of Faith. The janamsakhis were written almost one hundred years after his death when his teachings had become firmly established and his followers had bonded together in a new faith. What we see in the janamsakhis is the image of the Guru through the eyes of his followers who had been following his teachings for three generations. They do not give us the Nanak of History but they illustrate his teachings and bring them home more pithily than any bald sermonizing would have done. "The magic of Guru Nanak's personality has been and continues to be, of incalculable importance to the Punjab. The janamsakhis help us to appreciate some of this magic" (McLeod, W.H., *Exploring Sikhism*, p. 42).

The Nanak janamsakhis were the staple of my childhood. I spent endless evenings at my grandmother's knee listening to these wonderful stories. As a result, the janamsakhis became an integral part of my childhood, and consequently, of me. They coloured my thoughts and actions and have remained with me through all the ups and downs that have been my lot. Fanciful as these stories are, they are the basis of my perception of Nanak and his teachings. The Nanak of the janamsakhis will, for me, always be more real than the Nanak of History.

I can think of no better way to end this work than to retell some of my favourite janamsakhis. My readers may quarrel with my choice and may wonder why their favourite stories have not been featured here. I would have liked to recount all of the janamsakhis, but since this is not possible, the only yardstick I could apply was my own preference.

～

Nanak and Mardana were on their first journey, travelling in the foothills of the Himalayas. The monsoon had set in and the terrain had become difficult and tiring to traverse. The rain lashed their bodies and gusty winds threatened to tear the clothes off their backs. Even when it stopped raining they had to walk through slush, their legs often sinking in and making each step painful and laborious. And yet they trudged on as best they could. When they finally came down to the Gangetic plain, Mardana begged Nanak to stop for a few days of rest.

They entered a town, not too small, and yet not large enough to be called a city. The people were industrious, cheerful, and god-fearing, and when Nanak resumed his practice of *satsang* and *kirtan* on clear evenings, a fairly large congregation of men and women turned out to attend. Soon, Nanak's reputation as a wise and learned man spread beyond the town and people from neighbouring villages also came to listen and to participate in the *kirtan*. Among them was a shopkeeper from a neighbouring town. At first he came out of sheer curiosity, but once he had listened to Nanak's mesmerizing words and sung some of his beautiful hymns, all doubts and anxieties left him. He felt a sense of bliss and deep abiding joy. He looked for every opportunity to serve the Guru and the *sangat* in any way he could.

His family was so intrigued by the change in him that they came to listen to the Guru and they too became his ardent disciples. Soon a routine was set. The shopkeeper would close his shop early, and accompanied by his family, join the *sangat* in the courtyard of the house where Nanak had camped.

The shopkeeper now wore a perpetual smile on his face, he was never angry, and he had lost the desire to profit by unscrupulous means. He constantly recited God's name and often broke into one of Nanak's hymns almost without volition. The change in him was so great that it could not escape the notice of all those he came into contact with.

The neighbouring shop was owned by a handsome young man who was happy, cheerful, and industrious in his own way. His attitude to life was totally different from that of the first shopkeeper. He was in business to make profit by any means and he had no compunction whatsoever in exploiting his customers to the hilt. With this ill-gotten money he gave himself up completely to earthly pleasures. His philosophy in life was simple: You only live once, and life has so many pleasures to offer that one should enjoy them to the fullest. In spite of the great difference in their attitude to life, the two shopkeepers shared a cordial relationship.

One morning, the first shopkeeper was singing one of Nanak's hymns as he opened his shop. The second shopkeeper, who had already set himself up for the day, came out to greet his neighbour and heard him singing.

"What is that beautiful melody you are singing?"

"It is a hymn composed by Baba Nanak."

"How boring," the second shopkeeper said, crinkling up his nose in disdain. "Hymns are for the old and those weary of the world. What business can young people have with matters pertaining to religion? There will be time enough for that later."

"There is time enough for that even now. If you would but come once to listen to my Guru, I promise you it will change your life entirely."

"I am quite happy with my life as it is and do not wish to change it. But I am intrigued by the phenomenal change in you in recent days. I would like to hear the teachings that have changed you so profoundly."

So it was decided that that evening he would accompany the first shopkeeper to the *sangat*. But he was not to attain a state of grace so easily. As they were walking home together through the crowded streets, the second shopkeeper caught the eye of a pretty young woman sitting on a first floor balcony. Immediately attracted, he stopped to smile at her. His companion saw the woman's answering smile and the silent signal that passed between the two. The second shopkeeper gave a short laugh, turned to him and slapped him on the back, saying, "A greater bliss awaits me on that balcony, my friend. Your Guru will have to wait."

"Adultery is a sin. By indulging in the pleasure of the moment do not condemn your soul to eternal damnation."

"Who cares what happens to my soul when I am dead? For me, the present is enough." The second shopkeeper smiled a sly, wicked smile. "Come, my friend," he said in an urgent whisper. "Come with me and taste of the forbidden pleasure just once and I assure you, you will forget your Guru and the bliss that his teaching brings you. Like me, you too will not give a thought to sin and damnation of the soul."

The first shopkeeper shook his head sadly. "You know not what you do. There can be no bliss greater than being a disciple of my Guru."

"To each his own," the second shopkeeper shrugged. "You go to your bliss and I will go to mine."

The next morning the first shopkeeper was singing his hymns with that same radiant smile on his face. The second shopkeeper realised that his colleague's state of bliss was permanent while his own had lasted only till the satiation of his physical desire. His curiosity was aroused again and he wanted to visit the Guru to find out what inspired this divine happiness.

"I am sorry about last evening, my friend," he called out gaily. "But I promise I will come with you today and listen to your Guru's words."

But that evening as they walked down the cobbled street, he again caught sight of the beautiful woman. Once again his pulse quickened and the blood rushed to his temples and his entire being flushed with the excitement of anticipated pleasure. Once again he forgot about the Guru. "I am sorry, my friend," he said, "I cannot come with you today," and he went up to his mistress.

This pattern was repeated each day, and every morning the second shopkeeper could not but reflect upon how ephemeral his own happiness had been compared to that of his friend.

The first shopkeeper gave up talking to his friend about the sin he was committing and the damnation of his soul. It was as the Guru had said; a state of grace would come to his colleague only when God willed it so. Until that time, nothing on earth would bring him to the Guru. Each went his own way—the first following the path of grace and moving closer to spiritual salvation, the second following the path of sin and moving closer to eternal damnation.

One day, the second shopkeeper was to go to a neighbouring village to participate in a family function. It was agreed that he would meet his companions under the huge banyan tree that grew on the periphery of the town and they would proceed to the village together. The shopkeeper was the first to arrive and while he waited for the others, he began to look

159

around for something to occupy him. He found a stick and began to idly dig the ground near his feet. He was amazed to find something glittering in the earth as it caught the light of the setting sun. Picking it up, he cleaned it with his sleeve and was delighted to see that it was a gold coin. He was filled with excitement. He was sure that he had stumbled upon buried treasure.

He hurried to the nearest house, borrowed a pickaxe, and began to dig up the ground. When his friends arrived, they too were excited and offered to help. They forgot about the function, totally absorbed in unearthing the hoard of hidden gold. At last they stumbled upon a big terracotta jar but when their friend put his hand in it, he found only dirt and ash. Great was his disappointment but with his devil-may-care attitude, he flipped the gold coin in the air and turned to his friends. "At least I am richer than I was when I first stood under the tree. After all, a gold coin is a gold coin!" They laughed at this in agreement. They returned the pickaxe and hurried on to the neighbouring village to take part in the festivities and make up for all they had missed.

The other shopkeeper had not been as fortunate as his colleague. While returning from the *satsang*, a thorn went deep into his foot and when he was finally able to extricate it, the foot bled rather severely and had to be bandaged. The pain persisted and next morning he limped to his shop. His colleague saw him approaching and asked him why he was limping. When the unfortunate man told him about his mishap the second shopkeeper burst out laughing. "You are the one who talked about reward and punishment. You, who go daily to visit your Guru, listen attentively to his preaching, and then live by what you have learned, should have been rewarded with gold but instead have been punished by much pain. I, who according to you, sin every evening in the arms of my mistress and should have been punished with eternal damnation, have been rewarded with a gold coin. Do you think your Guru could explain that?"

The first shopkeeper only smiled. "If you can make time to visit my Guru, I am sure he will be able to explain how this fits in with the pattern of God's working."

So that evening, the second shopkeeper came into the Guru's presence. He listened to the *kirtan* and when the *sangat* moved away to partake of the *langar*, his friend led him up to the Guru and introduced him.

"Master, this is my friend and neighbour. He has a question to ask of you."

The Guru listened to the question carefully, looking closely all the while at his disciple rather than at the speaker. Then he smiled and turned to the second shopkeeper. "You are right to think the way you do—the gold coin can be considered a reward, and the thorn, a punishment. But there is another way of looking at it. Maybe you were destined to find a big jar full of gold coins but because you have sinned so often the gold coins were turned to dirt and ash and you found only a single gold coin. Your friend was destined to be impaled upon a sharp stake, but because of the good deeds that he has performed, only his foot was pierced by a thorn. Man's life is determined by the actions he performs. If his actions are bad he will only get a fraction of the good that destiny had in store for him. And if his actions are good, the harm that was destined for him is reduced."

∽

They were on their first udasi. It had been a long and tiring day through difficult terrain. Mardana and Nanak had not been able to obtain any rest or food during the day. Now, late in the evening, weary and hungry, with blisters on their feet, they came to the outskirts of what appeared to be a prosperous village. Nanak stopped to rest under a spreading tree and Mardana, unable to bear the intense pangs of hunger, went to scout for food and a place for the night. He stopped at the first house. He could smell the delicious aroma of food being cooked as he peered into the home of an obviously well-to-do family. Mardana's mouth watered at the prospect of obtaining a rich and delicious meal. He knocked at the door and a handsome, middle-aged man emerged from the house and came into the courtyard. As he came closer, Mardana realised he was handsome only in the arrangement of the features of his face and in the rich dress he wore. But there was meanness in his eyes and an ugly scowl upon his face.

"Yes?" he asked harshly. "What is it you want?"

"I am a weary traveller. I seek some food and a place to rest for the night."

The householder raised his hand as if to strike Mardana. "Go away! This is not a *dharamshala*. I work myself to the bone to feed my children, not to give away food to wasters like you. Go before I strike you." And as Mardana turned away, the door was slammed and bolted loudly behind him. Mardana made concessions for the man's behaviour; perhaps he was not as prosperous as he seemed to be, perhaps he had some vexatious problem on his mind. But it did not matter. It was a big village and Mardana was sure that not everyone would be as inhospitable as the man he had encountered. He was proved wrong. He received the same unpleasant response from every person he approached.

As Mardana despondently made his way back to Nanak, he could not help feeling that this rudeness and hostility seemed to be a special hallmark of the village. Nanak was deep in prayer, and not wishing to disturb him, Mardana sat quietly by his Guru and began to pray too. As he prayed, all the anger and bitterness at the treatment that had been meted out to him drained out of his heart and was replaced by calm acceptance. When Nanak finished praying he saw that Mardana had come back empty-handed and knew that they would have to go to bed hungry that night.

Night drew on and Nanak and Mardana wrapped themselves in their robes, curled up under the tree, and fell into an exhausted sleep. They were up early and after washing at a nearby well they again sat down to pray before proceeding on their journey. While they prayed, a delegation of the villagers came out to meet them. They were all sullen and sombre and many of them were armed with *lathis* and axes. "What do you want here?" the leader of the group demanded of Nanak belligerently.

Mardana opened his mouth to speak but Nanak held up his hand to indicate that he must hold his peace. "Night fell while we were travelling this road and we stopped to rest. All we wanted was a little food to assuage our hunger and perhaps a place that would shelter us from the elements for the night."

The leader grunted and waved his *lathi* in Nanak's face. In a voice loaded with suspicion and hostility, he said, "Well, the night is over now and you can resume your journey. Get to your feet and move on. There is no place for you here."

"Was it too much to expect a little kindness from you?" Mardana asked, unable to suppress his hurt.

"Kindness!" the leader scoffed. "Our first kindness is to ourselves, and this kindness lies in chasing away charlatans and parasites like you as quickly as possible from our village. Be gone before we take the law into our own hands."

Nanak smiled at the man "We have no desire to tarry. Come Mardana, we must be on our way." He got to his feet and retrieved the bundle with his meagre belongings. Mardana did the same as the group of villagers watched, angry and hostile. As Nanak turned to walk away from the village he held up his hand in blessing. "May your village prosper! May you find so much happiness and prosperity in your village that you and your children never feel the need to go beyond it!"

The crowd was perplexed by Nanak. He had been treated with the utmost rudeness and hostility and yet he had found it in his heart to bless the village and its inhabitants. They looked to their headman for a reaction but he was so confused with Nanak's response that he was lost for words. Mardana too wondered why such scoundrels deserved any blessings but he held his peace and they walked away from the village.

A few weeks later the two travellers came to a village where they received a warm welcome. The people vied with each other to attend to them. Each villager contributed his best to ensure that the Guru and his companion were made as welcome and comfortable as possible. After Nanak and Mardana had bathed and partaken of light refreshments, the villagers sat around Nanak for *sangat*. On the following morning, when Nanak got ready to leave, they fell at his feet and begged him to stay on for a few days. The village was blessed by his presence, they said. In fact, so far did their hospitality extend that even Mardana was overwhelmed by it. When it was time to leave Nanak blessed the villagers: "May your dreams and ambitions not be limited by the confines of your village! May destiny take you far and wide and may you scatter in all directions in the realisation of prosperity!"

Mardana was perplexed by the strangeness of this blessing. Those who had been rude and hostile to them had been blessed with great prosperity in their village and the wish that they would forever remain in the village, while for those who had been kind and generous there was the wish that they move out of their village and scatter far and wide. Mardana did not give voice to his musings because Nanak often said and did things which seemed strange. He knew that he would discover the significance of these two paradoxical blessings in due course.

As they went further on their travels, Mardana found this pattern of blessings being repeated. At last, unable to bear his lack of understanding any longer, Mardana turned to Nanak and asked for an explanation. "It's simple and obvious. Those who are rude and ill-mannered should remain confined to their village so that they do not poison the rest of the world with their rudeness, while those who are kind and generous should scatter and spread far and wide so that they illumine the world with their kindness."

~

During the course of one of his udasis Nanak passed through Lahore. The *Amil* of Lahore at the time was a wealthy merchant by the name of Duni Chand who was a good man but who took an inordinate pride in his phenomenal wealth. When Nanak came to Lahore, it was *sharad*, the period when all devout Hindus pray for their ancestors. As part of these prayers they organise feasts for Brahmins and other holy men in the belief that by feeding them, they feed their ancestors. The richer the Hindu, the richer and more extravagant the feasting. Duni Chand, being wealthier than almost everyone else, organised the most lavish feast of all.

Duni Chand heard of Nanak's arrival in Lahore and rejoiced at this news. He knew of Nanak's piety and wisdom, and though he had never met him, harboured great respect and admiration for the Guru. He went straightaway to where Nanak and Mardana were camping and begged the Guru to honour his home by camping there. Nanak always shunned the home of the rich and powerful and preferred to stay with the poorest of the poor. But Duni Chand remained adamant in his pleas and Nanak knew it would be churlish to refuse his offer of hospitality. So, much against his will, he allowed himself to be escorted to Duni Chand's *haveli*. All around him Nanak saw signs of great wealth and luxury. He was intrigued by the seven red flags that had been strung across the front door of the *haveli*, fluttering attractively every time they caught the wind. They were like captive souls seeking release, seeking to fly away high into the open expanse of the sky, never to return. Nanak asked his host the significance of these flags, and Duni Chand explained that each of them represented one lakh rupees of his wealth and that it was his endeavour to add another red flag to the string every year or two. Nanak was exceedingly uncomfortable and ill-at-ease in these lavish surroundings but having accepted his invitation, could not humiliate his host by moving out of his house.

In the evening, when Nanak and Mardana sang the sacred hymns, Nanak was pleasurably surprised to see that Duni Chand not only listened to the *kirtan* but also joined in the chorus. In the days that followed Nanak never saw this attention waver for a second. Duni Chand put aside all his work and attended only to Nanak and Mardana. Nanak realised that in spite of his obvious pride in his wealth, Duni

Chand was a man who was essentially good at heart. On his last night in the *haveli*, Nanak sent for Duni Chand and addressed him in private. "Duni Chand, you have been an exceptional host and you have overwhelmed me with your hospitality and kindness. Very rarely have I known a powerful businessman and officer of the Mogul court to completely put aside his work for me. I have come to trust you completely and I have a special favour to ask of you. I have something that is of great value to me and which I dare not carry on my travels for fear of losing it." Nanak took out a needle and held it up for Duni Chand to see. "Will you take charge of this needle and look after it for me? Guard it with the greatest care and return it to me when we meet again in the other world."

Duni Chand was bemused by this strange request—how could a humble needle be so important to the Guru? Mysterious were the ways of holy men, sometime beyond the comprehension of ordinary mortals like him. But if this needle was so important to the Guru he would guard it with his life and return it when they met in the next world. Duni Chand took the proffered needle and promised to keep it safe.

When Duni Chand turned in for the night, his mind kept going back to the charge that the Guru had given him. His wife saw the bemused expression on his face as he held the needle and asked, "What is it my lord? You seem perplexed. What is it that worries you?"

Duni Chand's wife was a sensible woman and he often turned to her for advice. "I am confused about this needle. The Guru leaves tomorrow. He has given me this needle for safekeeping until we meet in the next birth. What is so special about this needle? Is he trying to say something to me that I do not understand?"

Duni Chand's wife smiled at him and taking the needle from his hand, put it aside. "Of course there is something special about the needle—it is the smallest object that the Guru could find. What he is trying to tell you is extremely simple. Will you actually be able to take the needle with you when you die?"

Duni Chand thought for a minute. "No," he answered.

"And your wealth? If you are not able to take this tiny little needle with you, will you be able to take all the wealth that you are so carefully accumulating?"

Duni Chand understood at last what the Guru was trying to teach him. The food that he had fed to Brahmins and holy men could not cross the barriers of death and reach his ancestors just as all the money he had accumulated would not go with him when he died. Only his good deeds would live on. Far better to use his money for the benefit of others and earn merit in his next birth.

Next morning, before the Guru left, Duni Chand thanked him for opening his eyes to the futility of hoarding wealth. He sought the Guru's blessings and opened up his treasure chests, using all his money for the welfare of the poor. In the years to come Duni Chand became an ardent and devoted disciple of Guru Nanak and when the *dera* and township of Kartarpur were established, Duni Chand, as we already know, contributed a great deal towards these endeavours.

~

Camped beside the Tigris one evening, Nanak was visited by an old woman. She threw herself at his feet and began to weep. Nanak drew her up and wiped the tears from her eyes. "Sit beside me, Mother, and tell me the cause of your grief."

"I have waited twelve long years for you," she sobbed. Nanak was puzzled and waited for her to continue. She pointed to a jetty where passengers boarded a ferry to cross to the other side. "Twelve years ago I stood there," she said in a soft voice, "watching passengers climb into the boat. Among them was my twenty year old son, happy and excited to visit his sister. He waved to me as the boat pushed away from land. I stood watching as it went farther and farther, picturing in my mind's eye, the joyous reunion of brother and sister. Then, as I watched helplessly, the boat suddenly capsized. Some of the passengers were able to swim back to the jetty, others clung to the overturned boat. I ran to the edge of the jetty, jostled and pushed by the sudden onslaught of people rushing down to the water's edge. Some jumped into the water and I watched as they tried to rescue passengers. I scanned the faces of all the persons brought ashore but my son was not among them. Twenty-three people, including my son, never returned."

There was a cadence, a rhythm to her words, and the quiver of her voice lent poignancy to what she said. "I sat on the jetty late into the cold night, my eyes scanning the dark waters, my ears listening for a sound. But there was no cry, no one called my name. At last, when the night was old, I allowed a neighbour to draw me away from the river and lead me to my poor derelict hut. In the early hours of the morning I drifted off into a short fitful sleep and had a dream. In my dream I saw you, O holy one. You held up your hand and a light shone upon me, a light that filled my entire being with warmth. All sorrow left me and a voice whispered that a holy man would come from the East and restore my son to me." She paused, and when she spoke again the quiver had miraculously left her voice and a radiant happiness had replaced the poignancy. "And here you are. I know that my son will now come back to me—I know this is the reason for my long wait."

Nanak was moved by the intensity of the woman's faith. "Where do you think your son has been these last twelve years?" he asked.

"Why, in the custody of Allah!" the woman said without a moment's hesitation. "He has kept him safe and well so that he can return to me exactly as he left me."

"And do you think he has been happy with Allah?"

"Oh yes! He has known happiness unsullied by the shadow of grief or anxiety, happiness unknown to any human being," she said with great conviction.

"And you would be selfish enough to bring him back to this world where happiness is just an occasional episode in a long drama of pain and misery?"

The woman was silent and Nanak squeezed her shoulder gently. "Have you really lived without your son these twelve years?" he asked. "I can see him in your eyes, even now. I can see that in these twelve years there was not a moment when your son was not with you. Memories of his mischievous pranks made you smile and you cried when you remembered the times he was in pain. You gave him so much love while he was with you in flesh and blood, that he can never go away from you."

He could see the light begin to return to those tired old eyes. "You have not lost your son; you have only lost his body with all its inherent weaknesses. His spirit and his soul are always with you in all their strength and glory and will be with you till your dying day."

Realisation dawned upon the woman at last and she wept for the truth that the Guru had enabled her to perceive. When her weeping was done, she touched the Guru's feet and turned and walked towards her hut. At last she was at peace.

⁓

During his travels Nanak once came to the outskirts of a prosperous settlement situated by a river. He camped at a serene and picturesque site on a little hillock outside the settlement. People heard about the sage who had come to their town, and their curiosity aroused, they came to meet him. Nanak soon made a mark with his hymns, his simple way of life, and the sagacious words that he spoke to his listeners. His congregation grew till everyone in the settlement came each evening to listen to him; everyone except the richest and most powerful man in town. No one called him by his real name and he was always addressed and spoken of simply as "Karori," the owner of wealth and income running into *crores* of rupees. He did not take exception to the nick-name and was, in fact, secretly pleased by it.

Karori had everything that a man could desire—wealth beyond measure, a palatial home, a beautiful wife, and children. He dressed in the richest of clothes and jewellery, and ate of the choicest food. He had servants at his beck and call, who anticipated his needs even before he could give voice to them. There was nothing more that Karori could possibly want or desire and he was the envy of all who knew him.

But Karori had a secret; he could no longer get a good night's rest. He would toss and turn, and sleep would come to him in fitful snatches only to be rudely disturbed by strange nightmares. He found that he could no longer digest all the tasty dishes that he so relished. He was becoming increasingly short-tempered not only with his servants and his staff but also with his family.

His wife had begun to regularly attend Nanak's prayer meetings and the effect of these visits was soon visible. She was radiant and became increasingly gentle and kind with each passing day. Karori envied her this new-found happiness and serenity. One evening, when she returned from her daily prayer meeting, he gave voice to this envy.

"Then why don't you come with me?" she asked.

"Because your Nanak cannot help me—what relief can a purveyor of mere words bring when the most learned physicians have failed? He is no healer and I have seen enough of so-called holy men and *fakirs* to have nothing but contempt for them."

But in spite of this, when a few more days elapsed and he saw the deep and abiding joy on his wife's face, curiosity got the better of Karori, and putting aside his prejudices, he accompanied her to the *satsang*. He was drawn to Nanak's radiant presence and his divine words. He began to linger long after the *satsang* was over, till one day he and his wife were the only people left with Nanak. The evening shadows had lengthened and lights had begun to twinkle in the settlement, half a mile away from

Nanak's camp. Nanak smiled at Karori and even in the gathering darkness Karori felt the warmth of that smile.

"Something weighs upon your mind, my friend; one requires no clairvoyant power to discern that you are a troubled man. Tell me your troubles, perhaps I may be able to help. If not, the mere telling of your troubles to another may lighten your burden." And so Karori told him his problems and Nanak listened attentively.

"There is little that I can do or say to bring you relief. But there is something that you can do to help me. Even though your town is prosperous there are many who are poor. They come to listen to me only because of the promise of a frugal meal at the end of my *satsang*. I know for certain that this is all the nourishment that some of them get during the day. Could you find it in your heart to set up a community kitchen for the poor and the impoverished and provide them two simple meals a day? I ask this of you because I know that you are the only one in this town who is rich enough to be able to undertake this expense."

Karori was perturbed that the Baba, instead of paying attention to his problem, had burdened him with his own. But the Baba's last remarks made his heart swell with pride. Not for nothing was he known as Karori and he would use this opportunity of a community kitchen to further display his wealth. His head teemed with ideas and over the next few days all his thoughts and energies were focused on the community kitchen. So preoccupied was he that he did not notice that he was sleeping and eating better. Karori supervised the cooking and distribution of the food himself. Within a week he had got to know each of the indigent people who thronged his kitchen. For the first time in his life he saw them as individuals and found himself being drawn into their lives and concerned about their worries. Some had medical problems, some were involved in land disputes, while others struggled for a roof over their heads—the list of problems went on and Karori found himself involved more and more in resolving them. In addition to his kitchen he set up a dispensary and a special school for disadvantaged children. He would return home late at night, weary and exhausted, and after a hearty meal would fall immediately into a deep and untroubled sleep. He forgot his obsession with multiplying his wealth and delegated his business affairs to his *munshi*. People were amazed that he was no longer the proud, uncaring man they had known before. He had a kind word and a ready smile for everyone who crossed his path.

He did attend Nanak's *satsangs* fairly regularly but his preoccupation with his projects precluded spending much time with the Guru. But one evening, in spite of all the work that he had to attend to, he did linger on. Nanak smiled at him indulgently. "Come, Bhai Karori, come and sit beside me and tell me more about your indigestion and insomnia."

Karori knew that Nanak was teasing him. "Yes Master. That is what I came to tell you. Miraculously, my indigestion and insomnia have vanished and it is you who must take the credit for working this miracle."

"I only gave you the prescription. You worked it out yourself. In any case, both you and I know that there is no such thing as a miracle. The problems with your health were caused by your way of life and your attitude of mind. Your obsession with amassing wealth affected your sleep and your health. Once you started the free kitchen, you discovered the joys of giving and sharing. Your concern is now not for yourself but for others. Your obsession is no longer with how you can increase your holding of gold but the happiness and comfort that it can bring to the lives of others. You have subjugated the self to the service of mankind. You have attained a state of bliss, which many strive for but few achieve. You are now a true man of God."

~

Perhaps the most beautiful of the janamsakhis is the one concerning Nanak's last hours. Nanak lay under a tree on the riverbank just outside Kartarpur. Angad sat with Nanak's feet in his lap, his heart heavy with grief at the approaching end. All day, people from distant places came to see their Guru one last time. Nanak's breathing was heavy and he drifted in and out of sleep. As a wind struck up and rustled the leaves of the trees, Nanak opened his eyes and smiled at Angad. And Angad understood: Old leaves must fall off to make place for new ones to grow, just as the old must leave the world to make place for the young. Then the Guru's eyes became clouded again and he seemed to lose awareness of the world and of the people who sat around him.

A murmur started among the Guru's Muslim followers. "He is ours, our *pir*. When he dies his body must be handed over to us so that we can bury him with honour."

The Hindu followers were very upset by this claim. "No, no," they protested. "Nanak was born a Hindu. His father's name was Kalyan and his mother's name was Tripta. His teachings contain a great deal of the Hindu way of life. Besides, he never said he was a Mussalman. So how can you say he is yours? He is our Guru and we will perform the funeral rites in accordance with Hindu custom." The Guru opened his eyes and chuckled softly. Angad held up his hand and the quarrelling disciples fell silent.

"You are both right," Nanak said. "I belong to both of you. But there is a way to solve this difficulty. Each of you must bring flowers, lots of flowers, and put them beside me. The Muslims must put their flowers along my left side and the Hindus along my right. You must leave them there through the night. Then tomorrow morning you must look carefully at your flowers. If the Hindus' flowers are fresh then I belong to the Hindus and if the Muslims' flowers are fresh then I belong to the Muslims and they may do with my body as they wish." Nanak was tired. He closed his eyes again and drifted off to sleep.

The Guru's command was obeyed and both the Hindus and the Muslims brought many flowers and put them down as the Guru had directed. Then they sat to wait out the night. By the flickering light of the oil lamps, some prayed while others gazed at the Guru's face in these final moments. His breathing became softer and softer. It was almost dawn. It was the time that the Guru described as *amrit vela*, the time of nectar, his favourite time of the day.

The Guru opened his eyes one last time. In a faint voice he asked his followers to pray. He said one last prayer, then drawing the sheet over himself, he went into eternal sleep.

All through the morning, the disciples sat beside their Guru in silence. The Hindus and the Muslims carefully examined the flowers they had brought. The Muslims looked at their flowers and found they were still as fresh as when they had brought them. When the Hindus looked at their flowers they too found that they were as fresh as when they had been plucked. Both sides looked at each other in wonder. Even in death the Guru had underscored the lesson he had taught all through his life. There is no Hindu. There is no Mussalman. All men are equal and can make their lives as beautiful and fragrant as flowers through the good deeds that they perform.

171

ACKNOWLEDGMENTS

I would be failing in my duty if I did not acknowledge my deep gratitude to all those who have done work on Nanak before me. It was largely because of this tremendous work that my own task became so much easier and so much more enjoyable. I would like to make special mention of Mr. Khushwant Singh and his *A History of the Sikhs*, Mr. Navtej Sarna and his *The Book of Nanak,* and Mr. Roopinder Singh and his book *Guru Nanak: His Life and Teachings*.

I would also like to place on record my gratitude to Mr. Ashok Chopra for recommending my name for this project. I would like to thank Sonavi Desai for having had the faith to entrust me with this work and for doing such an excellent job with the editing: without this work, I am afraid, the book would not have been readable. Finally, I would like to thank Hema for undertaking the Herculean task of deciphering my terrible handwriting and typing out the manuscript.

Harish Dhillon
Mohali
20th September, 2005.

GLOSSARY

aarti	waving of lamps before an idol in a prayer service, accompanied by chanting of hymns
Acharya	term of respect for an extremely learned man.
Advaita	non-duality; the vedanta philosophy propounded by Shankara
Ahal–i-islam	followers of Islam
Ahal–i–kitab	followers of any religion whose precepts are contained in a religious book
allu vadi	dish made of potatoes and ground pulses
Amil	an official in the court of the governor who was entrusted the task of revenue collection
amrit vela	literally "the time of nectar"—the early morning hours embracing both pre-dawn and dawn
atman	Soul, also sometimes used in the sense of one's inner conscience
Baba	a term of respect for an older man
Babar Vani	a special hymn composed by Nanak mourning the destruction unleashed by Babar's invasion
bani	composition which contains precepts or teachings
Barah Mah	"Twelve Months"—A hymn by Nanak wherein he describes the passing of seasons
barat	a wedding procession
beri	a bush which bears "ber" or small berries
Bhai	Brother—term of respect and affection
bhajans	songs with religious connotations
bhakt	follower, worshipper
bhang	a kind of intoxicant
bhishti	water-carrier
brahm bhoj	a ritual meal organized for Brahmins on certain holy occasions, which has now come to mean any community meal at religious functions
Brahmin	a member of the highest among the four Hindu castes
chaddar	sheet, also a semi-woolen hand-woven shawl used in the winter

173

chapatti	round, thin Indian bread
chattai	reed mat used as a floor covering and as a sleeping mat
choga	loose, flowing ankle-length robe
chunni	a long length of cloth used as a scarf by women
crore	ten million
dal	lentil curry
dargah	tomb of a Muslim saint which has become a place of pilgrimage
darogah	Head Constable at a police station
Dar-ul-harb	country inhabited by infidels
dera	a center established by a spiritual or religious figure
dham	place of pilgrimage
dharamshala	charitable rest house, usually for travelers and pilgrims
dharma kand	the second stage of spiritual development where man performs noble and dutiful deeds which will help him along the road of spiritual realization.
divan	a low sofa
diwan	official in court, roughly equal to a chief minister
doli	palanquin to carry a bride to her husband's home
durbar	court
fakir	muslim man with spiritual leanings who has renounced the world
gachni	special brown mud used for providing a clean surface on the wooden slates that were used to practice writing
gadi	seat of succession
Gangajal	holy water from the Ganges
granthi	one who leads the prayer service and reads from the *Guru Granth Sahib*
gyan kand	the state in man's spiritual development where he has gained knowledge about the nature of the Supreme Power and all His creation.
hakim	a Muslim physician
Haj	pilgrimage to the holy city of Mecca, which all devout Muslims are expected to undertake at least once in their lifetimes
Haji	one who has performed the *Haj*
haumain	egoism, the self
haveli	large, palatial house
Hazoor	term of address used by subordinates or employees—has a connotation of subservience
hukam	the Divine Will
jagir	grant of land

janamsakhis	stories drawn from the life of Nanak
janeu	sacred thread which all high caste Hindu men wear
Japji	morning prayer composed by Nanak, at the beginning of the *Guru Granth Sahib*
jehad	holy war to be fought by Muslims against all forces which interfere with the true practice of their religion
jeziya	tax imposed by Muslim rulers on their non-Muslim subjects
juttis	leather or cloth slippers
kachcha	not yet ready (*kachcha* path is a dirt track)
kalandar	Muhammadan monk or recluse
kafir	non-believer
karma	result of past deeds; as per the theory of Karma a person's deeds in this birth will establish the state of their life in their next birth
karam kand	the path of action
kirtan	community singing of hymns
kos	unit measuring distance, roughly equivalent to two and a half miles
kotwal	constable
langar	community Kitchen
lathi	stick or baton
Maharaj	respectful term of address for a saint
Malik	governor
mantra	a chant of sacred words
marasis	class of professional musicians
moksha	freedom from the cycle of death and rebirth
maulvi	Muslim priest—each maulvi is attached to a mosque where he preaches
maya	illusion—in Hindu theology this world and life are regarded as illusory
mishri	sugar
mithya	illusion
modikhana	store house, treasury or granary
Mool Mantra	the opening of Nanak's Japji
mukham	destination, the abode of a saint
munshi	accountant and head-clerk
naam	the constant awareness of the Lord's name
namaz	the Muslim prayer, performed five times a day
nanakpanthis	followers of Nanak who are not baptized Sikhs
nankeh	home of the maternal grandparents
Navratras	the nine nights before Dassera
nath yogis	a sect of Hindu ascetics
pandal	temporary structure of bamboo and cloth

patti	wooden board, used as a slab in schools
patti likhi	writing on a *patti*—a name given to a poem composed by Nanak while still in school
patwari	keeper of revenue records in a village
phulkari	traditional embroidered shawl from the Punjab worn by the bride at her wedding
pinni	a sweet made from flour or ground pulses
pipal	a tree belonging to the Ficus family
piri	a low seat
pir	a Muslim holy man
prasad	consecrated food from a prayer service
puttar	child
qazi	a Muslim religious leader like the head of a diocese, a representative of the shariat in the administration
rabab	a stringed musical instrument played with a bow
raga	specific sets of notes on which compositions in Indian classical music are based
Rai	title used for a head or a leader
reetha	soap nut
rishi	an ascetic who lives in a hermitage and is a man of great learning
riyaaz	practice (in the performing arts of music and dance)
sach kand	the state (or domain) of truth
sacha sauda	true bargain—the transaction that Nanak conducted when he fed the holy men
sadhu	holy man
sangat	congregation
sanyas	state of renunciation
sanyasi	one who has renounced the world
sargun	possession of all virtues
satsang	community prayers
sawan	the month when the monsoon is at its strongest
seer	measure of weight (0.9331 kg)
serai	inn
sewa	service
shabads	hymns
shaheed	martyr
sharad	a period of sixteen days every year in September during which rituals are performed by Hindus for the souls of their ancestors
siddha	person who has attained certain spiritual powers
Siddhagosht	name given to a composition by Nanak which sums up his discussions with the *siddha yogis* in the form of a dialogue

siddha yogis	a perfect yogi; one whose experience of unity-consciousness is uninterrupted
suras	verses from the Qur'an
swami	holy man, usually head of a center of religious learning
tantrik	a practitioner of tantra
tera	yours; also the number thirteen
tehsil	administrative unit smaller than a district
thali	plate or salver
tilak	the red mark applied to the forehead by the priest as part of ritual prayers
udasis	itineraries; used as a term for Nanak's missionary travels
vaid	doctor practising Indian system of medicine
var	ballad
yagnopavitam	the ceremony in which a Hindu boy of a high caste is invested with the sacred thread
yogis	practitioners of yoga who believe that salvation can be achieved through the practice of mental and physical yogic exercises
zimmis	non-Muslims who were permitted to practice their religion on the payment of tax

BIBLIOGRAPHY

Anand, Reema, and Khushwant Singh, trans. *Rehras Evensong, the Sikh Evening Prayer*. New York: Viking, 2002.

Cunningham, J. D., and Patwant Singh. *History of the Sikhs*. New Delhi: Rupa, 2002.

Dhillon, Harish. *The Lives and Teachings of the Sikh Gurus*. New Delhi: UBSPD, 1998.

Duggal, K. S. *Sikh Gurus: Their Lives & Teachings*. New Delhi: UBSPD, 2005.

Duggal, Kartar Singh, trans. *The Holy Granth: Sri Guru Granth Sahib*. Hemkunt, 2004.

McLeod, W. H. *Exploring Sikhism: Aspects of Sikh Identity, Culture, and Thought*. New York: Oxford University Press, 2003.

Sarna, Navtej. *The Book of Nanak*. New Delhi and New York: Penguin Books, 2005.

Singh, Khushwant. *A History of the Sikhs*, vol. I: *The Sikh Gurus, 1469–1705*. New York: Oxford University Press, 1999.

Singh, Khushwant, trans. *Japjee: Sikh Morning Prayer*. New Delhi: Picus Books, 1999.

Singh, Kirpal, and Kharak Singh, eds. *History of the Sikhs & Their Religion*, vol. I, Dharam Parchar Committee SGPC, 2004.

Singh, Roopinder. *Guru Nanak: His Life and Teachings*. New Delhi: Rupa, 2004.

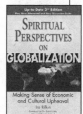
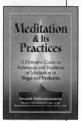

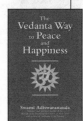

Sacred Texts—SkyLight Illuminations Series
Andrew Harvey, Series Editor

Offers today's spiritual seeker an accessible entry into the great classic texts of the world's spiritual traditions. Each classic is presented in an accessible translation, with facing pages of guided commentary from experts, giving you the keys you need to understand the history, context and meaning of the text. This series enables you, whatever your background, to experience and understand classic spiritual texts directly, and to make them a part of your life.

CHRISTIANITY

The End of Days: Essential Selections from Apocalyptic Texts—Annotated & Explained *Annotation by Robert G. Clouse*
Introduces you to the beliefs and values held by those who rely on the promises found in the Book of Revelation. 5½ x 8½, 192 pp, Quality PB, 978-1-59473-170-9 **$16.99**

The Hidden Gospel of Matthew: Annotated & Explained
Translation & Annotation by Ron Miller
Takes you deep into the text cherished around the world to discover the words and events that have the strongest connection to the historical Jesus.
5½ x 8½, 272 pp, Quality PB, 978-1-59473-038-2 **$16.99**

The Lost Sayings of Jesus: Teachings from Ancient Christian, Jewish, Gnostic and Islamic Sources—Annotated & Explained
Translation & Annotation by Andrew Phillip Smith; Foreword by Stephan A. Hoeller
This collection of more than three hundred sayings depicts Jesus as a Wisdom teacher who speaks to people of all faiths as a mystic and spiritual master.
5½ x 8½, 240 pp, Quality PB, 978-1-59473-172-3 **$16.99**

Philokalia: The Eastern Christian Spiritual Texts—Selections Annotated & Explained *Annotation by Allyne Smith; Translation by G. E. H. Palmer, Phillip Sherrard and Bishop Kallistos Ware*
The first approachable introduction to the wisdom of the Philokalia, which is the classic text of Eastern Christian spirituality.
5½ x 8½, 240 pp, Quality PB, 978-1-59473-103-7 **$16.99**

Spiritual Writings on Mary: Annotated & Explained
Annotation by Mary Ford-Grabowsky; Foreword by Andrew Harvey
Examines the role of Mary, the mother of Jesus, as a source of inspiration in history and in life today. 5½ x 8½, 288 pp, Quality PB, 978-1-59473-001-6 **$16.99**

The Way of a Pilgrim: Annotated & Explained
Translation & Annotation by Gleb Pokrovsky; Foreword by Andrew Harvey
This classic of Russian spirituality is the delightful account of one man who sets out to learn the prayer of the heart, also known as the "Jesus prayer."
5½ x 8½, 160 pp, Illus., Quality PB, 978-1-893361-31-7 **$14.95**

MORMONISM
The Book of Mormon: Selections Annotated & Explained
Annotation by Jana Riess; Foreword by Phyllis Tickle
Explores the sacred epic that is cherished by more than twelve million members of the LDS church as the keystone of their faith.
5½ x 8½ , 272 pp, Quality PB, 978-1-59473-076-4 **$16.99**

NATIVE AMERICAN
Native American Stories of the Sacred: Annotated & Explained
Retold & Annotated by Evan T. Pritchard
Intended for more than entertainment, these teaching tales contain elegantly simple illustrations of time-honored truths.
5½ x 8½, 272 pp, Quality PB, 978-1-59473-112-9 **$16.99**

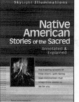

Sacred Texts—cont.

GNOSTICISM

The Gospel of Philip: Annotated & Explained
Translation & Annotation by Andrew Phillip Smith; Foreword by Stevan Davies
Reveals otherwise unrecorded sayings of Jesus and fragments of Gnostic mythology.
5½ x 8½, 160 pp, Quality PB, 978-1-59473-111-2 **$16.99**

The Gospel of Thomas: Annotated & Explained
Translation & Annotation by Stevan Davies Sheds new light on the origins of Christianity and
portrays Jesus as a wisdom-loving sage. 5½ x 8½, 192 pp, Quality PB, 978-1-893361-45-4 **$16.99**

The Secret Book of John: The Gnostic Gospel—Annotated & Explained
Translation & Annotation by Stevan Davies The most significant and influential text of
the ancient Gnostic religion. 5½ x 8½, 208 pp, Quality PB, 978-1-59473-082-5 **$16.99**

JUDAISM

The Divine Feminine in Biblical Wisdom Literature
Selections Annotated & Explained
Translation & Annotation by Rabbi Rami Shapiro; Foreword by Rev. Cynthia Bourgeault, PhD
Uses the Hebrew books of Psalms, Proverbs, Song of Songs, Ecclesiastes and Job,
Wisdom literature and the Wisdom of Solomon to clarify who Wisdom is.
5½ x 8½, 240 pp, Quality PB, 978-1-59473-109-9 **$16.99**

Ethics of the Sages: *Pirke Avot*—Annotated & Explained
Translation & Annotation by Rabbi Rami Shapiro Clarifies the ethical teachings of the
early Rabbis. 5½ x 8½, 192 pp, Quality PB, 978-1-59473-207-2 **$16.99**

Hasidic Tales: Annotated & Explained
Translation & Annotation by Rabbi Rami Shapiro
Introduces the legendary tales of the impassioned Hasidic rabbis, presenting them as
stories rather than as parables. 5½ x 8½, 240 pp, Quality PB, 978-1-893361-86-7 **$16.95**

The Hebrew Prophets: Selections Annotated & Explained
Translation & Annotation by Rabbi Rami Shapiro; Foreword by Zalman M. Schachter-Shalomi
Focuses on the central themes covered by all the Hebrew prophets.
5½ x 8½, 224 pp, Quality PB, 978-1-59473-037-5 **$16.99**

Zohar: Annotated & Explained *Translation & Annotation by Daniel C. Matt*
The best-selling author of *The Essential Kabbalah* brings together in one place the most
important teachings of the Zohar, the canonical text of Jewish mystical tradition.
5½ x 8½, 176 pp, Quality PB, 978-1-893361-51-5 **$15.99**

EASTERN RELIGIONS

Bhagavad Gita: Annotated & Explained *Translation by Shri Purohit Swami*
Annotation by Kendra Crossen Burroughs Explains references and philosophical terms,
shares the interpretations of famous spiritual leaders and scholars, and more.
5½ x 8½, 192 pp, Quality PB, 978-1-893361-28-7 **$16.95**

Dhammapada: Annotated & Explained *Translation by Max Müller and revised by*
Jack Maguire; Annotation by Jack Maguire Contains all of Buddhism's key teachings.
5½ x 8½, 160 pp, b/w photos, Quality PB, 978-1-893361-42-3 **$14.95**

Rumi and Islam: Selections from His Stories, Poems, and Discourses—
Annotated & Explained *Translation & Annotation by Ibrahim Gamard*
Focuses on Rumi's place within the Sufi tradition of Islam, providing insight into
the mystical side of the religion. 5½ x 8½, 240 pp, Quality PB, 978-1-59473-002-3 **$15.99**

Selections from the Gospel of Sri Ramakrishna: Annotated & Explained
Translation by Swami Nikhilananda; Annotation by Kendra Crossen Burroughs
Introduces the fascinating world of the Indian mystic and the universal appeal
of his message. 5½ x 8½, 240 pp, b/w photos, Quality PB, 978-1-893361-46-1 **$16.95**

Tao Te Ching: Annotated & Explained *Translation & Annotation by Derek Lin*
Introduces an Eastern classic in an accessible, poetic and completely original way.
5½ x 8½, 192 pp, Quality PB, 978-1-59473-204-1 **$16.99**

Spirituality & Crafts

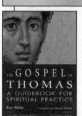

The Knitting Way: A Guide to Spiritual Self-Discovery
by Linda Skolnik and Janice MacDaniels
7 x 9, 240 pp, Quality PB, 978-1-59473-079-5 **$16.99**

The Quilting Path
A Guide to Spiritual Discovery through Fabric, Thread and Kabbalah
by Louise Silk
7 x 9, 192 pp, Quality PB, 978-1-59473-206-5 **$16.99**

Spiritual Practice

Divining the Body
Reclaim the Holiness of Your Physical Self   *by Jan Phillips*
A practical and inspiring guidebook for connecting the body and soul in spiritual practice. Leads you into a milieu of reverence, mystery and delight, helping you discover your body as a pathway to the Divine.
8 x 8, 256 pp, Quality PB, 978-1-59473-080-1 **$16.99**

Finding Time for the Timeless: Spirituality in the Workweek
by John McQuiston II
Simple, refreshing stories that provide you with examples of how you can refocus and enrich your daily life using prayer or meditation, ritual and other forms of spiritual practice. 5½ x 6¾, 208 pp, HC, 978-1-59473-035-1 **$17.99**

The Gospel of Thomas
A Guidebook for Spiritual Practice   *by Ron Miller; Translations by Stevan Davies*
An innovative guide to bring a new spiritual classic into daily life.
6 x 9, 160 pp, Quality PB, 978-1-59473-047-4 **$14.99**

Earth, Water, Fire, and Air: Essential Ways of Connecting to Spirit
by Cait Johnson 6 x 9, 224 pp, HC, 978-1-893361-65-2 **$19.95**

Labyrinths from the Outside In: Walking to Spiritual Insight—A Beginner's Guide
by Donna Schaper and Carole Ann Camp
6 x 9, 208 pp, b/w illus. and photos, Quality PB, 978-1-893361-18-8 **$16.95**

Practicing the Sacred Art of Listening: A Guide to Enrich Your Relationships
and Kindle Your Spiritual Life—The Listening Center Workshop
by Kay Lindahl 8 x 8, 176 pp, Quality PB, 978-1-893361-85-0 **$16.95**

Releasing the Creative Spirit: Unleash the Creativity in Your Life
by Dan Wakefield 7 x 10, 256 pp, Quality PB, 978-1-893361-36-2 **$16.95**

The Sacred Art of Bowing: Preparing to Practice
by Andi Young 5½ x 8½, 128 pp, b/w illus., Quality PB, 978-1-893361-82-9 **$14.95**

The Sacred Art of Chant: Preparing to Practice
by Ana Hernández 5½ x 8½, 192 pp, Quality PB, 978-1-59473-036-8 **$15.99**

The Sacred Art of Fasting: Preparing to Practice
by Thomas Ryan, CSP 5½ x 8½, 192 pp, Quality PB, 978-1-59473-078-8 **$15.99**

The Sacred Art of Forgiveness: Forgiving Ourselves and Others through God's Grace
by Marcia Ford 8 x 8, 176 pp, Quality PB, 978-1-59473-175-4 **$16.99**

The Sacred Art of Listening: Forty Reflections for Cultivating a Spiritual Practice
by Kay Lindahl; Illustrations by Amy Schnapper
8 x 8, 160 pp, b/w illus., Quality PB, 978-1-893361-44-7 **$16.99**

The Sacred Art of Lovingkindness: Preparing to Practice
by Rabbi Rami Shapiro; Foreword by Marcia Ford
5½ x 8½, 176 pp, Quality PB, 978-1-59473-151-8 **$16.99**

Sacred Speech: A Practical Guide for Keeping Spirit in Your Speech
by Rev. Donna Schaper 6 x 9, 176 pp, Quality PB, 978-1-59473-068-9 **$15.99**
HC, 978-1-893361-74-4 **$21.95**

Meditation / Prayer

Prayers to an Evolutionary God
by William Cleary; Afterword by Diarmuid O'Murchu

How is it possible to pray when God is dislocated from heaven, dispersed all around us, and more of a creative force than an all-knowing father? Inspired by the spiritual and scientific teachings of Diarmuid O'Murchu and Teilhard de Chardin, Cleary reveals that religion and science can be combined to create an expanding view of the universe—an evolutionary faith.

6 x 9, 208 pp, HC, 978-1-59473-006-1 **$21.99**

Psalms: A Spiritual Commentary
by M. Basil Pennington, ocso; Illustrations by Phillip Ratner

Showing how the Psalms give profound and candid expression to both our highest aspirations and our deepest pain, the late, highly respected Cistercian Abbot M. Basil Pennington shares his reflections on some of the most beloved passages from the Bible's most widely read book.

6 x 9, 176 pp, 24 full-page b/w illus., 978-1-59473-141-9 **$19.99**

The Song of Songs: A Spiritual Commentary
by M. Basil Pennington, OCSO; Illustrations by Phillip Ratner

Join the late M. Basil Pennington as he ruminates on the Bible's most challenging mystical text. Follow a path into the Songs that weaves through his inspired words and the evocative drawings of Jewish artist Phillip Ratner—a path that reveals your own humanity and leads to the deepest delight of your soul.

6 x 9, 160 pp, HC, 14 b/w illus., 978-1-59473-004-7 **$19.99**

Women of Color Pray: Voices of Strength, Faith, Healing, Hope and Courage   *Edited and with Introductions by Christal M. Jackson*

Through these prayers, poetry, lyrics, meditations and affirmations, you will share in the strong and undeniable connection women of color share with God. It will challenge you to explore new ways of prayerful expression.

5 x 7¼, 208 pp, Quality PB, 978-1-59473-077-1 **$15.99**

The Art of Public Prayer: Not for Clergy Only
by Lawrence A. Hoffman

An ecumenical resource for all people looking to change hardened worship patterns.

6 x 9, 288 pp, Quality PB, 978-1-893361-06-5 **$18.99**

Finding Grace at the Center: The Beginning of Centering Prayer
by M. Basil Pennington, ocso, Thomas Keating, ocso, and Thomas E. Clarke, sj
5 x 7¼, 112 pp, HC, 978-1-893361-69-0 **$14.95**

A Heart of Stillness: A Complete Guide to Learning the Art of Meditation
by David A. Cooper 5½ x 8½, 272 pp, Quality PB, 978-1-893361-03-4 **$16.95**

Meditation without Gurus: A Guide to the Heart of Practice
by Clark Strand 5½ x 8½, 192 pp, Quality PB, 978-1-893361-93-5 **$16.95**

Praying with Our Hands: 21 Practices of Embodied Prayer from the World's Spiritual Traditions   *by Jon M. Sweeney; Photographs by Jennifer J. Wilson; Foreword by Mother Tessa Bielecki; Afterword by Taitetsu Unno, PhD*
8 x 8, 96 pp, 22 duotone photos, Quality PB, 978-1-893361-16-4 **$16.95**

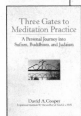

Silence, Simplicity & Solitude: A Complete Guide to Spiritual Retreat at Home
by David A. Cooper 5½ x 8½, 336 pp, Quality PB, 978-1-893361-04-1 **$16.95**

Three Gates to Meditation Practice: A Personal Journey into Sufism, Buddhism, and Judaism   *by David A. Cooper* 5½ x 8½, 240 pp, Quality PB, 978-1-893361-22-5 **$16.95**

Women Pray: Voices through the Ages, from Many Faiths, Cultures and Traditions
Edited and with Introductions by Monica Furlong
5 x 7¼, 256 pp, Quality PB, 978-1-59473-071-9 **$15.99**
Deluxe HC with ribbon marker, 978-1-893361-25-6 **$19.95**

About SKYLIGHT PATHS Publishing

SkyLight Paths Publishing is creating a place where people of different spiritual traditions come together for challenge and inspiration, a place where we can help each other understand the mystery that lies at the heart of our existence.

Through spirituality, our religious beliefs are increasingly becoming a part of our lives—rather than *apart* from our lives. While many of us may be more interested than ever in spiritual growth, we may be less firmly planted in traditional religion. Yet, we do want to deepen our relationship to the sacred, to learn from our own as well as from other faith traditions, and to practice in new ways.

SkyLight Paths sees both believers and seekers as a community that increasingly transcends traditional boundaries of religion and denomination—people wanting to learn from each other, *walking together, finding the way.*

For your information and convenience, at the back of this book we have provided a list of other SkyLight Paths books you might find interesting and useful. They cover the following subjects:

Buddhism / Zen	Gnosticism	Mysticism
Catholicism	Hinduism /	Poetry
Children's Books	Vedanta	Prayer
Christianity	Inspiration	Religious Etiquette
Comparative	Islam / Sufism	Retirement
Religion	Judaism / Kabbalah /	Spiritual Biography
Current Events	Enneagram	Spiritual Direction
Earth-Based	Meditation	Spirituality
Spirituality	Midrash Fiction	Women's Interest
Global Spiritual	Monasticism	Worship
Perspectives		

Or phone, fax, mail or e-mail to: SKYLIGHT PATHS Publishing
Sunset Farm Offices, Route 4 • P.O. Box 237 • Woodstock, Vermont 05091
Tel: (802) 457-4000 • Fax: (802) 457-4004 • www.skylightpaths.com
Credit card orders: (800) 962-4544 (8:30AM–5:30PM ET Monday–Friday)
Generous discounts on quantity orders. SATISFACTION GUARANTEED. Prices subject to change.

**For more information about each book,
visit our website at www.skylightpaths.com**